The Sin of Knowledge

*

The Sin of Knowledge

ANCIENT THEMES AND

MODERN VARIATIONS

*

THEODORE ZIOLKOWSKI

PRINCETON UNIVERSITY PRESS

PRINCETON AND OXFORD

Library of Congress Cataloging-in-Publication Data
Ziolkowski, Theodore.
The sin of knowledge : ancient themes and
modern variations / Theodore Ziolkowski.
p.   cm.
Includes bibliographical references and index.
ISBN 0-691-05065-1 (alk. paper)
1. Mythology in literature. 2. Adam (Biblical figure)—In literature.
3. Prometheus (Greek mythology) in literature.
4. Faust, d. ca. 1540—In literature. I. Title.
PN56.M95 Z56 2000
809′.9337—dc21   00-021204

This book has been composed in New Baskerville

The paper used in this publication
meets the minimum requirements of ·
ANSI/NISO Z39.48-1992 (R1997)
(*Permanence of Paper*)

www.pup.princeton.edu

Printed in the United States of America

10   9   8   7   6   5   4   3   2   1

TO MY GRADUATE STUDENTS

PRINCETON 1964–1999

WITH ADMIRATION

AND AFFECTION

✱ *Contents* ✱

List of Illustrations   ix

Preface   xi

PRELUDE
The Timeless Topicality of Myth   3

PART ONE
ANCIENT THEMES   7

CHAPTER ONE
Adam: The Genesis of Consciousness   9

  The Biblical Fall   9
  Near Eastern Sources   13
  The Paradox of Knowledge in Solomon's Jerusalem   17

CHAPTER TWO
Prometheus: The Birth of Civilization   25

  Hesiod's Trickster   25
  Aeschylus's Culture-Hero   32
  From Boeotia to Athens   39

CHAPTER THREE
Faust: The Ambivalence of Knowledge   43

  The Historical Faust   43
  The Growth of the Legend   49
  The Chapbook Speculator   52
  Marlowe's Power Seeker   60

INTERLUDE
From Myth to Modernity   69

PART TWO
MODERN VARIATIONS   73

CHAPTER FOUR
The Secularization of Adam   75

   Candide's Fall   75
   The Typological Impulse   77
   Romantic Tragicomic Falls   82
   American Ambiguities   92
   Modern Ironies   100

CHAPTER FIVE
The Proletarianization of Prometheus   111

   From Myth to Marx   111
   Modern Metaphors   115
   Marxist Myths   121
   GDR Ambiguities   127
   Three Major Re-Visions   132
   The Enemy of the People   141

CHAPTER SIX
The Americanization of Faust   149

   Modernizations of the Myth   149
   Faust and the Bomb   153
   Playful Fausts of the Fifties   156
   A Blue-Collar Faust   161
   Professorial Fausts   164
   Fausts of Politics and Poetry   174
   Fausts for the Nineties   177

POSTLUDE
On the Uses and Abuses of Myth   183

Notes   193

Bibliography   205

Index   217

❋ *Illustrations* ❋

1. Lucas Cranach, *Adam and Eve in Paradise (The Fall)*   2
2. Adam and Eve, fourth century   8
3. Prometheus, sixth century B.C.E.   26
4. Doctor Faust, 1594   44
5. Mike Figgis, *The Loss of Sexual Innocence*   74
6. Nuria Quevedo, *Prometheus*   110
7. Rockwell Kent, *Faust and the Earth Spirit*   150

Started 25 February 2013, 1900 D* in Helmand Province, Southern Afghanistan

* *Preface* *

Fᴏʀ in much wisdom is much grief: and he that increaseth knowledge increaseth sorrow." What thoughtful teacher or scholar or scientist has pondered those words of Ecclesiastes (1.18) without feeling at least a moment's scruple or doubt? Is our undertaking worth the malaise or even misery that it may entail? The doubts of a faith undermined by science? the unsettling of shared beliefs? the anxieties of civilization facing the threat of nuclear or biological extermination? the uncertainties of societies debating the pros and cons of recombinant DNA research, cloning, or the farming of body organs? even, at the most trivial level, the frantic pace of existences driven by television, the Internet, and cellular phones beyond the tranquillity and composure—the *leisure!*—necessary for civilized life? Can there be any man or woman engaged in intellectual work of any sort who has not at times questioned the validity of the enterprise? Nietzsche certainly did. In the self-critical preface written sixteen years after *The Birth of Tragedy* he wondered whether the systematic scientific pursuit of knowledge (*Wissenschaftlichkeit*) is not perhaps simply a flight from the unmitigated tragedy of life, a subtle defense mechanism against unadorned truth. Dostoevsky, whom Nietzsche once called the only psychologist from whom he had learned anything, observed in his *Notes from Underground* that consciousness itself is a disease—an observation repeated fifty years later by Miguel de Unamuno in *The Tragic Sense of Life.*

Yet we persevere, compelled by what Saint Augustine in his *Confessions* (10.35) called the human "appetite" or "desire" of knowing (*appetitus noscendi* and *libido noscendi*). To be sure, our understanding of "knowledge" has changed with the times. We live in an age—no longer an industrial age but what German sociologists call a *Wissensgesellschaft* or "knowledge society"— that believes fervently in Francis Bacon's maxim (in his *Sacred Meditations*) that "knowledge is power." This view is some-

[margin annotation: Science negates faith]

[margin annotation: there must be a degree of truth to this]

[margin annotation: Far too definitive; there is certainly exceptions to this]

xi

times trivialized. Many teachers have observed that students in the 1990s increasingly come to college not in search of the unsettling questions of a liberal education but with the expectation that the information acquired there will assure them financial success and "empowerment." This impression is confirmed by the recent surveys of first-year students conducted annually by the American Council on Education, and it has been dignified by the University of California at Berkeley through its establishment of a Xerox Distinguished Professorship of Knowledge—not in the College of Humanities but in its Haas School of Business.

On a more serious level, knowledge continues to be pursued even if it must be achieved according to the so-called devil's principle: What can be done, must be done. Edward Teller was simply stating a radical form of this conviction when he maintained in 1994 (as quoted by Roger Shattuck) that "[t]here is no case where ignorance should be preferred to knowledge—*especially* if the knowledge is terrible." As Byron's Adam rationalized his decision: "The snake spoke *truth*; it was the tree of knowledge, / It was the tree of life; knowledge is good, / And life is good; and how can both be evil?" (*Cain* 1.1.35–38).

Which is it to be? Shall we relentlessly pursue the power of knowledge at any cost or try to avoid sin and guilt by boycotting knowledge (as in our own decade the creationists have once again sought to do)? Between the extremes of conscienceless action and unquestioning faith or passive meditation lies the middle ground of anxiety, ambivalence, and doubt on which many thinking men and women seek to negotiate their lives.

FOR over two decades I have been pondering these issues and wondering, from my corner of the intellectual universe, why so many of the founding myths of humankind have focused on precisely that urgent question. And why so many writers of the past two centuries have been obsessed with the contemporary metamorphoses of that problem and its mythic shapings. For many years I have ended an annual lecture on Goethe's *Faust*

by reminding students that their professors all harbor, wittingly
or not, the ambition to play Mephisto to their Faust, to corrupt
their intellectual innocence through whatever knowledge they
profess. And why, after all, study literature if it does not pene-
trate our souls—if, as Rilke concluded his great sonnet on art
("Archaïscher Torso Apollos"), it does not force us to change
our lives? "Du mußt dein Leben ändern."

[handwritten margin note: How honest! The terrible ego at play from one who is given authority over another]

During the thirteen years I spent as dean of the Graduate
School at Princeton University I frequently had occasion to ru-
minate publicly about the value of higher education in an effort
to justify the enterprise. Why, if knowledge has often been portrayed as sinful and still generates doubts and anxieties both
personal and public, should we urge students to pursue graduate studies? If knowledge is purchased at the price of sin and
guilt, then to what responsibilities does that dear purchase
oblige us? That was the issue in a graduate commencement address that I delivered in 1980 at Brown University on "The Responsibilities of Knowledge," which took the Judeo-Christian
myth of the Fall as its leitmotiv. Around the same time the myth
of Prometheus suggested itself as the starting point of an inquiry into "Science, Frankenstein, and Myth," through which I
hoped to encourage students and colleagues in the sciences
and engineering to reflect on questions implicit in their work,
questions that unite the sciences and the humanities in a common concern. In yet another context I asked myself why it was
that so subversive a myth as the Faust theme, which amounts to
a vicious attack on universities, is placed at the center of many
humanities courses in our institutions. In this book I have
sought to organize and synthesize my thoughts on these seem-
ingly disparate topics into a serious jeu d'esprit—what Goethe
(in his last letter and with reference to his own *Faust*) called
"diese sehr ernsten Scherze"—unified by the common theme
that I call the sin of knowledge. For I believe that humankind's
continuing obsession with that theme exposes, from case to
case, the prevailing hopes and anxieties of the cultures that gen-
erate and reappropriate the myths.

The stories of Adam, Prometheus, and Faust—the authoritative myths embodying the sin of knowledge for their respective cultures—have inspired thousands of specialized books and articles, many of which I have gratefully consulted. It is neither necessary nor desirable to add yet another thematic history to the excellent studies by Butler, Dédéyan, Smeed, Trousson, and others listed in the bibliography. The three mythic models have sometimes been juxtaposed in various configurations and for various purposes by other scholars and critics. See, for example, the works by Heller, Kahler, Sewall, and Shattuck, as well as Bianchi and Kreitzer on Prometheus and Adam; Lecourt and Wutrich on Prometheus and Faust; or Hoelzel on Adam and Faust.

The present work differs from those cited in two important respects. First, in my treatment of the three basic myths I am concerned with the fundamental similarities underlying them and, specifically, with the reasons for the shift in each case from an earlier trickster legend to a vehicle for a culture's sudden and tragic awareness of the sin of knowledge. Methodologically, therefore, Part One considers in detail the foundational version of each myth, its sources, and its historical context.

Second, in my treatment of the modern variations I deal with aspects not covered to my knowledge in any of the existing thematic histories: notably, with the secularization of the story of Adam and the Fall into an image signaling the development of consciousness in modern narratives from Voltaire to the present; and with the reasons for the turn to the myths of Prometheus and Faust, respectively, in the post–World War II Marxist society of the German Democratic Republic and the late capitalist society of the United States. Methodologically, therefore, Part Two discusses in each chapter a variety of literary adaptations of the three themes. The representative pervasiveness of a myth in a given society can be demonstrated only to the extent that it permeates different genres at different cultural levels. Conversely, I mention only in passing certain classic works that are often exhaustively considered in the context of the three themes: for example, *Paradise Lost* or the great Romantic treatments of Faust and Prometheus. Milton's epic is a retelling of the Genesis story, not a metaphorical adaptation. Shelley's *Prometheus Unbound* is rarely a point of reference for the authors invoking that myth in the German Democratic Republic. And Goethe's *Faust* is merely one source for the postwar American writers, who also draw on the original chapbook, on Marlowe's drama, and on other versions for their material.

In sum, I offer the following observations not so much as a contribution to religion, myth, and literary thematology but as meditations on the problematic relationship of society to knowledge, of civilization to sin and guilt, of the individual consciousness to conscience. Accordingly the modern variations on the three basic themes should be understood as precisely that: variations, and not simply modern reworkings. Even though the basic structure of the myths—their "plot"—remains constant from case to case, or at least constant enough to be easily recognizable, the content or thematic import changes in such a manner as to reflect the concerns of the appropriating society. The sin of knowledge has quite different meanings for the inhabitants of tenth-century Jerusalem and of fifth-century Athens, for the citizens of the German Democratic Republic and of the postwar United States.

None of the following chapters has appeared previously in print. I developed the material of chapter 4 in the context of an undergraduate lecture course on European short fiction that I have taught for many years at Princeton. Chapter 6 was written as my contribution to a graduate seminar on the Faust theme that I have conducted three times over the past fifteen years. I have also had the opportunity to present the basic ideas of the book to a variety of audiences: notably at Trinity College in Hartford, Connecticut; in a commencement address at the University of Greifswald; and at the Sunday Evening Seminars in Wilmington, Delaware. On all these occasions I benefited from the responses that my presentations elicited. Finally, no manuscript ever leaves my study without the prior scrutiny and approval of my wife, Yetta Ziolkowski, who by that time understands my intentions as well as I do myself.

I am grateful again to Mary Murrell for her faith in this project as she heard about its progress and guided it through the editorial process at Princeton University Press. In Cyrus Hamlin, a broadly knowledgeable comparatist and one of our finest *Faust* scholars, my manuscript found its ideal reader, who responded with encouragement as well as helpful suggestions. I also benefited from the comments of Roger Shattuck, whose *Forbidden Knowledge: From Prometheus to Pornography* deals from a different perspective, and using different examples, with the mythic models that concern me. Once again a manuscript of mine has profited from Lauren Lepow's editorial acuity and empathy.

Adelaide Hagens and Lois Drewer from Princeton's Index of Christian Art shared their expertise in helping me to locate an appropriate illustration for chapter 1. Christa Sammons, curator of the Collection of German Literature in Yale University's Beinecke Library, generously provided me with a facsimile of the woodcut accompanying chapter 3. This is also the place, finally, to express my appreciation for the support I have received over the years from the superb reference staff of Firestone Library.

This book, like most of my others, has emerged directly from my teaching. Thematically it is even more immediately responsive than usual to the privileged and sometimes problematic relationship between student and teacher. The dedication is meant to acknowledge my appreciation to the splendid young men and women whom I first encountered in the graduate seminar room here at Princeton, and who, in the course of four decades, have become my friends and respected colleagues.

Theodore Ziolkowski
Princeton, New Jersey
October 1, 1999

The Sin of Knowledge

✳

Fig. 1. Lucas Cranach, *Adam and Eve in Paradise (The Fall)*, 1531.
Gemäldegalerie, Berlin. Courtesy of Staatliche Museen zu Berlin,
Preussischer Kulturbesitz.

The Timeless Topicality of Myth

ADAM, Prometheus, and Faust are always with us. In the summer of 1998 Hugendubel's bookstore in Berlin, facing the Kaiser Wilhelm Memorial Church whose bombed-out shell stands as a monument to the ravages of war, displayed new publications on a large table, on one corner of which reposed a heaping bowl of apples. A long, stuffed, rather jolly green serpent was suspended overhead. Confronted with this display, potential customers and readers found themselves thrust willy-nilly into the roles of Adam and Eve, tempted by the literary offerings to sacrifice their intellectual innocence yet again by consuming knowledge. An example of a different sort: the renowned Museum of Hygiene in Dresden features a life-size reproduction of one of Lucas Cranach's familiar paintings of Adam and Eve standing beneath the Tree of Knowledge. But here a sheet of clear plastic imposed directly in front of the painting contains various contraceptive devices, each in its proper position vis-à-vis the anatomies of the first man and woman. Again the implications leave nothing to the imagination. Germany is, of course, not alone in its exploitation of this cultural shorthand. We Americans are confronted daily with the corporate logo of Apple computers, urging us to take a bite from that corporation's electronic access to knowledge. As I write, the cover of the journal *Academe* (September/October 1998) features another painting by Cranach to illustrate an issue dedicated to sex and the academy. In that same month the on-line magazine *Salon* offered a cartoon based on Masaccio's *Expulsion from Paradise* with a sword-wielding angel; the heads of the two protoplasts were replaced by those of President Clinton and the First Lady, and the Eden in the background was symbolized by the White House. No citizen following the Sex-gate scandals of 1998 required an exegesis.

The biblical analogies are by no means unique. Prometheus has been called the only figure of classical mythology that has retained for the modern imagination a vital remnant of existential significance.[1] The evidence seems to validate that view. An element identified in 1945 and providing the energy source for luminescent watch dials as well as the miniature power source for space vehicles was labeled prometheum. In 1947, when Raymond A. Dart discovered in a South African cave at Makapansgat the remains of what he erroneously believed (from carbon traces) to be the first hominids to possess fire and forethought (for hunting and weapons), he named him Australopithecus prometheus. At Rockefeller Center in New York City an eight-ton bronze sculpture of Prometheus has since 1934 loomed over—not, to be sure, the business titans of Manhattan but—the swirling hordes of its ice-skating rink. The American titan was matched in monumentality by the two stone Prometheuses created in the 1930s by the German sculptor Arno Breker. In 1969 David S. Landes entitled his now classic study of technological change and industrial development in Western Europe from 1750 to the present *The Unbound Prometheus*. More recently Thomas P. Hughes called his analysis of the technological revolution during the Cold War years *Rescuing Prometheus*. The 1998 edition of *Books in Print* lists two densely printed columns of volumes in which Prometheus is "Rising," "Revisited," and "Reborn." An international journal of science policy is published in Italy under the title *Prometheus*; a major exhibition on gene technology was mounted in 1998 for the national Art and Exhibition Hall of the Federal Republic of Germany and publicized as "Prometheus in the Lab"; and that same year the German Historical Museum in Berlin cosponsored in Völklingen a 3.5-million-mark exhibition on the transformation of humanity's self-perception over time entitled "Prometheus: People, Images, Vision." For such reasons as these, in his 1995 encyclical letter on abortion, euthanasia, and the death penalty (§15),

4

Pope John Paul II lamented the existence in contemporary culture of "a certain Promethean attitude which leads people to think that they can control life and death by taking the decisions about them into their own hands." Clearly Prometheus, rejuvenated by the magic of molecular biology, still speaks to our imaginations as the twenty-first century begins.

The Bible and classical mythology do not provide the only sources for those vivid images that shape our cultural consciousness. Faust has long been a point of reference in Germany for advertisements (notably for wines and Mephisto footwear), political cartoons, and—during the inflationary years of the 1920s—even banknotes. But that great Reformation myth, which Oswald Spengler appropriated as a designation for Western civilization altogether, has made its way across the seas to become an international shibboleth for the demonic aspects of our technological world. Indications of the myth's familiarity can be seen in its appropriation by the comic book industry. Steadily in print since 1952, George Haimsohn's Madcap Classic *The Bedside Faust* presents in its cartoons a faithful rendition of seduction and betrayal. In his *Neo-Faust* (1989) the "Japanese Walt Disney" Osamu Tezuka portrays an aging biochemist who is rejuvenated and corrupted by a voluptuous female Mephisto. And the raunchy German "comic tragedy" by "Flix," with the startling English title *Who the Fuck Is Faust?* (1998), gives us Faust, Mephisto, and Gretchen "ready for the next millennium" in a contemporary Federal Republic, where among other adaptations the Walpurgis Night turns out to be a drug trip.[2] The legend attained perhaps its ultimate trivialization in the photo-novel by fashion designer Karl Lagerfeld (1995). Sixty black-and-white photos interspersed with movie-title cards featuring model Claudia Schiffer as Margaret, magician David Copperfield as Mephisto, and ex-model Veruschka von Lehndorff as Miss Lucy Fer, the owner of Martha's Garden nightclub in Monte Carlo, trace the adventures of a contemporary jet-set Faust, whose Gretchen ends up as a call girl in a high-priced bordello.

Adam, Prometheus, and Faust represent, in sum, three of the most familiar myths of our Western heritage. In other combinations one might well add Don Juan with his quest for sensual experience, Don Quixote with his idealistic efforts to elevate imagination over raw reality, or Hamlet with his ambivalence in the face of conflicting beliefs. But what links Adam, Prometheus, and Faust is the fact that each represents a response differing from culture to culture—Hebrew, Greek, Christian—to the specific issue of humankind's powerful, perennial, and sometimes sinful or unethical desire for knowledge and power. Hence their frequent appearance in connection with politics and science. To the extent that we understand these contents of our consciousness we can more fully appreciate the origins and growth of the culture in which we live. If we appreciate their origins and growth, in turn, we can better grasp the values by which we live and the conflicts inherent in them. A generation partial to channeling, UFO's, and other phenomena of New Age thinking has little reason to feel superior to the worshipers of Prometheus or to Faust's mystified contemporaries.

This is not to suggest, to state the obvious, that in a multicultural society such as ours other myths and images—notably African American, Latin American, Asian American, and Amerindian—have not colored our imaginations to an appreciable extent. But what ties us as Americans to the rest of the Western world are the materials of the Judeo-Christian tradition that have provided many of our moral and ethical values, and of the Greco-Roman culture that has shaped our language and our institutions. If we understand these myths in their genesis and transformations we understand something essential about ourselves.

6

PART ONE

ANCIENT THEMES

*

Fig. 2. Adam and Eve. Sarcophagus of Junius Bassus,
mid-fourth century. Rome, Vatican Grottoes. Courtesy of
Hirmer Fotoarchiv München.

CHAPTER ONE

Adam: The Genesis
of Consciousness

THE BIBLICAL FALL

Wно among us has not been moved by the familiar tale?
After God has accomplished the immense labor of creating
heaven and earth, he amuses himself by modeling from the
moist dust of the ground—almost playfully, it appears—a figure
into which, through divine CPR, he breathes life. What now to
do with this weakling on an earth still raw and inhospitable from
the Creation? As a home for his "Adam," whose name in Hebrew is the generic word for "man," he plants a garden in Eden,
a horticulturalist's delight in which thrives every variety of tree
both pleasing and useful: among them in the center the Tree
of Life and the Tree of the Knowledge of Good and Evil. He
informs his Adam-Man that he may eat freely from every tree
of the garden except, on pain of death, the Tree of Knowledge.
Then, to provide companionship for his new earthling, the divine potter shapes from the same clay, in sportive experimenta-
tion, various beasts of the field and birds of the air. Although
the man asserts his authority by giving names to all the cattle
and birds, he finds among them no helpmate suitable for himself. (According to ancient tradition, Adam's first and unsatis-
factory sexual intercourse was with the animals.)[1] So God anes-
thetizes the man and removes one of his ribs, from which he
clones a being similar to him. For an unspecified period—some
rabbinical readings grant them no more than that first day—
the two protoplasts live happily, and still in nameless generic
universality, in their nature preserve, neither aware nor
ashamed of their nakedness.

13 March 2013
Helmand Province, Afghanistan

But the serpent, wilier than any of the other creatures that God made and with no apparent motivation other than mischief, approaches the woman to ask why God has forbidden her and her mate to eat the fruit of the tree in the center of the garden, or even to touch it. "You will not die," the serpent assures her. Rather, if they should taste it, their eyes would be opened, and they would be "like God[s], knowing good and evil." Since the tree's fruit looks both nutritious and delicious (the biblical phrase anticipates the Horatian *dulce et utile*) and is reputed, moreover, to make wise, she samples a piece and takes some to her husband, who also partakes. Then their eyes are opened and, becoming suddenly aware of their nakedness, they cover themselves with makeshift aprons of fig leaves.

When next they hear God strolling in the garden in the cool of evening, they hide among the trees. But God summons them, and they confess that they concealed themselves out of shame for their nakedness. At this point the whole story, along with its sad but psychologically plausible finger-pointing, comes out. The man's eyes were opened to his nakedness because, at the woman's bidding, he consumed some of the forbidden fruit. The woman, in turn, pleads that she was just following orders: the serpent beguiled her. Thereupon God, in a most unholy burst of anger, curses everything in sight: the serpent is condemned to crawl forevermore on his belly, to eat dust, and to be trodden on by humankind; the woman, to feel sexual desire for her husband, to whom she shall be subservient, and yet to suffer great pain in bearing the children that result from their union; the earth, to bring forth thorns and thistles; and the man, hitherto the beneficiary of a lavish garden, to toil laboriously for his sustenance in the sweat of his brow. The man and his mate, finally, are condemned to eventual death and a return to the dust of the earth from which they were taken.

from broken trust comes our common condition

At this point, when they have been cast through sin from generic universality into human individuality, Adam names the woman Eve, thereby affirming his dominion over her in the same manner as previously over the animals. As a last gesture

10

of goodwill—he angers easily but does not hold grudges—God clothes Adam and Eve in garments of animal skin and then expels them from the garden into the arid wilderness beyond, lest they eat from the Tree of Life and thus achieve the immortality that he has prohibited. To ensure their compliance, he posts cherubim with flaming swords at the entrance to block the way back into the garden and to the Tree of Life.

THIS so-called second narrative of the Creation with the myth of Adam and Eve, the Temptation, and the Fall (Gen. 2.4–3.24) is one of the most familiar stories of Western culture. Saint Paul established a powerful tradition by identifying Adam as the "type" of natural man who was to be redeemed by the Second Adam, the "antitype" yet to come, in the person of Jesus Christ (Rom. 5.14). Just as sin and death entered the world through Adam's deed, so "one man's act of righteousness leads to acquittal and life for all men" (Rom. 5.18). Earlier he had preached to the Corinthians that death came by one man and resurrection by another. "For as in Adam all die, so also in Christ shall all be made alive" (1 Cor. 15.22). This "figural" analogy, which juxtaposes the Fall and the Redemption, Adam and Christ, and more generally the Old Testament and the New, is evident as early as the fourth century in images in Christian catacombs and on sarcophagi,[2] and it also informs those curious and closely related apocryphal books known as the *Apocalypse of Moses* and the *Vita Adae et Evae.*[3] It is not conclusively understood whether these Greek and Latin works, both of which were probably written sometime between the first and the third century of the common era and translated into many languages, go back to a Hebrew original or to Judeo-Greek or Aramaic sources. Both works, which profoundly influenced medieval views of Adam and Eve, recount the life of the first couple after their exile from Paradise and feature a quest for the Oil of Mercy to relieve Adam's suffering, followed by Adam's death, pardon, and burial. While both works end with Eve's death and burial, and although the *Apocalypse* includes a testament in which Eve

11

warns her children against sin by telling them about the Temptation and Fall, the *Vita* explicitly exonerates Adam and blames Eve for the expulsion from Paradise.

The familiar story was rehearsed again and again in such popular medieval texts as the ninth-century Old Saxon *Genesis*, the tenth-century Old English *Genesis B*, the eleventh-century Middle High German *Viennese Genesis*, and the twelfth-century Anglo-Norman mystery play *Jeu d'Adam*. At the same time, it provided images for scores of illuminated manuscripts as well as the bronze doors, reliefs, mosaics, statues, and stained-glass windows of medieval ecclesiastical buildings.[4] The tale of Adam and Eve was matched in popularity only by scenes from the lives of Jesus and the Madonna. Lucas Cranach's well-known paintings of the Temptation were paralleled in Reformation Germany by such dramatic representations as Hans Sachs's *Tragedy of the Creation, Fall, and Adam's Expulsion from Paradise* (*Tragedia von schöpfung, fal und außtreibung Ade auß dem paradeyß*, 1548). The age of the baroque in Catholic Spain as well as the Protestant Netherlands and England—from Lope de Vega's *La creación del mundo y primera culpa del hombre* (1618–1624) to Joost van den Vondel's *Adam in ballingschap* (Adam in exile, 1664) and John Milton's *Paradise Lost* (1667)—was obsessed by the subject. The fascination of the theme continued into the music, art, and poetry of the nineteenth century, and its popularity in the traditional genres was paralleled in folk art by its use on tiles, baking forms, and wedding chairs, and in songs and riddles ("Why did Adam bite the apple?" "Because he had no knife").[5] The myth of Adam and Eve provides without doubt several of the shaping images of the Western consciousness, which have demonstrated their continuing popularity in such twentieth-century media as advertisements and *New Yorker* cartoons.

FOR that reason it is all the more astonishing that, after their walk-on performance in the early chapters of Genesis (2–5), Adam and Eve do not reappear in the Old Testament. Adam is mentioned once by name at the beginning of the genealogy in

12

Chronicles (1.1). And Ezekiel (28.11–19), without naming him, laments the Son of Man who once walked blameless in Eden, the garden of God, until iniquity was found in him and he was cast out as profane. But the story itself apparently held no interest for the judges, the kings, the chroniclers, the psalmists, or the prophets. Nor, apparently, did Jesus know, or at least care about, Adam, who is mentioned only twice in the Gospels— once as one of the two unnamed protoplasts (Matt. 19.4–6) and once by name as the terminus a quo for the genealogy in Luke (3.38). Not the Gospels but the Pauline letters sound the keynote for the Christian obsession with the Adamic myth, and the early Christian theologians, eager to demonstrate the historical continuity between their upstart religion and the traditions of the Hebrew Bible, worked out the typological-figural analogies in elaborate detail. The myth of the Fall, one might almost conclude, became important only in light of the myth of Redemption.[6] Thus Milton exhorts his Heavenly Muse to sing

> Of Man's first disobedience, and the fruit
> Of that forbidden tree, whose mortal taste
> Brought death into the world, and all our woe,
> With loss of Eden, till one greater Man
> Restore us, and regain the blissful seat. . . .
>
> (*Paradise Lost*, 1.1–5)

NEAR EASTERN SOURCES

How, then, and why did the story make its way into Genesis? The concept of a fall from an earlier paradise appears in the myths of many peoples.[7] Etiological interest in the origin of things did not begin with modern cosmologists and the big bang theory; it is evident in the earliest legends of most cultures. This interest, combined with the Rousseauesque need to explain the deplorable human condition, suggested that humankind once lived in a happier state, from which it was

13

plunged—by disobedience, by fate, or by accident: for instance, by the unwitting violation of a taboo—into present misery.

While several of the elements, such as the creation of man from clay, belong to world folklore generally,[8] biblical scholars have long been aware that the Genesis account is based on cosmological legends and mythological elements known to various peoples of the ancient Near East[9]—in particular the image of a garden of the gods containing trees with mysterious powers. The anthropomorphic conception of a god strolling in his garden, as alien to the Hebrew tradition as is the walking and talking serpent, probably also came from another source. Notably, most of the characteristic motifs of the Genesis account are to be found, albeit in wholly different configurations, in the Mesopotamian epic of Gilgamesh.

In the Akkadian text of that epic, which was written around the turn of the second millennium B.C.E., Enkidu is created from the clay of the steppes by the love-goddess Aruru.[10] Enkidu, though not alone in the world, first lives in paradisiacal innocence (and sexuality?) among the wild beasts, with whom he jostles at the watering place, exemplifying the "absolutely undifferentiated human consciousness, corresponding to a psyche that has hardly left the animal level," according to C. G. Jung's definition of the trickster archetype in its purest manifestation.[11] A hunter, frightened by Enkidu's fierce demeanor, seeks counsel from Gilgamesh, who advises him to tempt the man of nature with a seductive harlot or temple prostitute. The hunter takes the woman to the watering place, where she exposes her breasts and "lays bare her ripeness." After Enkidu has mated with the temptress for six days and seven nights, the wild beasts of the steppe draw away from him. But while Enkidu's physical strength and speed—that is, his trickster qualities—are weakened by his encounter with human sexuality, "he now had wisdom, broader understanding," and the harlot tells him, in words anticipating the biblical serpent's, "Thou art wise, Enkidu, art become like a god!" Clothing him with half of her

14

garment, she leads him to Uruk, where, following a giant contest with Gilgamesh at the gates of the city, the heroes become blood brothers and embark on their epic adventures.

Initially it is Enkidu who, in his newfound understanding, fears death. Gilgamesh reassures him:

> "Who, my friend can scale heaven?
> Only the gods live forever under the sun.
> As for mankind, numbered are their days;
> Whatever they achieve is but the wind!
> Even here thou art afraid of death."

They undertake a successful expedition against the monster Huwawa in the hope of achieving at least the immortality of fame. However, when they slay the destructive Bull of Heaven, the gods ordain that Enkidu must die. After he has watched his friend waste away, Gilgamesh, now himself overcome by the fear of death, laments:

> "When I die, shall I not be like Enkidu?
> Woe has entered my belly.
> Fearing death, I roam over the steppe."

His wanderings bring him to Utnapishtim (the hero of the Mesopotamian flood myth), who reveals to Gilgamesh a secret of the gods concerning a magical thorned plant that bestows renewed youth (and hence, implicitly, immortality). Gilgamesh obtains the plant, which grows at the bottom of the sea, and intends to rejuvenate himself by eating it. But when he stops to bathe in a cool well, a serpent smells the plant's fragrance and carries it away. (The magic of the plant accounts etiologically for the serpent's subsequent ability to shed its skin and renew its own youth.) Gilgamesh weeps for his wasted labor, and a few lines later the epic breaks off.

Even this brief sketch of the principal episodes makes it evident that the epic contains virtually all the elements of the biblical account of the Creation, Temptation, and Fall although the roles are divided between two heroes, not concentrated in one.[12] Like Adam, Enkidu is created by a deity from the clay of the earth and spends his early days in naked innocence among the beasts of the field. Then, succumbing to a woman's temptation, he loses his innocence and acquires godlike knowledge. The motifs of a plant of life and the serpent that tricks Adam and Eve out of immortality occur after Enkidu's death in connection with Gilgamesh, who obtains the plant but is prevented from eating of it.

Several of these common Mesopotamian elements occur also in the later (fourteenth-century B.C.E.) Akkadian tale of Adapa, who is created by the culture-god Ea as "the *model* of men," and to whom is given wisdom but not eternal life.[13] When Adapa offends the supreme deity Anu and is summoned to heaven, Ea advises him not to eat or drink what will be offered to him, saying that it will be the bread of death and the water of death. But when Adapa refuses Anu's offerings, the gods laugh at him and return him to earth and mortality: for what he refused was in fact the bread and water of life.

Clearly, the Hebrew storyteller who wrote the second narrative was drawing on a common pool of ancient Near Eastern folkloric elements, which he combined in a new configuration but with profound psychological insight and with a wholly original emphasis. Man is still created from clay by a god and then lives, naked and innocent, among the beasts of the field. Tempted by a woman, he loses his innocence and acquires wisdom along with clothing. But at this point the emphasis is shifted. Enkidu is seduced solely by sexual desire; and there is no hint in the Akkadian epic that this trickster, though rejected by the animals, is scorned by the gods. Indeed, the parallel tale of Adapa suggests that wisdom is a power granted freely by the gods and not begrudged mankind. To be sure, both Gilgamesh and Adapa are cheated of immortality. But in the case of Gilgamesh it is the random gourmandise of the serpent that deprives him of the plant of eternal youth. And Adapa, despite

16

the wisdom bestowed upon him by Ea, is still offered by Anu the bread and water of life, which he loses because of the jealousy of a lesser deity.

THE PARADOX OF KNOWLEDGE IN SOLOMON'S JERUSALEM

The essential and characteristic difference between the biblical tale of the Fall and the Mesopotamian accounts is, simply, that Adam-Eve sins by eating from the Tree of Knowledge. From Paul (Rom. 5.19) by way of Dante (*Paradiso* 26.115–17) to Milton, to be sure, Christian theology has emphasized the fact of "Man's first disobedience": it was the act of disobedience that condemned Adam-Man; the means of that act, the tree, is of lesser importance. As Paul Ricoeur has summarized, "In the new and peculiarly Hebraic myth, the forbidden fruit stands for prohibition in general; compared to murder, eating forbidden fruit is a peccadillo" (248). The transformation of the original plant of youth into a forbidden Tree of Knowledge has major structural implications as well.

Motivation is, of course, important. In the biblical account the serpent is no longer the hungry creature of folklore, who achieves immortality by stealing the fruit of life, and not yet the evil Satan of later Christian interpretations. In a profound psychological sense it embodies a projection of Eve's very human curiosity and desire. Structurally, at the same time, it assumes the role of trickster that was originally held by Enkidu, but that can no longer be occupied by Adam in his new function as culture-hero and primogenitor of the human race.

As a result of its part in the sinful act the tree itself acquired a share in the guilt. (According to a widespread medieval legend reported in such sources as the *Legenda Aurea* of Jacobus de Voragine, it was the wood of that same tree, later transplanted to Adam's grave, on which Jesus was subsequently crucified.)[14]

17

Yet if Adam had chosen correctly, it is implied, he might with impunity have achieved immortality by eating instead from the Tree of Life. (As Frazer has demonstrated, trees functioned widely in folklore as embodiments of the life-spirit.)[15] It is the combination of knowledge and eternity that God begrudges him, unlike the Akkadian Anu, who offers Adapa the bread of life despite the wisdom he has already received. Adam-Eve's sin, in short, is the desire for knowledge.

This poses an interesting dilemma. Why should the people who subsequently prided themselves for centuries on being the People of the Book have placed at the beginning of history a myth suggesting that the fall of humankind was due to the desire for knowledge? Despite the widespread presence of trees in the other Near Eastern gardens of delight—no wonder, after all, in light of the regional topography with its wildernesses and oases—and despite the frequent occurrence of trees or plants of life, as in the Gilgamesh epic, only Hebrew mythology has a Tree of Knowledge.[16] (It is worth stressing at this point that the qualifying phrase "of Good and Evil," far from restricting the knowledge communicated by the tree to matters of morality and conscience, is intended to suggest the entire extent of human knowledge, of consciousness generally. The opposing terms simply convey the idea of everything between those two extremes.[17] The exegetical history of the phrase over the past century reveals that every generation has interpreted it in a manner appropriate to the times: for example, the scientific reading of positivism, the ethical reading of the 1920s, the sexual reading of the 1960s and 1970s.)

Why should it have been a tree of *knowledge* through which sin was introduced into the world? The question becomes all the more urgent in light of the assumption that the Israelite narrator changed it from what, according to Adapa and other tales, was originally probably a tree of *death*.[18] The authorship and dating of the second narrative remain problematic. (It is called the second narrative because a later postexilic scribe known as P, presumably feeling that the primeval account did

18

not do full justice to the dignity of the Creation, added the now familiar chronology of the first chapter of Genesis.) Known as the "J Source" and attributed to a scribe known as "the Yahwist" (for his use of the tetragrammaton YHWH to designate God), the document has been variously dated, and current opinion suggests that the major units of the source—primeval history, patriarchs, exodus, wilderness, conquest of Canaan—may in fact have been compiled at different periods during the four hundred years extending from Solomon through the Babylonian Exile.[19] It is generally agreed, however, that the section of interest here—the "prologue" or primeval history of pre-Israelite mankind covered in Genesis 2–11—whether compiled by a "school" or written by a single narrator, was composed during the so-called Solomonic enlightenment of the mid–tenth century.[20] And internal textual evidence suggests certain conclusions that bear out such a dating.

Generally speaking, myths of a past Golden Age and of man's fall from that happy state are produced by cultures that have reached a certain level of sophistication, that are interested in origins and look back with a degree of nostalgia at an imagined simpler, happier existence. (The focus on origins is implicit in the now traditional name "Genesis," which was assigned to that book by the translators of the Septuagint; the Hebrew Bible knows it simply as "Bereshith" ["In the beginning"], the first of the five books of Moses.) If the Yahwist lived in Solomon's glittering Jerusalem, then he was acquainted with a society that had advanced well past the culture of simple shepherds and peasants that characterized the era of the patriarchs, the settlement of Canaan, and the judges.

Prior to the political consolidation achieved by David and Solomon the twelve tribes were still essentially seminomadic with a social organization dominated by clanlike families. It was the sense of crisis produced among the tribes by the Philistines in the eleventh century—the defeat of the Israelites, the destruction of Shiloh, and the capture of the Ark of the Covenant—that first produced the clamor for a monarchy embracing all twelve tribes. This impetus, in turn, enabled Saul to begin the process of unification that entailed the revival of the national religion along with the abolishment of the worship of such foreign deities as Baal and Astarte. The consolidation was completed by David (ca. 1004–965 B.C.E.), who unified the seminomadic tribes still riven by internecine warfare and moved the seat of government to Jerusalem, which was established as the administrative center of the new monarchy. When Solomon (ca. 965–928 B.C.E.) built the Temple as a home for the Ark of the Covenant, the new urban capital became, in addition, the religious center of the nation. The historical consciousness that characterizes the Yahwist and produced his interest in origins constitutes a natural corollary to the process of consolidation.[21]

Yet even during this process of consolidation signs of stress were evident, as signaled by the seductions, rapes, treachery, political assassinations, fratricides, and other crimes reported in Samuel 2, along with Solomon's own flagrant apostasies. During Solomon's reign the people chafed under the heavy taxes imposed by a burgeoning bureaucratic administration to support the resplendent court life and, in particular, under the corvée that required citizens to contribute free labor to the elaborate public projects. Following the accession of Solomon's son Rehoboam the resistance to further economic burdens resulted in the schism of the monarchy into the two kingdoms of Israel and Judah.

Living with such stresses as these and witnessing the commercial activity of the monarchy, the moral decay of the kings, the lavish imports of silver and cedar, the flourishing trade in horses, the fleets of ships sailing to Mediterranean ports—achievements so spectacular, indeed, that Solomon was pursued through antiquity and the Middle Ages by a reputation for sorcery[22]—the writer of the primeval history had ample reason to feel that his society, for all its political power and urban sophistication, represented a decline away from what must have been a simpler, better life in Israel's nomadic and peasant past. Indeed, his text betrays more than a trace of the alienated intellectual familiar in modern times from Rousseau to communitarian thinkers of the present. In his self-conscious ruminations he turned naturally to originary thoughts, to meditations on the meaning of the past. If Max Weber was correct in his belief that reason and understanding tend to disenchant the world, perhaps the use of myth to explain the origin of things represents an attempt to "reenchant" a world grown rational and colorless—to restore myth to a world newly conscious of history. (As Nietzsche reminds us, in *The Birth of Tragedy* [1:23], myth tends to disappear when history emerges.)

myth and history

The Yahwist's text suggests that he wonders specifically what happened to account for the fact that men must work so hard to eke out a living from an intransigent soil, that women are condemned to subservience and to the pains of childbearing, that humankind is ashamed of its nakedness, that a hostility exists between humankind and the animal world, with whose skins we conceal our nakedness, and that the serpent must crawl on the ground. Above all, why are men and women condemned to death, not blessed with immortality?[23] (His etiological curiosity is suggested by such phrases as "therefore" or "that is why," which punctuate the Yahwist's narrative at certain points.) Life in Solomon's Jerusalem was more glorious than anything the Jewish people had experienced. Yet at what cost had that glory been achieved? Sigmund Freud points out in *Civilization and Its Discontents* (1930) that, when God caused misfortune after misfortune to strike the people that considered themselves his favorite child, they never gave up the belief in their special relationship, nor did they question his power or righteousness. "Instead, they produced the prophets, who held up their sinfulness before them; and out of their sense of guilt they created the over-strict commandments of their priestly religion"(21:127). But they also produced thinkers like the Yahwist, who looked back in time to seek the causes of that guilt.

21

Freud famously argues that "the price we pay for our advance in civilization is a loss of happiness through the heightening of the sense of guilt" (21:134). Yet what else is civilization but knowledge? It was political knowledge that unified the twelve tribes, engineering knowledge that made possible the building of the Temple, economic knowledge that produced the conspicuous consumption in Jerusalem, military knowledge that defeated the Philistines. Paradoxically, it is knowledge itself that induces the tendency to thought and reflection generating the etiological and originary speculations of the Yahwist. Hence it is no accident that the tree whose fruit precipitates the Fall is specifically a tree of knowledge—not anything as simple as the sexual knowledge that estranges the trickster Enkidu from the animals, but the more profound knowledge of the world that puts men and women on the same level as the gods, *scientes bonum et malum*, and thereby alienates them as individual human beings from the general creation to which they originally belonged.[24] The Yahwist is obsessed with the sin of knowledge.[25] He is, after all, also the author of the episode recounting the building of the Tower of Babel, another incident in which humankind challenges the authority of an irascible God who carefully guards his privileges. The Lord realizes that the ambitious construction project "is only the beginning of what they will do; and nothing that they propose to do will now be impossible for them" (Gen. 11.6). That the whole enterprise is attributable to intelligence and knowledge is suggested by the circumstance that it is their unified language that makes everything possible. Rashi, in his commentary on the passage, identifies the builders of the tower simply as "the sons of Adam, the first man." It is likewise consistent with the understanding of early Christianity that the builders, translated as "the sons of men" in the Revised Standard Edition, are called "sons of Adam" (*filii Adam*) in the Latin Vulgate. Saint Augustine, in his *Confessions* and elsewhere, routinely uses the expression *filii Adam* to designate man in his state of sinfulness. For it was precisely in their acquisition and application of knowledge and human reason that they revealed themselves as the descendants of that first sinner.

The narrator of the primeval history, living in the sophisticated intellectual climate of Solomon's Jerusalem and reflecting historically on origins, etiologically on the state of his present culture, and psychologically on the sources of modern malaise, appropriated motifs from the common pool of Near Eastern folktales concerning Creation and Fall and collated them in such a manner, most conspicuously through Adam's name, as to make universal what had been local legends and to lend a new dimension of moral meaning to primitive myths that had held little but entertainment value for nomadic desert peoples[26]—in sum, to transform the trickster Enkidu into the culture-hero Adam (and simultaneously to give the serpent a new importance by projecting upon it the role of trickster). We should always remind ourselves that the primeval history deals with humanity as a whole; the specific history of the Israelites begins only in Genesis 12 with the legend of Abraham. It is no longer fate, accident, or violation of a meaningless taboo that causes the fall of the entire human race from its state of primal bliss, but specifically the acquisition of knowledge that alienates humankind from its place in a unified creation, separating subject from object, man from nature. Here, for the first time in human consciousness, knowledge is sin.

The myth has been read in this manner at least since the Enlightenment. In his "Conjectures on the Beginning of Human History" (*Mutmaßlicher Anfang der Menschengeschichte*, 1786), which is essentially a reading of Genesis 2–3, Immanuel Kant argued that "man's emergence from that paradise which reason represents to him as the first abode of his species was nothing other than his transition from a rude and purely animal existence to a state of humanity, from the leading-strings of instinct to the guidance of reason—in a word, from the guardianship of nature to the state of freedom."[27] Half a century later, in his world-weary essay entitled "Experience," Emerson defined the Fall of Man simply as the discovery that we exist.

23

"Once we lived in what we saw; now, the rapaciousness of this new power [consciousness] engages us." And Arnold Toynbee, searching for the factor that has occasionally shaken mankind out of "the integration of custom" into "the differentiation of civilization," suggests that the Fall "symbolizes the acceptance of a challenge to abandon this achieved integration and to venture upon a fresh differentiation out of which a fresh integration may—or may not—arise" (65–67).

CHAPTER TWO

Prometheus: The Birth of Civilization

NIETZSCHE believed that the myth of Prometheus displays
the same characteristic significance for what he labeled "Aryan"
culture as does the myth of the Fall for "Semitic" culture, and
that "there exists between the two myths a degree of relationship like that between brother and sister" (1:58). In the seminal
chapter 9 of *The Birth of Tragedy* he goes on to explain that in
both myths humanity achieves its loftiest goal only through a
sacrilegious act and must bear the consequences of suffering
and misery which the offended deities visit upon the human
race. But he points out what he regards as an essential difference between the twin myths. The dignity that the Greeks attribute to Prometheus's theft of fire contrasts vividly with the Semitic myth of the Fall, in which idle curiosity, deceitfulness, sed-
uctibility, lasciviousness—in short, a series of what Nietzsche
terms essentially female emotions—are regarded as the source
of evil. In sum, the Aryans understood sacrilege as male, while
the Semites considered sin as female. We need not accept
Nietzsche's racial and gendered understanding of the two myths
in order to appreciate his analysis of the fundamental similarity
between the stories of Adam and Prometheus. The two, as we
shall see, occupy analogous positions in the ethical and historical
consciousness of the cultures that brought them forth.

HESIOD'S TRICKSTER

It is paradoxical that the myths which have dominated Western
thought for so many centuries—right down, as we noted earlier,
to our own decade—should have had such inconsequential beginnings. According to common handbook knowledge, the culture-hero who brought to humankind the tools of civilization

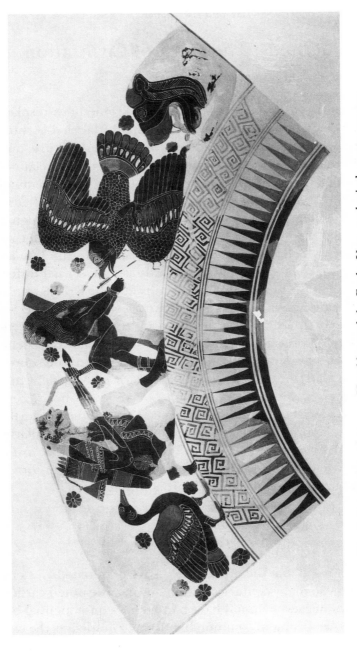

Fig. 3. Prometheus between Herakles and the Eagle. Vase, early sixth century B.C.E.
Courtesy of the National Archaeological Museum of Athens.

began his career as a local fire-demon whose sparse cults occupied a peripheral place in archaic and classical Greece.[1] In Lucian's satirical dialogue *Prometheus on Caucasus* (ca. 170 C.E.) Prometheus complains to Hermes and Hephaestus, as they busily nail him to his crag, that temples of Zeus, Apollo, Hera, and the other gods are everywhere to be seen, but "who ever saw a temple of Prometheus?" In Athens, to be sure, he was the patron deity of potters, whose craft involves fire; he had an altar in the Academy along with Hephaestus, an originally Near Eastern deity who eventually displaced Prometheus as fire-god, and Athena, eponymous patroness of the arts and crafts. Like them, he was honored with a festival, the Prometheia, which featured a torch-race in which teams of runners carried sacred fire from his altar in the Academy (outside the city walls) to the potters' quarter within the city—a ritual of annual purification and renewal of the fire (which was believed to become sullied by use). Outside Athens, however, Prometheus seems to have played no significant role in the religious life of Greek antiquity. While Homer probably was acquainted with the story—he refers to Prometheus's father Iapetus along with the other Titans—he never mentions the Fire-Bringer himself.[2]

Prometheus's initially lowly status in the hierarchy of gods is evident when we first encounter him in the late eighth century, where in Hesiod's *Theogony* and *Works and Days* he is little more than a trickster, much like the tricksters in scores of myths around the world—for instance, the Amerindian Coyote or the Polynesian Maui—who steal fire for humankind.[3] Hesiod, a near contemporary of Homer, had interests quite different from the more heroic ones of the bard of the *Iliad* and the *Odyssey*. If we can credit his account in *Works and Days*, he was a landowner in Boeotia, whither his father had immigrated from Aeolia. Not the exploits of kings and noblemen concerned his imagination, but the religious traditions of his native province and the homely virtues of justice and hard work required of the farmers and shepherds on the slopes of Mount Helicon. Above all—and this amounts to an obsession on the part of Hesiod,

27

who witnessed hunger, oppression, and social turmoil at first hand in his native Boeotia[4]—he wondered why men must live lives of suffering and toil, illness and injustice. This is where Prometheus enters the picture, for in both works the evils that humankind must endure are attributed directly to him.

Hesiod's *Theogony* portrays the creation of the world, the birth of the gods, and the succession of heavenly dynasties with an emphasis on the orderly evolution from chaos to law, not on the adventures of the gods.[5] Prometheus's name first occurs in a routine genealogical listing. A member of the second generation following the initial coupling of Gaia (earth) and Ouranos (heaven), Prometheus is one of the four sons of the Titan Iapetus and Klymene. Zeus for unspecified reasons condemns each of the sons to various punishments: prideful Menoitos is cast into Erebos; stout Atlas is sent to the earth's end to support the sky on his shoulders; Epimetheus is so foolish that it is apparently punishment enough for him to be left among the mortals; and Prometheus is shackled to a pillar where daily an eagle comes to devour his liver, until at last Herakles shall kill the bird and deliver Prometheus from his torments. At this point Hesiod interrupts his genealogical account with some eighty lines of narrative to explain why Prometheus was singled out for this punishment.

Once when the gods and mortal men were meeting at Mekone—it is not clear whether they were gathered to mark the permanent separation of men from gods or to define the conditions of their continued coexistence—Prometheus sought to trick Zeus. As he carved up the ox for a feast, he concealed the choicest pieces beneath a hide covered with the ox's gut; then he decorated the bones with tempting white fat and offered the two portions for Zeus's choice. Although Zeus was aware of Prometheus's plan, he wittingly selected the bones covered with fat and then vented his anger at Prometheus. It was apparently Hesiod's intent to justify etiologically the custom of burning bones in sacrifice to the gods: hence the necessity of Zeus's choice of the less appetizing portion. At the same time, Zeus's wrath, even though with his all-encompassing intelligence he is aware of Prometheus's plan from the outset, can be explained by his outrage at Prometheus's "deceitful skills" (*doliês technês*, line 560), which for Hesiod, as we shall see, mark the beginning of a human history of moral deterioration. Zeus decides to punish Prometheus—not directly but by depriving his beloved mortals of the fire required for civilized life on earth. (Specifically, he withholds from hardwood trees, like the ash, the fire that could be extracted from them by drilling.)

At this point, however, Prometheus deceives him a second time by stealing fire (Hesiod does not tell us from whom) in a fennel stalk and presenting it to mankind. The furious Zeus now vents his fury on Prometheus as well as his human beings. It is not clear why Zeus transfers his anger from Prometheus to the mortals—perhaps simply because they are guilty by association (with Prometheus and Zeus's enemies, the Titans) or to define the difference between men and gods. (The legend that Prometheus himself created humankind from clay is much later in origin.) In any case, to punish mankind he sends among them the first (still unnamed) woman, created from clay by Hephaestus and glamorously outfitted by Athena. There is no need to discuss Hesiod's notorious misogyny: suffice it to say that he regards women, a "beautiful evil" (*kalon kakon*, line 585), as a burden on mankind. They are eager to share men's wealth but want no part of their hardships; they nag and plague their husbands with their malice—a proper punishment, in Hesiod's mind, for the stolen fire. Prometheus, in turn, for his cunning audacity is chained to a pillar as a feast for a liver-devouring eagle, while Hesiod returns to his main story: the Titanomachy and the further genealogies of the gods.

This topic—the hardships of human existence precipitated by Prometheus—continued to obsess Hesiod, who returned to it in *Works and Days*, albeit from a wholly different standpoint. In the *Theogony* Prometheus appears midway in the divine genealogy as a god cast out for reasons described in lavish detail; in the human context of *Works and Days*, in contrast, he stands at the beginning of human history as the source of man's grief and misery.[6] The earlier work culminates with the institution of law and justice among men; the later one takes a violation of law and justice as its occasion. The work, a handbook of moral homilies and practical advice for farmers, is written in the form of a letter to Hesiod's brother Perses, who apparently sought by bribing public officials to cheat Hesiod out of his fair share of their patrimony. This incident enables Hesiod to introduce at the outset his recurrent theme of equity and hard work—a theme that, in turn, generates the statement that in former times a good day's work produced enough to sustain a man for an entire year. As a result of Prometheus's iniquity, however, Zeus deprived men of fire and devised the troubles that have beset them ever since.

> "Son of Iapetos, there is none craftier than you,
> and you rejoice at tricking my wits and stealing the fire
> which will be a curse to you and to the generations that follow.
> The price for the stolen fire will be a gift of evil
> to charm the hearts of all men as they hug their own doom."
>
> (Lines 55–59)

He then recounts the story, this time in greater detail, of Pandora and her vessel of grief, sent by the gods to bring disease to men during the day and pain in the stillness of night.

To drive home his point, Hesiod now relates the traditional myth of the four ages of mortals—gold, silver, bronze, and iron—into which he inserts a fifth in order to account for the heroic age of the demigods who sailed to Troy. The earlier ages lived with hearts unburdened by care. Hesiod concludes his account with the wish that he had not been born into the fifth (iron) age, when men have no rest from toil and care. Nor has the worst yet come: in the future, family virtue will deteriorate; public standards of law and morality will be violated; envy will corrode all satisfaction. This miserable state of affairs is attributed to Prometheus's trickery and disrespect for the gods, with whom hitherto mankind had lived in peace and harmony. If the present state of humanity reflects a decline in moral values, leading to the inheritance feud in Hesiod's own life, then the beginning of the process of moral decay goes back to Prometheus and his deceitful ways.

> But Zeus was angered in his heart and hid the means to life
> because Prometheus with his crooked schemes had cheated him.
>
> (Lines 48–49)

For Hesiod, then, Prometheus is still far from being the noble culture-hero and is no longer, or not yet again, the "patron saint of the proletariat."[7] Instead, he is the amoral trickster whose deceitful ways set mankind on the slippery slope of moral degeneration, and who is responsible for all the suffering and worry with which humankind is burdened. (Hesiod is centuries removed from Lucian, whose Prometheus excuses himself by arguing that his offense was, after all, nothing but a joke among friends.) Writing some two centuries after the Yahwist, Hesiod shares a view of society and human history that is remarkably like the Genesis account of the Fall.[8] In both cases man originally inhabited a paradise or golden age in which nothing was prohibited except the means of progress (knowledge and fire, respectively); as a direct consequence of his theft of the forbidden object, the trickster (the serpent or Prometheus) is punished (by being condemned to crawl in the dust and to be trodden upon by humankind or by being shackled to a pillar and tormented by an eagle) while man is expelled from his initial beatific state into a world of harsh reality, which he shares with a woman who is a living symbol of his guilt: because she is either responsible for his sin or sent in retribution for his violation. For Hesiod as well as the Yahwist, the "progress" of mankind has been accompanied by a pronounced increase in hardship and a loss of moral value. Both are interested in cosmogony, but Hesiod's polytheism has more in common with other legends from India to Iceland.[9]

31

It is difficult to agree with those interpreters who see in Hesiod's Prometheus an analogy to Christ.[10] In eighth-century Boeotia, at least, and in his first literary metamorphosis beyond a local fire-demon, Prometheus is anything but a savior-figure. His crime and punishment suggest the wish-dream of Hesiod for the scheming brother who was cheating him out of his fair portion. His name suggests crimes of premeditation more than prudent forethought.[11] For Hesiod, as we see from the reverent invocation at the beginning of *Works and Days*, Zeus is a benevolent deity of justice, not a capricious tyrant from whom a heroic Prometheus must save mankind. Like the God of Genesis, he can be driven to sudden wrath by devious behavior, but he is also capable of forgiveness, both of Prometheus and of humankind. (He permits Herakles to kill the tormenting eagle, and he sends justice into a desolate world.) Hesiod is no more a political revolutionary than is the Yahwist. In Hesiod's Boeotia as in the Yahwist's Jerusalem, knowledge (fire) is still a problematic commodity, whose sinful acquisition has brought more misery than happiness into the world. It is symptomatic that, more often than not, this unpromising Prometheus was reduced to a figure of fun in the comedies of Aristophanes (*The Birds*) as well as in Lucian's satires.[12] For a different view we must wait more than two centuries until Greek religious beliefs began to give way to the sophisticated rationalism of fifth-century Athens.

AESCHYLUS'S CULTURE-HERO

Between Hesiod and *Prometheus Bound,* and despite the popularity in sixth-century vase art of representations of his torment by the eagle, Prometheus leaves virtually no mark in extant Greek literature, and on the two occasions when he does show up it is in comic roles.[13] (It has been plausibly suggested that this legend of the potter's patron would have had little appeal for the ruling aristocracy of the sixth century.)[14] Consequently we are not prepared for the drastic change in his persona that we encounter in *Prometheus Bound*. The play is problematic for at least three reasons. First, although it has been attributed to Aeschylus since at least the third century B.C.E., some scholars have questioned whether a play so critical of the gods was written by Aeschylus at all.[15] Second, if it does belong among the some ninety plays attributed to Aeschylus, it is uncertain—again, for religious and stylistic reasons—whether it is early or late. Finally, there is strong disagreement about the relationship of this play to two other Promethean works also ascribed to Aeschylus in antiquity and of which fragments have come down to us: *Prometheus Unbound* (*Prometheus Lyomenos*) and *Prometheus the Fire-Bringer* (*Prometheus Pyrphoros*). While most scholars believe that the works constituted a trilogy, the *Prometheia*, of which the extant *Prometheus Bound* was the first play and *The Fire-Bringer* the last,[16] several recent critics have argued for the sequence *Fire-Bringer, Bound*, and *Unbound*.[17] (So few fragments remain of *The Fire-Bringer* that it cannot be determined whether it was supposed to tell the story of Prometheus's initial theft of fire, or whether it was intended to depict his eventual admission as a local patron deity to the Academy in Athens.) I write with the assumption that the play was written by Aeschylus toward the end of his life, and that it was the second play in a trilogy: that the first play dealt with the theft of fire for which Prometheus is punished by Zeus, and that the third dealt with his liberation by Herakles and his reconciliation with Zeus.

The play begins as Zeus's henchmen, Power and Violence, drag Prometheus to the summit of a ravine in remote Scythia, where, for the crime of bringing fire to mankind, he is bound to a rock with unremovable chains by his reluctant kinsman, Hephaestus. After their departure and following a monologue in which Prometheus laments his fate, he is visited by the daughters of Oceanus, who have been drawn to the scene by the clamor of Hephaestus's hammering. In this first episode Prometheus tells the chorus of Oceanides how he helped Zeus to seize power from his father, Kronos, and rescued the human race, which Zeus was intent on destroying. Then Oceanus himself appears, urging Prometheus to prudence (actually: subservience) and promising to speak on his behalf to Zeus. But when Prometheus warns him that his efforts might incur the wrath of Zeus, Oceanus takes his own advice and prudently departs. Following the chorus's ode, and without the appearance of another character, Prometheus delivers a long speech to the chorus (the so-called Culture Speech) in which he recounts the various boons that he brought to suffering humanity and hints at a secret that will one day obtain his release. The next choral ode is followed by the unannounced arrival of the cow-headed Io. She relates in a long monody how she was lured from her father's home and into the arms of Zeus by dreams and oracles; how she was then transformed into a heifer by the jealous Hera and guarded by hundred-eyed Argus; how finally she was driven by a tormenting gadfly from her Peloponnesian home and across Greece to this remote corner of the world. At her request, Prometheus foretells the lengthy wanderings that will carry her across Europe and Asia to Egypt, where one day she shall bear Zeus a child, from whose lineage shall finally emerge the great hero, Herakles, whose arrow will liberate Prometheus from the eagle that torments him.

Following Io's departure and the chorus's next song, Prometheus confides to them that he alone knows the secret that can save Zeus from destruction: the name of the woman with whom Zeus's union would produce a son mighty enough to cast him from his throne. At that point Zeus's messenger, Hermes, arrives to demand that information, threatening Prometheus that otherwise he will be cast for aeons into the void and then resurrected again to have his liver consumed daily by a voracious eagle. But Prometheus, knowing that his life depends on his keeping the knowledge to himself, refuses defiantly to reveal his secret. As the play ends, a storm of thunder and lightning sunders the rock to which Prometheus is bound and dashes him into the chasm. In *Prometheus Unbound,* presumably, Prometheus, having been brought back up from the underworld, is liberated by Herakles from the eagle that has been gnawing on his liver, and then reconciled with Zeus, to whom in return for his release he finally reveals the name of the fateful mistress: Thetis (who goes on to marry Peleus and to bear the mightiest mortal warrior, Achilles).

Such a recapitulation, of course, does no justice to the grandeur of this play. Because of the immobility of its principal character—the shackled Prometheus is presumably unable even to gesture!—it is reduced even more than is normally the case in Greek tragedy to the sheer power of language. The effect of the language is heightened, moreover, by the remoteness of the stark setting and the temporal displacement: it takes place close to the beginning of human history. The audience is more than usually dependent on language for a sense of time and place.[18] We feel the effect at the beginning, where Prometheus's silence is more eloquent than any words. (This initial silence anticipates his subsequent refusal to name the threat to Zeus's hegemony.)[19] In the opening lines, as Prometheus is dragged through the pathless wilderness to the ends of the earth, Power does not even mention his name, referring to him only in the third person as "this villain." As Hephaestus goes about his grim task, he begins to address Prometheus in the second person, still without naming him directly, although he identifies him as the son of Themis. (It is not until line 66 that his name is first mentioned.) For eighty-seven lines the tension mounts almost unbearably until finally, after the departure of his tormentors, Prometheus speaks, imploring the forces of nature—air, water, earth, and sun—to witness the evils he must endure.

Another brilliant example of Aeschylus's language and stagecraft is evident in the introduction of Io as the counterpart to Prometheus. Whereas Prometheus is immobile, bound as he is to his rock, Io is the epitome of hectic, frenzied motion, driven almost to madness by the stings of her gadfly. When she first arrives, interrupting the chorus's ode, she speaks with a lyric intensity (lines 561 ff.) that only gradually resolves itself into the calmer iambic trimeter of normal dramatic dialogue. And by the time she rushes out again (lines 877–86) her language has collapsed once more into frenetic rhythms that reflect the symptoms of her virtually epileptic condition: spasms, palpitations, rolling eyes, incoherent speech.[20] As we shall see, the language also incorporates such central themes as the political situation of *new* gods, the injustice of Prometheus's treatment, and the cultural symbolism of fire.

Even this brief recapitulation reveals that Aeschylus's treatment lacks two of the major plot elements of Hesiod's accounts. In the *Theogony*, over half of the story (67 of 109 lines) is devoted to Prometheus's deception of Zeus at the feast at Mekone and to the aftermath involving Pandora; the theft of fire takes up only nine lines. *Prometheus Bound*, in contrast, contains no allusion to the feast at Mekone; Prometheus's only guilt is the gift of fire to humankind. Nor does Aeschylus refer to Pandora or Epimetheus; Prometheus alone must pay the penalty for his crime. These plot changes alert us to major shifts in thematic emphasis.

Most conspicuously, with the disappearance of the plot elements mentioned above, our attention is focused wholly on Prometheus, who is no longer simply a trickster; his defiance of Zeus bestows upon him a nobility of character wholly lacking in Hesiod. Various factors contribute to this shift. First, Zeus is repeatedly identified as a *new* god—one who, having seized power violently and not by any rights of hereditary kingship, governs as a "tyrant" (line 10). Indeed, as we learn from Prometheus himself, he helped Zeus and the "new gods" (line 439) in the conspiracy to overthrow Kronos and cast him down into Tartarus. Unlike Hesiod's wise and benign Zeus, this Zeus is in no way superior to Prometheus in intelligence or morals. Those whose rule is new govern harshly, as Hephaestus reminds Prometheus (line 35). The chorus knows that Zeus is ruling "lawlessly" with "new" (that is, nontraditional) laws. (The terms characterizing his rule anticipate those with which Sophocles will later characterize Creon's rule in *Antigone*.) The fact that Zeus is a "new" ruler—a fact reiterated leitmotivically (e.g., lines 995 and 960) throughout—serves to delegitimize his behavior, to emphasize its unjust violence, and to enhance Prometheus's own dignity. As he points out, it is not shameful to suffer ill at the hands of one's enemies (lines 1041–42).

Second, Prometheus is motivated not by the trickster's simple delight in deceiving Zeus but by a genuine love of humankind—by what is twice (lines 11 and 28) called his "philanthropic turn." In his first monologue Prometheus sees himself being punished for his "excessive love of humankind" (line 123). Immediately after seizing power and without any apparent motivation, as Prometheus informs the chorus, Zeus intended to annihilate the existing race of mortals and create a wholly new one in its place (lines 232–33), and only Prometheus among the gods sought to save them. For this he now suffers his punishment. To be sure, Prometheus has flaws of his own, notably his hubris: he is repeatedly characterized as being just as intractable and outspoken as Zeus. (The vocable *authadia*, "willful stubbornness," recurs almost leitmotivically.) Yet the nobility of his behavior stands in sharp contrast to the trickery of Hesiod's fire-god.

As far as fire is concerned, it is no longer simply a primitive tool for cooking but, rather, symbolic of the general enlightenment that Prometheus has bestowed upon humankind. (For this reason Bachelard coined the phrase "Prometheus Complex" to designate the human desire to know more than our fathers and our teachers.) To be sure, it is specifically for the theft of fire that Prometheus is being punished. At the outset Power identifies him (lines 7–8) as the one who stole "the flame of all-working fire" and gave it to mortals. He is perplexed because Hephaestus is not equally angered at the deity who made free with his particular prerogative, fire (line 38). Before Prometheus is interrupted by the arrival of Oceanus, he boasts to the chorus of his gifts to humankind: he caused them to stop thinking about death by instilling in them blind hope (lines 248–50); and above all else he gave them fire, by means of which they would learn many arts and crafts (lines 252–54). Later Prometheus introduces himself to Io as "the giver of fire to mortals" (line 612). But the references to fire and hope, the two remnants from Hesiod's account, strike us almost as incidental.[21] In his great Culture Speech (lines 436–506), Prometheus begins by pointing out that humankind was still childlike (literally *nê-pios* or "incapable of speech") until he rendered it "mindful" (*ennoos* or "possessing *noûs*"). "Seeing, they saw not, and hearing they understood not." Prometheus taught them the crafts of building and carpentry, the science of astronomy, the skills of counting and writing, the knowledge of animal husbandry and sailing and mining, the gift of healing and soothsaying and sacrifice. In sum: "all the arts and crafts [*technai*] came to men from Prometheus." This thematic emphasis is borne out by the language of the play, throughout which words referring to teaching and learning (*[ek]manthanô, epistomai, [ek]didaskô, deiknumi, exeuriskô,* and others) are conspicuously present. What in Hesiod was merely the wit or cleverness of a trickster has ripened into true knowledge and wisdom.

This speech clearly presents a different view of human history from that of Hesiod. Rather than a humankind declining from a glorious golden age to the present deplorable iron age, Aeschylus sees humanity progressing by means of knowledge—the crafts, arts, and sciences—from blindness and ignorance to its present loftiness. It has even been suggested that Aeschylus's view of human progress is close to the position of modern dialectical materialism.[22] But that is probably too simple a reading for so subtle a dramatist and thinker as Aeschylus, a thinker keenly aware of the problematic conflict in his society between the old and the new. Accordingly, it is perhaps not unreasonable to sense in the earlier reference to "blind hopes" (line 250) that Prometheus presented to humankind, along with the skills derived from fire, an expression of Aeschylus's "skeptical irony" with regard to the promises of technology.[23] Hans-Georg Gadamer is probably correct in his view that cultural consciousness is inevitably accompanied by cultural criticism.[24] For that reason, Plato in his retelling of the myth in *Protagoras* (320d–322d) reports that men, with the technical skills given to them by Prometheus, were able to improve their lot; but without political wisdom they continued to injure one another. "Zeus therefore, fearing the total destruction of our race, sent Hermes to impart to men the qualities of respect for others and a sense of justice, so as to bring order into our cities and create a bond of friendship and union."

In the absence of Pandora and her jar of troubles, humankind itself has not suffered as a result of Prometheus's deed. If we take the chorus in its traditional role as spokesperson for the contemporary audience, then Aeschylus surely expected the citizens of his mid-fifth-century Athenian democracy to side with the culture-hero Prometheus against an upstart ruler who wanted to withhold knowledge from humankind and now condemns the culture-bringer unjustly.[25] We have already noted that the chorus speaks of the new laws through which Zeus rules unjustly (lines 150–51). And in his last words a defiant Prometheus summons the elements once more to witness what injustices (*endika*) he suffers. Here, for perhaps the first time in literature, we encounter what becomes the classic model for the conflict between the rebellious intellectual and political authority.[26]

FROM BOEOTIA TO ATHENS

What accounts for this pronounced, even fateful shift from Prometheus as a fire-demon whose trickster behavior brings misery upon humanity, and who is justly punished for his iniquities, to the culture-hero whose gift of knowledge is regarded as a boon, and whose punishment humankind regards as the injustice of a violent ruler-deity? The late-sixth-century B.C.E. Athens that

Aeschylus (ca. 525–456) knew as a young man resembled in many respects King David's Jerusalem in which the Yahwist was writing.[27] Under the half-century rule of the tyrants Peisistratus and his son Hippias (561–510) it had developed from one among many minor Aegean city-states into a cultural center supported by prospering agriculture, manufacture, and commerce. Challenged in its political and economic power only by Sparta, it was also becoming the leading center of archaic Greek culture. Hippias's brother Hipparchus, a patron of the arts, invited Anacreon and Simonides to Athens. However, the art for which it was so prominent—the temples on the Acropolis, the gleaming statues, the red-figured vase painting, the poetry contests and dramatic performances—still stood principally in the service of religion. The shrines were dedicated to Athena and other deities; Peisistratus commissioned the temple of Olympian Zeus; poets and musicians traveled to Athens in order to take part in the religious festivals; tragedy itself was a product of the Great Dionysia Festival. This combination of political power, religious authority, and artistic genius conspicuously resembled tenth-century Jerusalem.

But during the first decades of the fifth century, following the ouster of the tyrants, dramatic changes began to take place. Athens emerged from the Persian Wars (490–479) as the richest and most powerful empire of the Mediterranean world. The economic and political changes were accompanied by a constitutional democratization that had begun in 507 with the reforms of Cleisthenes. The postwar government under Pericles, Ephialtes, and their associates completed the process, dismantling the traditional powers of the Areopagus. (The violent conflict between old and new that these changes entailed is evident in *Prometheus Unbound*, as they are also most conspicuously in Aeschylus's *Eumenides*. As a member of the old aristocracy of Eleusis, Aeschylus was to a certain extent ambivalent about the reforms that, along with their improvements, also swept away many revered institutions.)

While the constitutional reforms, recorded by Aristotle in *The Constitutions of Athens*, shaped political thought in the West for the next twenty-five hundred years, the simultaneous intellectual reforms were no less epoch-making. The striking political changes awakened a new sense of history, as demonstrated by the popular success of Herodotus's account of the Persian Wars, which was then closely succeeded by the more scientific historiography of Thucydides. The consciousness of history, as we have already seen in connection with the Old Testament, is normally accompanied by an interest in origins. Meanwhile, developments in philosophical discourse marked the pronounced shift of fifth-century Athenian thought from that of Hesiod in eighth-century Boeotia and of the Yahwist before him. Perhaps the main characteristic of this thought was the turn from religion to philosophy, from divine machination to human reason. Philosophical reasoning had been emerging in the Greek cities of Asia Minor since the middle of the sixth century. It was from the Ionian city of Clazomenae that Anaxagoras (ca. 500–ca. 428), a younger contemporary of Aeschylus, came to Athens around 480 as the city's first philosopher.

What is distinctive about Anaxagoras's thought, and relevant in the present context, is his consistent effort to explain natural phenomena, and specifically cosmogony and the origins of matter and life, with no reference to the gods. According to Anaxagoras, the force that sets the elements of cosmic being into motion and that animates biological being is *noûs* or "mind."[28] "For *noûs* is the finest and purest of all things and possesses knowledge of everything and has the greatest power. And *noûs* has rule over everything that possesses soul, the greater as well as the smaller beings" (frag. 12). "Mind is eternal" (frag. 14). It was this insight that revolutionized philosophy by establishing the dualism between mind and matter that has occupied thinkers ever since. There is no direct evidence that Aeschylus was familiar with Anaxagoras and his thought.[29] But given the fact that ancient biographical references to Anaxagoras frequently

41

begin by identifying him as the thinker who put *noûs* over all being,[30] it seems unlikely that a contemporary would not have been aware of his ideas. And if we recall how Prometheus prides himself on first instilling "mind" (*ennoos*) into a humankind still existing in an animal-like condition, it is hard to believe that Aeschylus did not share the views of Anaxagoras's intellectual circle. That certainly seems to be Schelling's assumption when, in a discussion of *noûs*, he calls Prometheus "that principle of humanity which we have named mind."[31] The gifts that Prometheus bestows upon humankind and that are rehearsed in his great Culture Speech are wholly the product of "mind" (that is, fire or enlightenment), and not of the gods. To be sure, Aeschylus never denies the gods. But Prometheus is notable above all for his defiance of the "new" gods. For this reason Aeschylus and the Athenian public were able to regard Prometheus not as a mere trickster but as the bringer of culture.

If we now compare Aeschylus's Prometheus with the Yahwist's Adam, we see how far human thought has come in some five hundred years. The anxious sinner of Genesis has metamorphosed into the proud rebel of Greek tragedy. What distinguishes this "Aryan" view in contrast to the Semitic myth of the Fall, according to Nietzsche, is precisely the dignity that it ascribes to crime: "active sin" is the Promethean virtue (1:59). Consciousness is no longer a sin whose possession is punished by a wrathful Yahweh and that precipitates the Fall of humankind. It is, on the contrary, the gift that makes possible the birth of civilization, a civilization accompanied, to be sure, by all the ambivalence that has surrounded the arts and sciences ever since.

CHAPTER THREE

Faust: The Ambivalence of Knowledge

THE HISTORICAL FAUST

THE REFORMATION and Counter-Reformation were not kind to the mythic heroes who emerged from the vitality of Renaissance Europe, and whose quests for individual freedom and action threatened the foundations of traditional Christian values as well as medieval social forms and beliefs.[1] Don Juan's search for sensual experience is punished by his consignment to the gaping jaws of hell. Don Quixote's idealistic efforts to elevate imagination over raw reality end in mockery and death. Hamlet's indecisiveness, reflecting an irresolute modernity confronted with the conflicting values of a new era, leads to his death by, appropriately, an inwardly corrosive poison. And there is no Goethean redemption for the Reformation Faust, who, howling in agony and horror, is hauled off to hell by the devil's henchmen in fulfillment of his contract. The novels, plays, and chapbooks recounting the adventures of these exemplary figures fascinated enormous audiences, who trembled and gloated over their frustrated attempts to overreach the realities and restrictions of their day.

The chapbook *Historia von D. Johann Fausten* (1587), the earliest of these roughly contemporaneous works and quite possibly the most popular book printed in Germany after Martin Luther's translation of the Bible, went through some twenty-two editions in the decade following its publication despite local prohibitions; was immediately turned into rhymed couplets by a Tübingen student;[2] was published in 1588 in London as an illustrated broadside of twenty iambic quatrains; was swiftly translated into English, French, and Dutch; and in 1599 was

Fig. 4. Title page of Faust chapbook. Frankfurt am Main, 1594. Courtesy of The Beinecke Rare Book and Manuscript Library, Yale University. (The illustration is identical with that of the first illustrated Faust chapbook: Strassburg, 1588.)

expanded fourfold by Georg Rudolff Widman, who added moralizing notes and lengthy disquisitions. It can therefore claim for its time the degree of authority represented by Aeschylus's *Prometheus Bound* for fifth-century Greece and by the Genesis stories for Solomon's Jerusalem.

The differences among these Renaissance myths are conspicuous, as we readily determine if we consider our modern appropriation of their names. A "Don Juan" is a seducer, a libertine; a "quixotic" individual is an impractical romantic; a "Hamlet-like" person is one rendered impotent by irresoluteness. But "Faustian," thanks to Oswald Spengler, designates not simply an individual who makes a compromise with evil forces in order to achieve his ends, but also an entire technological age that applies intellect often destructively to the subordination of nature.

Faust differs from his Spanish and Dano-English mythic counterparts, not to mention Adam and Prometheus, in another essential respect: he was an actual historical personage, with whose notoriety such contemporaries as Martin Luther (1483–1546) and Philipp Melanchthon (1497–1560) were well acquainted. His story therefore represents a wholly different process of mythification from those of Don Juan, Don Quixote, and Hamlet. In "Faust," as in the New Testament accounts of Jesus, we witness the accretion of legend around an actual, albeit minimal historical nucleus. *That* someone known as Faust existed is a fact; but who he was and what he actually did is less obvious.

Faust is mentioned at least twice in Luther's *Table Talks*, on both occasions as a sorcerer assumed to be in league with the devil. Luther's comments make it clear that the theologian, if not personally acquainted with the magician, was familiar with his reputation.[3] The Hellenist Melanchthon, in his commentaries on the Scriptures, also refers twice to Faust as an exemplary magician. More personal is a passage from the *Locorum Communium Collectanea* (1563), in which Melanchthon's student Johannes Manlius assembled extracts and quotations from his lectures. Melanchthon came from Bretten, a small town in

southwestern Germany near Karlsruhe, and in one of the con-
versations reported by Manlius he remarked that he knew "a
certain man by the name of Faust from Kundling, which is a
small town near my birthplace." He goes on to report that Faust
studied magic at Cracow, wandered around Europe pro-
claiming mysteries and providing spectacles, and finally died
in the Duchy of Württemberg under suspicious circumstances,
lying near his bed with his face turned toward his back. "Thus,"
Melanchthon concludes, "the devil had killed him." Today it is
widely assumed that Faust was in fact born in Kundling (pres-
ent-day Knittlingen) around 1480.[4] (Knittlingen has been since
1967 the base of the International Faust Society, its publication
Faust-Blätter, and its museum and archive.) Another generally
reliable mid-sixteenth-century Swabian source, the so-called
Zimmerische Chronik maintained by Count Froben Christoph von
Zimmern, reports that Faust died around 1540 in the town of
Staufen (south of Freiburg near the Swiss border). Zimmern
regards the story of Faust as so remarkable that, around 1565,
he expresses the hope that someone will relate it fully and con-
sistently in a dedicated account.

Other contemporary documents attest at first hand to the life
and career of an early modern trickster going under the name
of Faust or its Latinized form, Faustus. The earliest and most
extensive of these is a letter written on August 20, 1507, by
the polymath Johannes Tritheim, a friend and teacher of the
occultist Agrippa von Nettesheim and abbot of a Benedictine
monastery at Würzburg, to his friend Johannes Virdung, professor of mathematics and court astrologer at Heidelberg.[5] Tritheim's letter, a response to Virdung's inquiry about a certain
Georgius Sabellicus, also known as "Faustus junior," amounts to
a long diatribe in Latin. Faustus, "who has presumed to call
himself the prince of necromancers, is a vagabond, a babbler
and a rogue, who deserves to be thrashed so that he may not
henceforth rashly venture to profess in public things so execra-
ble and so hostile to the holy church." In the town of Gelnhausen he boasted to the monks that he was so learned and

blessed with such a prodigious memory that, if all the works of Plato and Aristotle should be lost, he would be able to restore them with even greater elegance than the originals. In Würzburg he bragged that he could repeat all the miracles of Jesus at will. Yet when Tritheim arrived in Gelnhausen, "he fled from the inn and could not be persuaded to come into my presence." This blasphemer was not content to mystify the monks. When he was appointed schoolmaster in Kreuznach, he began to indulge in "the most dastardly kind of lewdness with the boys" (*nefandissimo fornicationis genere cum pueris*) and had to get out of town to avoid prosecution. Ending his letter, Tritheim assures his friend that he has conclusive evidence for his assertions. So when Faust comes to Heidelberg, "you will find him to be not a philosopher but a fool with an overabundance of rashness." The credibility of Tritheim's letter has been questioned:[6] Tritheim never states that he actually encountered Faust face-to-face; and the harshness of his tone could be attributed to the fact that Tritheim, who prided himself on his own accomplishments in "white" magic and astrology, was simply trashing the competition.

But for all the uncertainty regarding his name and place of birth, there is too much supporting evidence to leave any doubt regarding the reputation of the trickster known throughout Germany as Georg (Jörg) Faust or Faustus. The matriculation records of Heidelberg University report that on January 15, 1509, a certain Faust—this time exceptionally with the forename Johannes—was awarded a bachelor's degree, a statement consistent with Virdung's expectation in 1507 that Faust would be coming to Heidelberg. On February 12, 1520, "Doctor Faustus" was in Bamberg, where he received the appreciable sum of ten gulden for casting a horoscope for the bishop. Eight years later, on June 17, 1528, the soothsayer "Dr. Jörg Faustus of Heidelberg" was banished from the city of Ingolstadt, and on May 10, 1532, the records of the city council of Nuremberg indicate that a temporary residence permit was denied to "Doctor Faustus, the great sodomite and necromancer." (In both cases it is

47

likely that the towns were taking standard precautionary mea-
sures to protect their citizens against itinerants, "cunning folk,"
and fortune-tellers who drifted back and forth across Europe in
the sixteenth century.)[7] The precautions were not unwarranted,
because many people, not only uneducated monks and peasants but also gullible noblemen, were taken in by his hoaxes
(as was the case in subsequent centuries with such charismatic
charlatans as Cagliostro and Rasputin).[8] Educated humanists
were doubly incensed at the pretensions of the boastful faker.
In 1511 Conrad Mutianus Rufus reported the arrival of the
soothsayer Georgius Faustus in Erfurt. While the Erfurt humanist was not impressed by Faust's chatter and vauntings, he
conceded that the common folk marveled at him (*Rudes ad-
mirantur*). And in 1536 the philologist Joachim Camerarius re-
proached a friend in Würzburg for being impressed by Faust's
"breeze of empty superstition" (*vento uanissimae superstitionis*)
and cheap fairground tricks (*praestigijs*).

From official records and personal accounts of this sort, most
scholars conclude that a man named Georg Faust was in fact
born around 1480, probably in Knittlingen; that he may have
studied at least briefly in Heidelberg; that he traveled around
Germany as a kind of fairground hustler, casting horoscopes,
soothsaying, and performing magical feats and conjurations of
a sort readily produced by skilled prestidigitators; that he was
widely regarded as a charlatan by sophisticated humanists; that
he was several times accused of sodomy and pederasty and run
out of town; that his notoriety made him persona non grata in
respectable communities; and that he died around 1540, probably in Staufen. The mysterious circumstances of his death as
reported by Manlius—house-shaking noises and a corpse with
its head twisted 180 degrees to the rear—add a further dimension to his character: they may well have resulted from an explo-
sion produced by alchemistic experiments.[9]

How do we get, within fifty years, from this social undesir-
able—a trickster, mountebank, sexual predator, and altogether

one of the most unsavory characters of his age!—to the fascinating necromancer of the chapbooks and the tragic hero of Marlowe's drama? The question of actual identity, of compelling interest to would-be biographers of the historical Faust,[10] turns out to have little relevance in this connection since hardly more than his name and general notoriety were appropriated for the further development of the legend.

THE GROWTH OF THE LEGEND

Several factors are at work here. We know from the accounts by Tritheim, Mutianus Rufus, and others that, despite the contempt in which this trickster was held by the educated elite, Faust had considerable appeal among credulous monks and the simple folk in the inns that he frequented. Astrology was still a "science" esteemed by such educated humanists as the bishop of Bamberg, who commissioned Faust to cast his horoscope. "White" magic, based on the natural philosophy of the period and its belief in correspondences between the macrocosm of the universe and the microcosm of man, was a theologically acceptable subject professed at such universities as Cracow. But Faust obviously went on to practice black magic or necromancy. We learn from the testimony of no less an authority than Martin Luther that such feats of magic as Faust was reputed to perform could be accomplished only through the assistance of the devil. (This was consistent with the medieval belief that power and erudition were often acquired with the aid of fiendish powers. The legends attached to such figures as Pope Silvester II, Roger Bacon, Michael Scot, and others attest to this association, as does the etymological derivation of our words "glamour" from "grammar" and "charm" from *carmen*, or the use of "spell" for both the orthography of a word and the state of enchantment.) Luther's own firm belief in the reality of the devil was frequently attested—among other examples, by the ink spot at Wartburg

49

Castle that according to legend resulted when the Bible translator hurled his inkpot at Satan. And Luther was representative
rather than exceptional in a century still entangled in superstition and obsessed with the devil.

It was necessary for confidence men and tricksters like Faust
to walk a very narrow line here. The sixteenth century in Germany was hardly a safe time for those claiming magical powers
and traffic with the devil. The notorious *Malleus Maleficarum* of
1487, compiled by the Dominican monks Heinrich Institoris
and Jakob Sprenger from the magiological literature of the
times, initiated a period of steadily intensifying persecution by
persuading secular courts to support the church in the prosecution of witches and sorcerers.[11] It would not have been prudent for any sorcerer to make open claims of fiendish assistance: one always ran a very real risk of being burned at the
stake. Yet even during his lifetime, as we know from Luther's
remarks, Faust did not discourage reports of his allegiance
with the devil. It was good for business among the common
folk, who often preferred witchcraft to orthodox religion.[12] Religious chaos prevailed in the transition from a medieval Europe
unified by one faith to an early modernity riven by contesting
religious beliefs and unsettled by the scientific discoveries of
the Renaissance. Given the general sense of social crisis, many
people turned away from organized religion to alternative
means of access to the supernatural, including satanism and
witchcraft. (The analogy to our own society in the late twentieth
century hardly needs to be stressed.) It was among such spiritu-
ally rootless people that Faust found his willing audience. Soon
after his death, as we know from Melanchthon's account and
from the *Zimmerische Chronik*, the rumor began to spread that
his violent death was inflicted by Satan himself, with whom
Faustus had been in league. By the 1580s, the decade that produced the first literary treatments of the Faust legend, the witch
panic in Germany, with its trials and burnings, had reached its
peak. For that reason it is not unreasonable to believe that the

myth of Faustus is at least partially a product of the trials for witchcraft.[13]

Paradoxically, Faust was saved from the oblivion into which most contemporary necromancers and astrologers fell at least in part by his very notoriety.[14] In 1539, around the time of his death, Philip Begardi, a physician in Worms, attested that many people had complained to him that they had been cheated by Faustus. What better way for humanists to discredit false learning and for theologians to stigmatize black magic than to portray as an object lesson such a blatant and sordid example? Accordingly his name began to show up with increasing frequency in works of an edifying nature. In his *Sermones Convivales* (1548) the Swiss clergyman Johannes Gast related several tales about Faustus's tricks in monasteries and colleges, only to conclude that the wretch came to a deplorable end, "for he was slaughtered by the devil and his body on the bier kept turning its face downward even though it was five times turned on its back." Johannes Weier, a Dutch physician who led a campaign against superstition, drew on the sources discussed above for a passage concerning Faust that he introduced into the fourth (1568) edition of his influential work *De Praestigiis Daemonum* (On the deceptions of demons). "John Faust was born in the little town of Kundling and studied magic in Cracow, where it was formerly taught openly; and for a few years previous to 1540 he practiced his art in various places in Germany with many lies and much fraud, to the marvel of many." He goes on to relate a lengthy example of Faust's villainy "on the condition that the reader will first promise not to imitate him." The following year, in his popular treatise on ghosts (*Von Gespänsten*, 1569), the Swiss preacher Ludwig Lavater adduced Faust as an example for sorcerers who boast great wonders but then receive their just deserts from the devil. Among the various other edifying works from the second half of the sixteenth century that cite Faust, one is of particular interest: Augustin Lercheimer's "Christian reflections" on sorcery (*Christlich bedencken und erjnnerung von*

Zauberey, 1585). Lercheimer, a professor of Greek and mathematics at Heidelberg, rehashes the standard information: Faust was born at Knittlingen, studied at Cracow, was accused of sodomy at Kreuznach, and was strangled to death by the devil in a village in Württemberg. Of interest, in particular, is the new detail that Faust spent a year in Wittenberg, where he was personally rebuked by Melanchthon for his sins. But Lercheimer, who had himself studied at Wittenberg and heard the local stories about Faust, goes on as a loyal alumnus stoutly to deny the allegation that Faust was associated in any official capacity with his alma mater or that he died in Wittenberg. "I have pointed out these particular things because it has vexed and grieved me greatly, as it has many other honest people, to see the honorable and famous institution together with Luther, Melanchthon, and others of sainted memory so libelled."

The Chapbook Speculator

In the course of the fifty years following his death Faust had become notorious as a negative exemplum for a life of sexual degeneracy, charlatanry, and sorcery. Inevitably, stories so varied and popular began to be collected. In the university town of Erfurt a group of tales relating Faust's adventures among the students was assembled;[15] in Nuremberg around 1570 a schoolmaster named Christoph Rosshirt recorded another set of tales in a manuscript notebook.[16] In the early 1570s many of these stories were gathered into the so-called Wolfenbüttel manuscript, a work that appears to have been circulated widely in expensive manuscript copies.[17] (Because this manuscript is so close to the subsequently printed text, it is commonly assumed that both of them go back to a slightly older common source, though probably not in Latin as formerly believed; the author seems to rely wholly on German works.) But none of these earlier compilations were published. It was not until 1587 that

Johann Spies in Frankfurt am Main, hitherto known primarily as the publisher of Lutheran tracts,[18] brought out the *Historia*, which enjoyed an instantaneous popular success and provided the basis for the myth of Faust that was to engage the Western consciousness and conscience for the next four hundred years. (Although the popular chapbooks were normally illustrated— sometimes, as in the case of Sebastian Brant's *Ship of Fools* of 1494, by artists as distinguished as Albrecht Dürer—Spies, a Lutheran of the conservative iconolastic school, omitted illustrations.)

The author of the *Historia von D. Johann Fausten, the notorious Sorcerer and Nigromancer* is unknown, although the text makes it persuasively evident that he was theologically trained; some attribute it to Spies himself. The book purports to have been written by Faust's research assistant or *famulus*, Christoph Wagner, on the basis of Faust's own account and incorporating passages from his master's works as well as his written pact with the devil. (During the two centuries following his death various works attributed to Faust were in circulation: for example, *Praxis Cabulae nigrae* [The practice of black magic] or *Höllen- zwang* [Hell-incantation].)[19] It is clear from the title page on- ward that the book was intended as a cautionary work of Chris- tian homiletics fully consistent with Spies's other publications and representative of the vast literature of sorcery and witch- craft current at the time.[20] Specifically, it is identified as a "terri- ble case, repugnant example, and well-meant warning for all arrogant, presumptuous, and Godless men and women."[21] The message is reinforced with a quotation from the New Testa- ment: "Submit yourselves therefore to God. Resist the devil and he will flee from you" (James 4.7). In his dedication the pub- lisher reminds the reader that stories about Doctor Faustus have circulated in Germany for many years and created a demand for an authoritative account. Astonished that no one has previously composed this terrible story "as a warning for all Christendom," he now undertakes to publish the account allegedly communi- cated to him by a friend in Speyer as "a remarkable and terrible example in which one can not only see the devil's envy, deceitfulness, and cruelty toward the human race, but can also perceive clearly whither false security, presumptuousness, and excessive curiosity can ultimately drive a person." The author adds his own sermonizing preface "to the Christian Readers," claiming that "without any doubt sorcery and black magic constitute the greatest and most serious sin in the eyes of God and the whole world." He presents the example of Doctor Faustus and his horrendous end in order to acquaint reasonable men and women with the devil and his enterprises in the hope that "no one will be tempted by these stories to idle curiosity and imitation." Fortified by these warnings, the reader then proceeds to the sixty-eight chapters recounting the life, adventures, and death of Doctor Faustus.[22]

The enterprise was not without its perils. The Tübingen student who versified Spies's book later that year was jailed, along with his publisher, in the student *carcer,* and the entire edition (down to a single remaining copy) was destroyed as immoral—no doubt because versification was believed to turn what was intended as a moral treatise into mere entertainment.[23] The French translator, Pierre Victor Palma-Cayet, encountered an even stranger fate. A onetime convert to Calvinism who subsequently returned to Catholicism, he included a few anti-Protestant remarks in his *Histoire prodigieuse et lamentable du Docteur Fauste* (1598) and was thereupon prosecuted by the Protestants for witchcraft and for having himself signed a pact with the devil.[24]

It is a fair assumption that the chapbook's popular appeal was due mainly to the two long central sections of the book, which amount to a catalog of Faust's various adventures and tricks: his trip to hell and journeys around the world, his conjuration of such figures as Alexander the Great and the heroes of the Trojan War, the "horning" of a knight with antlers, the consumption of a peasant's horse and wagon along with its load of hay, his chopping off and restoring the heads of four other magicians. (The famous ride on the wine keg, along with other feats, was added to later editions from the Erfurt and Nuremberg collections.) These often tedious episodes, based on information culled from standard contemporary reference works—for example, the medieval encyclopedia known as *Elucidarius* and Hartmut Schedel's world chronicle (*Buch der Croniken*, 1493)—and using anecdotes borrowed from a variety of other sources, such as Luther's *Table Talks*, are only tenuously related to the homiletic theme of the work.[25]

We would hardly be reading the *Historia* today if it amounted to no more than a random collection of pranks associated with numerous sorcerers of history and legend. Here for the first time the hitherto disparate anecdotes are located within a biographical framework with a pronounced temporal rhythm, which makes the narrative sequential rather than merely serial.[26] In this primitive bildungsroman Faust is always keenly aware of the point he has reached in the rigorous chronology of twenty-four years allotted to him by his pact with the devil. Moreover, the few circumstances of the historical life have been altered to accommodate the Lutheran message. For instance, Faust's birthplace is shifted from Knittlingen, in the southwestern and Catholic Palatinate, to Roda near Weimar in central-German (and Lutheran) Thuringia. In the first sentence we learn that Faust, the son of peasants, was sent to Wittenberg (the headquarters of liberal Lutheranism and hence opposed by the more orthodox faction to which Spies belonged)[27] to a prosperous relative, who enabled him to study theology and made him his heir. But already the second sentence warns the reader that Faust, through no fault of his devout family, soon departed from righteous ways. Blessed with intelligence and memory, he became a doctor of theology and later a doctor of medicine. But his desire for knowledge led him to the study of magic so that he could conjure up the devil, who manifested himself in the gray garb of a friar (chap. 2). Unafraid, Faust laid down his terms: that the devil serve him and answer all his questions; that he not withhold any knowledge Faust should demand; and that he respond with the truth to all interrogations (chap. 3).

At this point we begin to realize that the character and personality of the historical Faust, hitherto known simply as a trickster, have been drastically altered along with his birthplace. There is no hint here of sodomy or cheap magic. This chapbook Faust, like any Renaissance humanist, is driven initially by the desire for knowledge, albeit a sinful knowledge transcending the traditional school teachings. It is this new theme of sinful knowledge that sets the *Historia* apart from all previous accounts of the historical Faust.[28] In earlier stories it was simply assumed that Faust must have been in league with the devil in order to gain his magical powers; there was nothing about his desire for knowledge. But the *Fürwitz* mentioned repeatedly in the *Historia* (chap. 2) is that same *curiositas* that had been maligned in Christian theology at least since Augustine. (In book 10 of the *Confessions*, for instance, Augustine speaks of a form of temptation that is even more dangerous than the temptations of the flesh: the desire for experience and knowledge [*experiendi noscendique libido*] that he calls *curiositas*.)[29] He is specifically called a *Speculierer* (chap. 1), a term used in the Reformation to designate those who sought knowledge outside the Bible.[30]

After further negotiations (chap. 4) Faust signs a contract to that effect with the devil, whose name, he learns, is Mephostophiles. (This is the first occurrence of the name that—in a variety of spellings—was to be linked with Faust's own name through the centuries.) Having determined "to speculate the elements" ("die Elementa zu speculieren," that is, to understand the basis of all being) and having realized that he cannot obtain such knowledge from human sources, he elicits from Mephostophiles, a servant of the Hellish Prince in the Orient, the promise to serve him in his quest for knowledge and experience. In return, Faust pledges that after twenty-four years Mephostophiles can claim him body and soul. He signs the contract with his own blood even though, when he pricks his left hand, his very life fluid warns him by flowing out to shape the words: *O homo fuge* (chap. 6).

The contract with the devil, along with the traditional period of twenty-four years, is new with Spies's *Historia*. Earlier accounts, including those that depicted Faust's dire end at the hands of the devil, made no mention of any formal agreement. The author, confronted with the desire to link into a sequential narrative a series of otherwise unrelated incidents drifting through the sixteenth century, and with the need to provide a source for Faust's sinful knowledge, had to find a way of committing the devil to Faust for a sustained period of time. The motif of satanic assistance had been familiar in Christian legendry at least since Simon Magus in the New Testament (Acts 8.9–24), the apocryphal *Acts of the Holy Apostles Peter and Paul*, and the *Clementine Recognitions*.[31] Melanchthon was perhaps the first to introduce Faust into this tradition when he related that Faust sought in Venice to imitate Simon Magus's attempt to fly—with the same unfortunate result.[32] Another frequently cited Christian analogue to Faust is the legend of Saint Cyprian of Antioch, the subject of Calderón's sacramental drama *El Mágico Prodigioso* (1637), who summoned up the devil to assist him in the seduction of a virgin. Impressed by the maiden's virtue and the power of God to repulse the efforts of the devil, Cyprian is ultimately converted to Christianity and martyred for his faith.[33] Most directly relevant is the enormously popular legend of Theophilus, deacon to the bishop of Chartres (in the widely known version related in the *Legenda Aurea*).[34] Removed from his position by the bishop's successor, the despairing Theophilus consults a magician who conjures up the devil, with whom the deacon signs a pact in blood. But after being restored to his office, Theophilus repents and, with the assistance of the Virgin Mary, forsakes his hellish helpmate and is liberated from his pact and redeemed. This blood-signed pact was appropriated as the basis for Faust's agreement with the devil.

The first sixteen of Faust's twenty-four years (chaps. 11–32) are spent mainly in the pursuit of knowledge—theological, astronomical, and cosmological—through disquisitions and travel. During these years Faust's activities remain entirely on the level that one might reasonably expect from a curious and serious Renaissance scholar. It is only toward the end of his allotted period—as a result of boredom?—that he descends to the pranks whose account is interrupted only once, in the seventeenth year (chap. 52), when a pious old man, a devout physician and Faust's neighbor, appeals to him to forsake his evil ways. But when Faust, moved by his appeal, contemplates an abrogation of his contract, the devil appears and forces him with terrible threats to sign an even more exigent pact, again in blood. This hedonistic period of Faust's life culminates in his second conjuration of Helen of Troy and their conception—outside wedlock, of course, a sacrament from which he is excluded by his diabolical pact—of a son, Justus Faustus (chap. 59).

If Faust is motivated by a desire for sinful knowledge and experience and assisted in their acquisition through a pact with the devil, then the wages of his sin must be shocking enough to convince the Christian reader that his example is not worth imitating. This is the purpose of the final chapters, which recount the events of the last year. Faust makes his will and testament, assigning all his property and powers to his *famulus* Wagner (chaps. 60–61). When he realizes that he has only one month left, he begins to lament his fate (chaps. 62–64), whereupon Mephostophiles scoffs at him in words that at times pervert sayings of Martin Luther (chap. 65), reminding Faust that he had been unwilling to content himself with the natural gifts and skills that God had bestowed on him. Following a final lament, in which he regrets that he has no "mighty fortress" against hell and damnation (chap. 66), a spirit appears with the contract in hand and notifies him that the devil will come the following night to claim him. Accompanied by his students, Faust goes to the (otherwise unknown) village of Rimlich near

Wittenberg, where they share a meal that clearly travesties the Last Supper (chap. 67). In his final "Oratio ad Studiosos" (chap. 68) Faust confesses that all the learning they have admired in him has resulted from his pact with the devil. He urges them to take his dreadful end as an admonition to keep God before their eyes, to implore him to protect them from the devil's deceit and treachery, and not to turn away from him "like the Godless and damned man that I am, who have despised and renounced baptism, the sacrament of Christ, God himself, the whole Heavenly Host." He warns them to retire to their beds and not to be frightened by the horrible noises they will hear in the night. The students, amazed that their professor had exposed himself to such perils of body and soul "merely for the sake of roguery, curiosity, and sorcery," regret that he did not confess earlier so that they might have helped him to extricate himself from his predicament. Faust asks them to pray that, even as the devil takes his body, God may save his soul.

Shortly after midnight a mighty windstorm shakes the house to its foundations. The innkeeper flees, but the students remain outside Faust's room, where they hear a terrifying whistling and hissing as though the house were full of serpents. (The author is obviously drawing on the rhetoric of hellfire and damnation familiar from contemporary sermons.) Faust cries *Mordio!* and screams for help. Then suddenly—silence. At daybreak the students enter their professor's room and find it covered with blood, his brain cleaving to one wall, against which the devil had hurled him, and his teeth and eyes scattered about. Finally they discover Faust's body outside on the dungheap, a terrible sight to behold, for his head and all his limbs are hanging disjointed. "Thus ends the true Historia and Sorcery of Doctor Faustus, from which every Christian—and especially those of arrogant, haughty, curious, and defiant mind and head—should learn to fear God and to flee sorcery, conjurations, and other work of the devil."

Through its bold appropriation of the blood-signed pact with the devil and its inevitable fulfillment, the *Historia* unified the

59

many varied accounts of Faustian magic and trickery and gave them a biographical framework consistent with the new Renaissance self-consciousness. By shifting the action to Wittenberg, by its frequent citation of Luther's words, and by its indirect critiques of Catholicism (e.g., the devil always appears in friar's garb), Spies's chapbook makes explicit its conservative Lutheran orientation. At the same time, as the representative of an organized church, Spies was attacking the popular occultism, satanism, and witchcraft of the sixteenth century, a populist trend objectionable to Catholics and Protestants alike. Above all: by motivating Faust with the desire for knowledge and experience, secular as well as theological, the Reformation author took aim with considerable anti-intellectual animus at the main ideals of the Renaissance, thereby raising Faust from the lowly ranks of itinerant fairground magicians, from the status of a mere trickster, and elevating him into the company of Renaissance overreachers—and into the lofty order of those earlier seekers after sinful knowledge Adam and Prometheus.

MARLOWE'S POWER SEEKER

For all its popularity in Germany, France, England, and the Netherlands at the end of the sixteenth century, it is unlikely that the story of Faust would have survived to become one of the great myths of modernity had Marlowe never written his *Tragical History of the Life and Death of Doctor Faustus.* Long after the cautionary chapbooks had lost their audiences, Marlowe's play made its way across Europe—albeit in the frequently trivialized form presented by English traveling players, who often had to resort to pantomime because they did not speak the Continental languages—and in the puppet shows based on those stage performances that can be viewed in Germany's marketplaces still today. These performances contributed appreciably to the spread and continued popularity of the theme.[35] It should be stressed at the outset that, despite the incomparably greater literary quality of Marlowe's powerful drama, the essential shift in Faustus's character from trickster to seeker after knowledge had already taken place in the German source.

The reasons for the appeal of this story to Marlowe are obvious: in temperament and reputation—accused of blasphemy, atheism, and even pederasty, and himself to be the victim of a violent death—the Elizabethan dramatist was not unlike the Reformation necromancer. While the circumstances surrounding the composition and text of Marlowe's play are still debated, it seems likely that he wrote it in 1592, shortly before his death in 1593 in a tavern brawl. The play has come down to us in two versions, one published in the quarto of 1604 (A) and a longer one in 1616 (B) containing several additional episodes not written by Marlowe. The earlier text without the distracting buffoonery was long regarded as the more authentic one. Today most scholars believe that the B-text is based on a manuscript that antedates A, which is now considered to be a version abbreviated for the use of traveling troupes.[36] Marlowe's source was most likely *The Historie of the damnable life, and deserved death of Doctor John Faustus*, which was "newly imprinted" in 1592 (on the basis of a first edition presumably published earlier that year). The *Historie*, rendered into English by an anonymous known to history only as "P. F. Gent.," amounts to more an adaptation than a translation of the German *Volksbuch*, omitting as it does a good part of the theological disquisitions, generally muting the homiletic tone of the German tract, and providing an altogether more readable account.[37] But the major transformation occurred when Marlowe adapted the episodic narrative of the prose chapbook to the requirements of the Elizabethan stage.

For this purpose Marlowe cut his source drastically, introduced a chorus to provide narrative continuity, punctuated the Faustus plot with contrasting comic scenes that have the effect of relativizing Faust's absolute aspirations, and added allegorical features borrowed from the late medieval morality plays still being performed in sixteenth-century England: notably the

Good and Evil Angels, the pageant of the Seven Deadly Sins, and the hell-mouth through which Faust is dragged off at the end. Above all, he modified character and circumstances in such a way as to expose the tragedy implicit in the medieval cautionary tale. This shift is attributable in no small measure to the dramatist's modern point of view. The author of the chapbook, taking it for granted that there are some things which the good Christian is not supposed to know, assigns the guilt squarely to Faust's *curiositas*. Marlowe, as we shall see, has a different attitude.

The technical shortcomings of the play have been thoroughly catalogued in the course of two centuries of criticism.[38] Marlowe was confronted with the daunting challenge of representing persuasively the twenty-four years between Faust's pact and his death within the short stage-space of three hours. Even those critics who have praised the grandeur of the opening and closing scenes have been embarrassed by the often vulgar buffoonery of the middle sections in the pope's Rome and at the emperor's court in Innsbruck (largely appropriated from the chapbook).

If we disregard the slapstick and stage business of acts 3 and 4, we quickly realize that Faustus is still motivated by the *curiositas* of the chapbooks and engaged, at least initially, in the quest for knowledge. The opening chorus adheres to the traditional theme. Faustus excelled in the study of theology, we are told in the prologue,

> Till swoll'n with cunning, of a self-conceit,
> His waxen wings did mount above his reach
> And melting, heavens conspired his overthrow!
> For falling to a devilish exercise
> And glutted now with learning's golden gifts
> He surfeits upon cursed necromancy.
>
> (Prologue, 20–26)

The famous opening scene goes beyond the source to provide a psychological explanation for Faust's turn to magic, which in the chapbook was simply stated as a fact. To achieve this, Marlowe exploits a conventional topos of the Renaissance: the skeptical survey of scholarship, which would have been familiar to Marlowe, the Cambridge undergraduate, from such contemporary works as Cornelius Agrippa's scandalous 102-chapter satire on pedantry and the shortcomings of traditional scholarship in his *De incertitudine et vanitate scientiarum et artium* (1532). ("Cunning Aprippa" is mentioned in the text [1.1.111–12].)

That Marlowe's Faustus is driven by intellectual curiosity is now a critical commonplace.[39] (It seems perverse to write off his genuine intellectual aspirations as those of a "frivolous academic opportunist.")[40] The great opening monologue, which goes well beyond anything Marlowe found in his source, focuses our attention on the question of knowledge and surveys the inadequacies of the traditional four faculties and disciplines by specifying and quoting the works of Aristotle, Galen, Justinian, and Jerome—the classic representatives of philosophy, medicine, law, and theology. Yet we soon become aware of three significant differences vis-à-vis the concept of knowledge in the German and English chapbooks.

The first difference is evident if we consider the ambivalent image of the book. Faust is a true intellectual to the extent that he seeks the answers to all of life's questions in books, which provide from the opening speech to his final words the governing image of the play. Yet from the moment he puts the traditional books aside to take up his "negromantic books" (1.1.48) the vocable takes on pronouncedly negative associations. In the eyes of the Good Angel it is precisely "that damnèd book" (1.1.67) which symbolizes his corruption. Books, and the learning they signify, become attributes of hell: Mephostophilis presents Faust with a book whose magic will produce gold, change the weather, and summon armed henchmen (2.2.161–67); and Lucifer gives him a book that will enable Faust to assume whatever shape he wishes (2.2.183–84). Even the Chorus sounds like a postmodern semioticist for whom the world is a text when it speaks of Faustus's attempt

> To find the secrets of astronomy
> Graven in the book of Jove's high firmaments. . . .
>
> (3. Prologue)

It is consistent with this symbolism that Faust, lamenting his fall, cries out, "O, would I had never seen Wittenberg, never read book" (5.3.47–48). Accordingly, his last words (5.2.197), before the devils drag him off through the hell-mouth, are famously "I'll burn my books!" In case the audience has missed the point, the epilogue sums up the anti-intellectual message that certain kinds of knowledge are sinful. There the Chorus exhorts us, regarding the hellish fall of this learned man,

> Only to wonder at unlawful things,
> Whose deepness doth entice such forward wits
> To practice more than heavenly power permits.

Yet Marlowe goes beyond the conventional opposition of lawful and forbidden, of the good Christian and the "forward wit" motivated by *curiositas*, of heaven and hell.

For, in the second place, his play exemplifies in a manner not present in the *Volksbuch* an ambivalent tension between the Reformation and Renaissance attitudes toward knowledge. Although the Good Angel condemns Faustus's books and sinful knowledge, the students who discover Faustus's remains resolve to give him a proper burial out of respect for his intellectual achievement.

> Well gentlemen, though Faustus' end be such
> As every Christian heart laments to think on,
> Yet for he was a scholar once admired
> For wondrous knowledge in our German schools,
> We'll give his mangled limbs due burial. . . .
>
> (5.3.13–17)

Similarly the Chorus, rather than condemning Faustus outright, initially solicits our "patient judgments" and at the end

64

laments "the branch that might have grown full straight" had it not been bent by its desire for sinful knowledge.

There is no need to deal here with the vexed biographical question of Marlowe's religious skepticism or even atheism: the play contains its own religious context. (Indeed, there is no better example to illustrate the danger of citing a work as evidence of the author's own beliefs.) The students are clearly prepared to respect Faustus's intellectual *curiositas* quite apart from his unfortunate end, to distinguish the intellectual from the moral, to undertake what Erich Heller has called "the mind's absolute emancipation from the vigilance of moral judgment" (16).

This distinction is justified by suggestions within the play that Faustus is not solely responsible for his damnation. For, as we learn in the prologue, "heavens conspired his overthrow."[41] And Mephostophilis later confesses that it was he, when Faustus took up the Bible, who turned the pages and led Faustus's eye to the passages that set him off on the path to perdition (5.2.100–103).

As though to underscore Faustus's innocence, Marlowe invented two characters, the magicians Valdes and Cornelius (whose presence and function incidentally suggest Marlowe's firsthand familiarity with the practice of magic). That they have long been conspiring to seduce Faustus into witchcraft is indicated by Faustus's greeting when they first appear:

> Know that your words have won me at the last
> To practice magic and concealèd arts.
>
> (1.1.98–99)

Hence it is not accurate to state that "[n]o god urged him on, no oracle foretold his fate."[42] In fact the Chorus foretells his fate, and the two magicians urge him on.

In a third and crucial departure from the chapbooks, Faustus's turn to magic is not motivated principally by the quest for pure knowledge, be it lawful or sinful; indeed, when he first appears he is already "glutted . . . with learning's golden gifts" (Prologue, 23). No, Faustus as a true Renaissance man longs for power—a longing that Marlowe had already personified in the figure of his Tamburlaine: that power which Marlowe's contemporary, Francis Bacon, defined as the virtual synonym of knowledge: *nam et ipsa scientia potestas est.*[43] As Faustus turns to the words and images of his "negromantic books," he meditates:

> O, what a world of profit and delight,
> Of power, of honor, and omnipotence
> Is promised to the studious artisan!
> All things that move between the quiet poles
> Shall be at my command: emperors and kings
> Are but obeyed in their several provinces
> But his dominion that exceeds in this
> Stretcheth as far as doth the mind of man. . . .
>
> (1.1.51–58)

To be sure, Faust wants the spirits to "resolve me of all ambiguities" (1.1.76) and to "read me strange philosophy" (1.1.83). But his dreams rapidly pass beyond intellectual curiosity to other "desperate enterprises": he plans to wall Germany with brass, to cause the Rhine to circle Wittenberg, to clothe the students in silk, and to drive the Spanish ruler from the Low Countries. His lust for power is seconded by the magicians Valdes and Cornelius, who assure Faustus that with the knowledge of magic they can compel spirits to "fetch the treasure of all foreign wracks" as well as "all the wealth that our forefathers hid / Within the massy entrails of the earth" (1.1.139–41). Similarly the Bad Angel urges Faust to "think of honor and of wealth" (2.1.23), not knowledge.

Faustus asks few of the traditional theological questions: he is curious about the hell to which by the pact he has just consigned himself (2.1). Yet Mephostophilis's astronomical information, to his dismay, goes hardly beyond the "slender questions" that even a Wagner might decide. Whenever the answer would require mention of God, as in the matter of the world's creation, Mephostophilis refuses to respond. Instead, the devils try to distract him with such entertainments as the pageant of the Seven Deadly Sins. Accordingly, his first charge to Mepho-stophilis, in sharp distinction to the Faust of the chapbook, is "[t]o do whatever Faustus shall command" (1.3.36), and specifically to accomplish deeds of raw power: "Be it to make the moon drop from her sphere / Or the ocean to overwhelm the world" (1.3.37–38). Significantly, the terms of the contract specify—again in contrast to the chapbook—deeds, not knowledge. The buffoonery that dominates the subsequent scenes at the courts of the pope and the emperor must not blind us to the fact that acts 3 and 4 introduce Faust to the two principal realms of earthly power, and that the struggle between the two popes symbolizes what has been called "the drama's pervasive theme of contested authority."[44]

Marlowe was, of course, constrained by the traditional plot sequence and the narrative elements of his source: because the beginning and end were fixed, the twenty-four years had somehow to be filled in. The sublimity of the play results from its language—Marlowe's "mighty line" praised by Ben Jonson—and not from the plot.[45] Yet even the beauty of the traditional conjuration of Helen (5.1.96–115)—"Was this the face that launched a thousand ships . . . ?"—cannot mask the fact that the Helen he embraces is, in the last analysis, a fiendish succuba pandered by the devil. Faustus's longing for her love is not noble but rather, as the final episode in a pattern of alternating despondency and sensual pleasure, a desperate flight he undertakes into lust in order to forget his swiftly approaching death.[46] Similarly, the concluding lament (5.11.140–97) is anticipated both in the *Weheklag* of the source and in the pronounced temporal momentum of the twenty-four years. It is not the fact of the lament or its topic that is original but Marlowe's brilliant concentration of the powerful rush of time into "one bare hour," which moves irrevocably forward toward midnight despite Faustus's appeal to the stars and the clock to stand still.

The language also contains words that call to mind the other two mythic heroes. When Faustus speculates that "[a] sound magician is a demi-god" (1.1.59), and when the Bad Angel tempts Faustus with the words "Be thou on earth as Jove is in the sky, / Lord and commander of these elements!" (1.1.73–74), it is difficult not to recall the serpent's words to Eve: *Eritis sicut dii, scientes bonum et malum.* And when Faust is dragged off with thunder through the hell-mouth, we think involuntarily of Prometheus being blasted into the abyss by Zeus's thunderbolt. But how much of this is in Marlowe's mind and text, and how much is in our own critical imagination?[47] While Faustus allows himself to be tempted like Adam-Eve, his last-minute groveling before God has nothing in common with the Titan's proud defiance of Zeus.

Marlowe has advanced far enough beyond the Middle Ages to perceive the tension between religion and science, to understand the ambivalence of knowledge and its potential for power, and to be moved by the tragedy of a man tempted by knowledge and power to overreach his limits. But his Faustus, even as he prefigures a modern intellectual consciousness, remains mired in a medieval morality and is finally judged by its standards. It remained for later ages to redeem a Faust who has developed in the course of some fifty years from a historical and then legendary trickster by way of a Reformation seeker after knowledge to a power-crazed Renaissance tragic hero.

From Myth to Modernity

Our SURVEY of the three themes has revealed that myths concerning the sin of knowledge typically emerge during periods of social crisis produced by the tension between conflicting sets of values and beliefs. Men and women are tantalized by the new knowledge yet prohibited by existing authority from enjoying it. Or, having partaken of the new knowledge, they are tormented by the losses that seem inevitably to accompany its gains. The legend of Adam assumed its place in Hebrew lore at the moment when thoughtful people in tenth-century Jerusalem were coming to terms with the rapid shift from a nomadic culture of firm religious faith to a more sophisticated, less devout urban civilization. Prometheus first appeared among the peasants of a Boeotia suffering under feudal lords and embittered by the signs of moral degeneration. He asserted his claim on the Greek imagination when fifth-century Athens was making the shift from tyranny to democracy and enjoying the fruits of rationality while agonizing over the loss of traditional values. Faust emerged from the strife and social chaos in a sixteenth-century Germany forsaking the intact faith and social order of a medieval world challenged by the intellectual advances of the Renaissance and the moral claims of Lutheranism. (The fact that Faust was originally a historical personage while Adam and Prometheus were generated from local folktales does not vitiate the fact that the process of their development to mythic authority is precisely analogous.)

All three mythic heroes violate divine prohibitions against the new knowledge: Adam disobeys God and eats from the Tree of the Knowledge of Good and Evil; Prometheus deceives Zeus and steals the Olympian fire that becomes the source of all civilizing arts and crafts; and Faust rejects God to contract with the devil for access to theological and cosmological secrets that transcend the limits allowed by official church doctrine. All three are punished grievously for their offenses: Adam is banished from Paradise into 930 years of earthly toil and misery, followed according to Dante (*Inferno* 4) by centuries in limbo until his redemption by Christ in the Harrowing of Hell; Prometheus is blasted into the abyss and later tormented for 30,000 years by the liver-gnawing eagle until his rescue by Herakles; and Faust is carted off to hell for all eternity by the devil's henchmen. In all three cases woman is assigned a role reflecting conspicuously misogynistic attitudes: for the Yahwist, Eve is the curious weakling who succumbs to the temptation of knowledge and seduces Adam from the paths of righteousness; for Hesiod, Pandora is the "beautiful evil" sent to plague mankind for receiving the gift of fire; and for the author of the Faust Book, Helena—the only woman permitted to Faust, who is precluded by his contract from the holy sacrament of marriage— is a conjured succuba whose lips suck forth his soul.

In the last analysis all three mythic figures assume for their cultures the role of scapegoat who must suffer so that humankind may endure. Adam is cast out of Paradise, but he becomes the father of the human race. Condemned for his sin by the Hebrews and then rapidly forgotten, he is resurrected by Christian theologians on the grounds that his *felix culpa* both necessitates and makes possible the subsequent redemption by Jesus. Prometheus suffers his agonies so that humankind may continue to enjoy the benefits of fire and enlightenment. Faust goes off to hell so that his students and, through them, all Christendom may understand the wages of sin and avoid the pursuit of forbidden knowledge.

The structure of the myth, with its protagonist morphing from trickster to tragic hero whose quest for sinful knowledge brings about his fall and punishment, is remarkably constant in every case, although each myth reveals a different relationship between the hero myth and the trickster legends from which it evolved—"trickster" understood, as we have seen, in its broadest spectrum of meanings. The Gilgamesh epic contains both the Jungian trickster in the person of Enkidu and, in Gilgamesh himself, the rudimentary culture-hero outwitted by the hungry snake. The Genesis account, which conflated Enkidu and Gilgamesh into the culture-hero Adam, had to strip Adam of Enkidu's trickster qualities, which were externalized and projected onto the serpent, who could then be opposed to humankind. The myth of Prometheus, like that of Adam, is set at the beginning of human history. In his earliest form Prometheus, as the traditional fire-stealing trickster, is opposed to the mankind upon whom his behavior brings misery. But as society's view of knowledge changed and became positive, the trickster metamorphosed into the tragic hero of Aeschylus, and Zeus was burdened with the role of humankind's tyrannical enemy. Faust exemplifies a similar evolution from trickster to (tragic) hero: the myth is based on an actual historical figure who was in fact a fairground trickster vis-à-vis his own society. But as the story of Faust evolved from history through legend into myth—first as a negative exemplum and then as a tragic hero—Faust, like Adam and the later Prometheus, had to be stripped of his trickster aspect; the narrative generated a new trickster in the person of the devil, who tempts and opposes him, the representative of humankind, as once the serpent tempted Adam.

The nature of the forbidden knowledge also varies from culture to culture.[1] Adam's newly acquired knowledge of good and evil represents the fall out of a primal innocence into consciousness and conscience. Prometheus's fire symbolizes the next step—from simple consciousness to the rational enlightenment on the basis of which all civilization is built. Faust's forbidden desire, in the context of a culture already conscious and civilized, goes beyond the moral and intellectual knowledge of Adam and Prometheus to a modern lust for power. It is these specific associations that characterize the modern variations of the ancient myths, which are not simply appropriated with their original meaning. Rather, the structures of their stories are adapted to suit the specific historical circumstances of the appropriating society: Adam and the Fall provide a metaphor for the movement from innocence into consciousness and conscience in young men and women of the modern world; Prometheus as the culture-bringing hero is appropriated as the ambivalent image for a Marxist society pursuing and then questioning its technological prowess; and Faust exemplifies a modern capitalist society willing to seal a pact with evil in the quest for knowledge and its power. The modifications of the myth, in sum, provide a key to the anxieties and hopes of the society that recognizes itself in the mythic model. The result, of course, may sometimes fulfill what Valéry's Faust quips: "They have written so much about me that I no longer know who I am" (21).

PART TWO

MODERN VARIATIONS

*

Fig. 5. Adam, Eve, and the serpent, in *The Loss of Sexual Innocence*, written
and directed by Mike Figgis, 1999. Courtesy of Mike Figgis.

* CHAPTER FOUR *

The Secularization of Adam

CANDIDE'S FALL

VOLTAIRE'S *Candide* (1759), known to many Americans through Leonard Bernstein's musical, if not from Voltaire's original philosophical tale, begins when the hero is expelled from the Westphalian castle of the Baron of Thunder-ten-tronckh after the Baron catches him in sexual dalliance with his daughter Cunégonde. Beginnings of this sort—the expulsion of the hero or heroine from a haven of comfort and security into a life of adventure and danger—belong to the familiar pattern of picaresque narratives from Cervantes by way of Dickens to Günter Grass. But our attention is aroused when, in the first sentence of chapter 2, we are told that Candide has been ejected from an "earthly paradise" ("paradis terrestre"), for the Baron's crude castle, which is distinguished by nothing more than the fact that it has a door and windows and a tapestry in the great hall, suggests anything but a paradise.

However, "paradise" turns out to be a central motif of the story. In the course of his wanderings Candide experiences two more "paradises": the true earthly paradise of Eldorado (chaps. 17 and 18), where men and women are happy, free, and equal, but which Candide leaves for the cynical reason that as a happy man there he would simply be like everybody else; and the realistic paradise of the conclusion (chap. 30), where Candide learns that mortal man can fend off the three great evils—boredom, vice, and poverty—only by cultivating his own garden. The story is tied down, then, at beginning, middle, and end by three versions of paradise: the false paradise of Thunder-ten-tronckh, the earthly paradise of Eldorado, and the realistic paradise of

Candide's garden near Constantinople (which is explicitly compared to the Garden of Eden). These three paradises provide the organizing framework of the action. The first half is governed by Candide's association with his tutor Pangloss, the prophet of optimism: yet almost every incident—war, pillage, rape, murderous butchery, earthquakes—contradicts Pangloss's conviction that theirs is the best of all possible worlds. The second half is dominated, in turn, by Candide's association with the Manichaean scholar Martin, whose experience has convinced him that God has abandoned the world to evil. Yet, again, reality demonstrates that good often prevails: in particular, those thought dead reappear, and Candide is able through his wealth to help many others. In each half of the book, then, reality overcomes ideology: Candide moves first from a position of naive optimism to realism and then from excessive pessimism to realism. His garden represents ultimately the only paradise possible in the real world of good and evil.

Given what turns out to be the governing importance of the paradise image, we look again at the first chapter and discover a number of telltale hints. The Baron is called "My Lord" ("Monseigneur"), and Candide's own name suggests his primal innocence. Candide and Cunégonde, who are much taken with each other, are persuaded by Pangloss that they do indeed dwell in the best of all possible worlds, in which there is a sufficient reason for every happening. The trouble begins when Cunégonde happens to observe Dr. Pangloss in the bushes giving "a lesson in experimental physics" to her mother's maid: witnessing the learned doctor's "sufficient reason" as well as its causes and effects, she returns home filled with the desire for such knowledge ("désir d'être savante") and dreaming that she might provide the sufficient reason for young Candide. When she and Candide find the occasion, she drops her handkerchief and he picks it up; she takes his hand "innocently," and he "innocently" kisses hers. One thing leads to another: their lips touch, their eyes are inflamed, their knees tremble, and their hands wander. Observing this "cause and effect," the Baron expels Candide from his childhood paradise, and the adventures begin.

By this point every reader realizes that Voltaire is playing games with the story of Adam's Fall: an innocent young man, living in a place explicitly designated as a paradise, is tempted by a young woman who is motivated by a desire for forbidden knowledge; when their behavior is witnessed by the "Lord," the youth is expelled from paradise into a life of toil and misery. The author brilliantly exploits the myth of the Fall to alert us to the symbolic dimensions of Candide's fall from innocence into the knowledge of good and evil exemplified respectively by the teachings of Pangloss and those of Martin.

We must not take Voltaire's achievement for granted. His adaptation of the myth of the Fall differs radically from the reverent retellings popular in biblical epics and dramas from Joost van den Vondel's *Adam in Ballingschap* (Adam in exile, 1664) or John Milton's *Paradise Lost* (1667) down to Friedrich Klopstock's *Messias* (1748) or *Der Tod Adams* (Adam's death, 1757), published only two years before *Candide*. The authors of those classic works adapt the biblical material seriously as a vehicle for their own religious convictions. Voltaire, in contrast, exploits the material to lend explicitly satirical dimensions to his picaresque philosophical tale. Several significant developments in European intellectual history had to take place before such a use was conceivable.

THE TYPOLOGICAL IMPULSE

Voltaire is not simply retelling the biblical story of the Fall; he is employing an exegetical technique familiar to centuries of biblical scholars and known as typology or figuralism.[1] The entry in Hastings's standard *Encyclopaedia of Religion and Ethics* (12:500–504) defines typology as "the science, or rather, only

77

too often, the curious art of discovering and expounding in the records of persons and events in the Old Testament prophetical adumbrations of the Person of Christ or of the doctrines and practices of the Christian Church." Erich Auerbach's classic essay "Figura" represents a second, more general sense, which assumes a similar relationship between past and present without limiting it to the Bible: "Figural interpretation establishes a connection between two events or persons, the first of which signifies not only itself but also the second, while the second encompasses or fulfills the first."[2] In either sense the faith of the exegete posits a mystical relationship between two historically discrete events. A certain "type" (person or event) in the Old Testament is said to find its corresponding "antitype" in the New Testament, as when Joseph's being sold by his brothers is fulfilled in Jesus' betrayal by Judas. Or, according to the term favored by the Latin exegetes, an incident in the New Testament is anticipated by a "figure" in the Old Testament, as Jesus carrying his cross up to Golgotha is prefigured by Isaac, who must carry the wood upon which he is to be sacrificed. In all such cases Christian faith juxtaposes *umbra* and *veritas*, seeing, for instance, the "shadow" of the innocent shepherd Abel, slain by his brother, realized in the living "truth" of Jesus, the shepherd of men, who is slain by his brothers. The essential relationship is characterized by the fact that both figures and types are believed by Christian faith to be real historical events or persons. It is this sense of historical reality that distinguishes figural or typological understanding from other forms of allegory, in which one pole of the relationship is generally an abstract notion.

Although typological or figural interpretation was not unknown to pagan and Jewish antiquity, the early Christian church seized most eagerly upon the method since it enabled the exegetes to create instant history for their upstart religion by showing that Jesus and his teaching constituted fulfillments or antitypes of figures and types contained in the venerable Hebrew Bible. The prefiguring shadow of the Law was believed to have given way to the eternal truth embodied and fulfilled in the person of Jesus Christ. (Hence the frequent occurrence in the Gospels of such phrases as "That it might be fulfilled.") This characteristically Christian mode of interpretation reached three pinnacles of popularity and influence—in the Alexandrine period, again in the twelfth century, and finally in the seventeenth century—and maintained its authority until it was undermined by eighteenth-century rationalism and wholly discredited by the scientific Bible criticism of the nineteenth century. Yet strong traces of typological thinking can still be detected in the works of post-Enlightenment writers like Goethe and his contemporaries, who emerged from the German Pietist tradition. The figural mode was preserved by such American writers as Emerson, Hawthorne, and Melville, who received the Calvinist belief in typology by way of the Puritan theologians Samuel and Cotton Mather, Edward Taylor, and Jonathan Edwards.[3]

Although strict constructionists from Saint Jerome to Martin Luther and Calvin always insisted that typological interpretation must be restricted to the relationship between the two biblical testaments, the mode of thought became so fashionable, indeed so ingrained, that it was frequently opened up to include extrabiblical types. It is, of course, still a standard device of Sunday sermons, which focus on an incident in the Bible that is seen to foreshadow or parallel a contemporary dilemma. And it was soon appropriated by writers as well. In *The Sorrows of Young Werther* (1774), for instance, Goethe exposed his hero's religious obsession by causing him ultimately to fall into a delusional state in which he stages his life's final events so as to post-figure the circumstances leading up to Jesus' death in the Gospels.[4] Voltaire, who was familiar with this mode of thought from his Jesuit education at the Collège Louis-le-Grand in Paris, is making use of typological analogies between Adam and Candide that he would confidently have expected readers of his generation to recognize. At the same time, it is clear that Voltaire is using figuralism satirically, not seriously. And in order for that satirization to occur, yet another development had to have taken place.

New questions concerning the understanding of the Bible had already been raised by the humanists of the Renaissance and the theological thinkers of the Reformation. But by the second half of the eighteenth century the historicity of the Old Testament was being seriously challenged by contemporary scientific developments and by the rationalism of the Enlightenment. This process has been often rehearsed, as in the first chapter of Karl Barth's classic exposition of Protestant theology in the nineteenth century, *From Rousseau to Ritschl.* Whereas, for instance, the natural philosophers of the seventeenth century made it their task to explain nature as a manifestation of God's wonders, the scientists of the late eighteenth century began to understand that the geological evidence simply could not be made to support the story of the Creation as recounted in Genesis,[5] and Bishop Ussher's calculations, according to which the world was created in 4004 B.C.E., began to give way to more realistic estimates.

Around the same time biblical scholars began to put criticism of the Old Testament on a scientific basis. Notably Johann Gottfried Eichhorn, professor of Oriental languages at the University of Jena, in his *Introduction to the Old Testament* (*Einleitung in das alte Testament*, 1780–1783), established modern biblical criticism by applying to the Old Testament the rigorous philological methods recently developed by the classicist Christian Gottlob Heyne.[6] In particular, Eichhorn proposed that many incidents in Genesis, which had previously been assumed to have a historical basis, should in fact be attributed to the ingenuity of myth or legend. While accepting the assumption that Moses wrote the first five books of the Old Testament, Eichhorn argues that Moses based his depiction of the Creation on an oral tradition or legends (*Sagen*) going back hundreds or even thousands of years. And he regards Gen. 2.4–3.24 as an interpolation from foreign sources.[7] It was mythic thinking of this sort, as we have already noted, that enabled Kant, in his "Conjectures on the Beginning of Human History," to reason that the departure of man from Paradise represents nothing but the transition from a crude animal existence into the state of humanity, from instinct into reason—from the constraints of nature into freedom. To be sure, he continues, this transition, which for the species was a huge step forward, was not necessarily the same for the individual. Before the awakening of reason there were no commandments or prohibitions, and hence no violations of them. But as reason developed, conflicts arose. The individual was not yet capable of dealing with the new vices that were alien to his original state of innocence. "From the moral point of view, therefore, the first step beyond this state was a *fall*; and from the physical point of view, this fall was a punishment, for it led to a host of hitherto unknown evils."[8]

Voltaire emerged from this tradition of a rationalism that went beyond skepticism to cynicism. In his many writings on the Bible he employed all the tools of satire to ridicule the contemporary commentators who still sought to justify a literal reading of the Bible and to expose the contradictions and impossibilities of their naïveté.[9] He conceded that the Bible contains fascinating stories which reflect the manners and customs of the ancient Near East; but as a historical document it possesses absolutely no authority. By implication, then, the story of Adam's Fall from Paradise is pure fiction with no claim to historicity or religious authority. As one of literature's most familiar plots, however, as the archetypal tale of the universal fall from innocence, it can be exploited by the techniques of typology to lend dimensions of meaning to a work like *Candide*. With his use of Adam's Fall at the beginning of his narrative to signal the fall from innocence into consciousness and specifically into the knowledge of good and evil, Voltaire established a pattern that was to repeat itself many times in literary masterpieces of the next two centuries. As the Marxist playwright Peter Hacks put it two centuries later in the afterword to his own comedy

81

on the subject, the essential truth of the Christian legend is accessible only to those who no longer regard it as literally true. "Only those who are not required to believe can make use of it."[10]

ROMANTIC TRAGICOMIC FALLS

Heinrich von Kleist's *The Broken Pitcher* (*Der zerbrochne Krug*, first performed in 1808 and published in 1811) is a classic of the German theater and one of its few great comedies. The play was initially inspired by an engraving by Jean Jacques Le Veau (after a painting by Debucourt) that Kleist saw in 1802 in the apartment of his friend Heinrich Zschokke in Bern: labeled *The Judge, or The Broken Pitcher* (*Le juge, ou la cruche cassée*), it depicts an old woman angrily exhibiting a broken pitcher to a village magistrate as a younger woman and various other figures look on. The scene inspired the two friends to a literary competition that resulted in Kleist's dramatic masterpiece and Zschokke's less impressive novella of the same title.

In Kleist's courtroom drama all the action has taken place when the play begins: the denouement is devoted to the analysis and understanding of those actions.[11] During the preceding night the corrupt justice of the peace in a seventeeth-century Dutch village near Utrecht visited a beautiful and virtuous young woman in the attempt to seduce her by threatening to have her fiancé, Ruprecht, assigned for military service to the East Indies. (The threat is both illegal and outside his power, but the unlettered young woman has no way of knowing that.) Ruprecht, paying a surprise visit to his girlfriend, caught the judge in her room but failed to recognize him in the dark. Fleeing through the window, the judge knocked down an earthenware pitcher and injured his leg on the grape trellis outside, where his wig was ensnared. Before the intruder made his escape, Ruprecht managed to hit him twice on the head with a metal door latch. The girl's mother, Frau Marthe, aroused by the clamor and finding Ruprecht in the room, mistakenly accused him of breaking her pitcher.

On the following morning Frau Marthe appears in court to sue Ruprecht for the pitcher, while Ruprecht in turn has become convinced that his fiancée is a common slut. (The broken pitcher is among other things an image for her alleged loss of innocence.) Just as the hearing is about to begin, the judge's secretary, Licht, announces an impending visitation by Councillor Walter, a judicial inspector from Utrecht. The court session turns into a comedy of multiple errors and deceptions as the judge and the young woman for their own separate reasons, he out of guilt and she out of shame and the pressure of blackmail, try to keep the truth from emerging even though all the clues—the prints of the judge's clubfoot in the snow, his injured leg, the gashes on his head, his lost wig—point to the true culprit. As the judge exploits his considerable skill in local court procedures to hide or explain away the facts, Walter, astonished at the unorthodox proceedings, seeks to discover the truth and to carry out his official inspection of the court records and finances. The truth is ultimately uncovered, along with the fact that the judge has also misused court moneys. The comedy ends and order is restored when the judge takes flight and Walter appoints the toadying and ambitious Licht (meaning "light") as his temporary replacement (to bring Enlightenment into the backward village).

The play, still one of the popular works of the German stage, has many fascinating dimensions. As the imaginative exposition of a painting, it provides a textbook example of the relationship between literature and art. It amounts to a brilliant literary parody as a humorous inversion of Sophocles' *Oedipus Rex*, to which Kleist explicitly refers in his preface to the play: in this courtroom drama the judge is attempting to conceal crime (his own) rather than to uncover it. It also reflects metaphorically the contemporary controversy in Kleist's Prussia between the traditional practices of customary law and the rational new General Provincial Code (*Allgemeines Landrecht*) of 1794.[12] In addition to these rich dimensions, another one becomes evident when we take into account the names of the judge and the young woman: Adam and Eve.[13]

The biblical analogies emerge in the first scene (even more strongly in the stage variant than in the published version) when Licht enters to find Judge Adam bandaging his leg. Adam claims that he injured his leg when he stumbled that morning on the floor of his room, but Licht, fully aware of the judge's ways, comments that he is related by name to an ancestor who, at the beginning of time, fell and became famous as a result of his Fall:

> Ihr stammt von einem lockern Ältervater,
> Der so beim Anbeginn der Dinge fiel,
> Und wegen seines Falls berühmt geworden.
>
> (Lines 9–11)

The judge—with much punning on the word "fall"—continues to insist on his version, saying that he stumbled just as he was getting out of bed: "I still had the Morning Song on my lips."[14] This opening dialogue between the judge and his secretary ends when Licht observes skeptically that his accident was "the first Adam's Fall that you have made from a bed" ("Der erste Adamsfall, / Den Ihr aus einem Bett hinaus getan," lines 62–63).

As the action continues, the comic resonances of the Adamic Fall are enhanced by the fact that the German word for a court case is the homonym "der Fall." Accordingly, as Adam and Walter investigate the "case" of the broken pitcher, they are also dealing, the one wittingly and the other at first unwittingly, with the judge's "fall" out of Eve's window the night before—a literal fall that has plunged him into a confrontation with good and evil. Eve presents a different case: while her attractions do indeed tempt Adam into invading her garden and then her bedroom and cause his "fall" from the window when he is caught there by Ruprecht, she is initially innocent and finds herself in her predicament simply because she was foolish enough to "fall" for the pressuring scheme of the judge (his threat to have Ruprecht assigned to the East Indies). Yet it is also true that, through this affair, she loses her innocence, if not necessarily her virginity, and becomes Adam's accomplice in the attempt to deceive the higher authority: for in the person of Judge Adam she has been exposed to good and evil in a manner from which she was previously sheltered. Even Ruprecht, prompted by circumstances to doubt Eve's innocence, falls out of innocence into consciousness.

Kleist does not exploit all of the more obvious possibilities of the plot: in Zschokke's novella, for instance, the broken pitcher itself is decorated with images of Adam and Eve and the Fall, whereas Frau Marthe's pitcher displays scenes from the history of the Netherlands. The text contains, however, along with various biblical allusions (for instance, to the Tower of Babel and to Sodom and Gomorrah), frequent references to the devil. At one point it is even suggested by a neighbor woman that the figure she saw emerging from Eve's garden during the night, to judge from the prints of his clubfoot in the snow and from his awful stench, was none other than the devil. Accordingly, in Kleist's tantalizingly ambivalent version of the Fall, the judge plays the role not simply of the fallen Adam but also of the devil who corrupts Eve's innocence, while Councillor Walter is thrust into the role of the godlike authority who removes Adam from the Paradise-like sinecure of his position as village magistrate.

Kleist (1777–1811) was so greatly intrigued by the legend of the Fall that one scholar has ventured the proposition "that Genesis 3 is nothing less than the fountain-head of Kleist's poetic world in its entirety, and that the intricate criss-cross of strains combining to furnish its symphonic weave can be traced back to that tonic chord above all."[15] His most explicit reference to the theme occurs in his essay "On the Marionette Theater" (1810; 2:338–45). The dialogue deals, through a variety of examples, with the loss of innocence, grace, and spontaneity through consciousness. Kleist's interlocutor begins with the paradox that marionettes, whose movements are all controlled by a single center of gravity, display far more symmetry, lightness, and mobility than human dancers for the simple reason that they lack all conscious posing and coyness. When Kleist expresses his astonishment, his partner suggests that he has not read the third chapter of Genesis with sufficient attention. "If one does not know this first period of all human cultivation, one cannot suitably discuss the following periods, much less the most recent one." Kleist replies with an example of his own: a young man of cultivation and grace, who noticed in a mirror one day, as he placed his foot on a stool to dry it, that his position resembled the famous classical sculpture of the youth removing a thorn from his foot. From the moment when he became consciously aware of his pose, however, he lost his effortless charm of movement. Not only was he unable again to capture the natural position of the sculpture; in his entire person he lost one trait after another. Kleist concludes that in the animal world, where reflectiveness is weak, natural gracefulness emerges smoothly and dominantly; but in the human world, which has been corrupted by consciousness, innocence is lost and its paradise can never be recaptured. Whereupon his friend offers the example of two points that cross and then, after moving in opposite directions through infinity, meet once again: by analogy, when cognition has gone through an infinity, grace reappears. It manifests itself most purely in bodies that have either no consciousness or absolute consciousness: in the marionette or in God. "Therefore," Kleist concludes questioningly, "we would have to eat again from the Tree of Knowledge in order to fall back again into the state of innocence?"

It was Kleist's tragic dilemma, which drove him only a year after the publication of his play to death by suicide, that he lived in the period between the fall and the recapture of innocence through a higher consciousness—between the worlds of the marionette and of God. Dismayed by his encounter with Kant's *Critique of Pure Reason*, which convinced him that there can be no epistemological certainty in this world, Kleist and his fictional creations cling for security to such moral certainties as

86

their faith in themselves and others (*Vertrauen*) or to such social certainties as the Prussian legal code, which Kleist read with the same attentiveness, and with the same degree of faith and skepticism, that he brought to the Bible. (Like most members of his generation, Kleist was *bibelfest*, and references to the Bible show up frequently in his works and especially in his letters.) For a time he even seriously entertained the Candide-like notion of buying a farm in Switzerland, where he might might find security and stability in cultivating his own garden.[16]

In *The Broken Pitcher* he shows the dilemma of a young couple whose innocence is betrayed by the very person in whom society (the village) should be able to place its faith: the judge, the representative of law. Once that innocence is lost, they find support in the higher authority of the state (Utrecht). But innocence once lost can never be recovered. Ruprecht's faith in his betrothed has suffered, however wrongly, its first crack. Eva's confidence in the state has been only tentatively restored by Walter. There is no assurance whatsoever that the village will be better served by the cynical, scheming Licht than it was by Adam. Kleist's play reenacts the events of the Bible, where the fall of humankind is redeemed only when we have once again been restored to paradise—a state attainable neither by the figures of his tragicomedy nor by Kleist himself.

E.T.A. HOFFMANN (1776–1822) was Kleist's near contemporary and, like him, a legally trained advocate of the Prussian legal system. Kleist, however, was no fan of Voltaire and other French *philosophes* of the Enlightenment. In 1801 he expressed his doubts in a letter to his fiancée about the handsomely bound volumes of Rousseau, Helvetius, and Voltaire that he had seen in the libraries of revolutionary Paris. "What good have they done? Has a single one achieved its goal? Have they been able to hold back the wheel that rushes inexorably plummeting toward its abyss?" (2:681). Kleist's obsession with the story of the Fall, to the extent that it had a source outside himself and his own fascination with the Bible, probably came from Kant's

"Conjectures on the Beginning of Human History" and from works of art. Hoffmann, in contrast, admired Voltaire and in particular *Candide*, calling it in his diary for January 7, 1804, "the very norm of a good novel" (65–66), which conceals its philosophical composition behind a veil of caricatures, and which is spiced by human folly represented in the most vivid coloring.

Hoffmann's "fairy tale from modern times," *The Golden Pot* (*Der goldne Topf*, 1814), appears at first glance to be so utterly Romantic that it could have nothing in common with an Enlightenment classic like *Candide*. Like many Romantic narratives, *The Golden Pot* revolves around a central myth of redemption. (The mythic aspect of the tale has attracted the attention especially of Jungian critics.) For his deeds of passion and violence, we learn, the elemental spirit Salamander was once upon a time cast out of the primal paradise of Atlantis and exiled to earth in the human form of Archivarius Lindhorst; he may not return until all three of his daughters have found and married young men who still believe in the wonders of nature and poetry. At that time Salamander will be redeemed and may return to the glories of Atlantis. Thus far the myth, which is recounted in the eighth of the twelve "vigils" (chapters) that constitute the narrative.

The actual story, which like most of Hoffmann's tales takes place on the often confusing borderline between reality and fantasy, involves one such suitor, the student Anselmus, who lives in the Germany of Hoffmann's day. Because his talents suggest that he may aspire to the lofty position of court councillor, the ambitious Veronica, daughter of Deputy Rector Paulmann, has set her sights on him. Anselmus is engaged by Archivarius Lindhorst to copy manuscripts in his library, and in the course of these activities he falls in love with Lindhorst's daughter Serpentina. In alternating "vigils" we see how Anselmus is torn back and forth between the world of Veronica, which is located in the realistic setting of taverns and drawing rooms in the Dresden of 1812, and the realm of Serpentina, situated in the fantastic setting of Lindhorst's house and library, where magical transformations and psychedelic experiences take place. Veronica enlists the aid of a woman with reputedly witch-like powers in her effort to win back the affections of Anselmus. But eventually he succumbs to Serpentina's charms and departs with her—the first of Lindhorst's three daughters—to the kingdom of Atlantis. (Hoffmann suggests, but does not clearly state, that Anselmus's disappearance from Dresden is the result of a suicidal plunge into the Elbe River.) Veronica happily weds Registrar Heerbrand, who has himself just been appointed court councillor.

In the last "vigil" the narrator introduces himself into the story, explaining that, after portraying Anselmus's fantastic experiences, he has become so depressed by the miserable circumstances of his own life that he is unable to complete his account. Then he receives a note from Lindhorst, inviting him to his house, where the archivarius reveals a vision of Anselmus happily living with Serpentina on his estate in the kingdom of Atlantis. The narrator, having recorded this final vision, is again dismayed at the thought of his own wretched reality in his garret room. But Lindhorst reminds him that he, too, has a stake in Atlantis through his poetic visions. "Is Anselmus's bliss anything other than a life in Poetry, to which the sacred harmony of all being reveals itself as the most profound secret of nature?" And on this note, which suggests that the narrator himself will become the suitor of Lindhorst's second daughter, the fairy tale ends.

This account seems to have little to do with Voltaire or, for that matter, with Genesis. Yet within the first few pages we realize that Hoffmann has mastered the lessons learned almost ten years earlier from *Candide*. We first meet Anselmus at three o'clock in the afternoon of Ascension Day, as he rushes through the Black Gate (an actual gate leading out of the northern suburb of Dresden Neustadt) and collides with an ugly old woman selling apples and pastries from her basket. As her wares are scattered across the road, Anselmus confusedly hands her his wallet with its paltry coins and, in embarrassment at his clumsiness, rushes on, while the old woman curses and shouts after him, "Just run, run, you child of Satan—you'll soon fall into the crystal." (The crystal, which for Hoffmann and other Romantics had negative connotations of seduction and imprisonment, anticipates Anselmus's illusion later in the story that he is imprisoned in a crystal jar on a shelf in Lindhorst's library.) Now, unless we are willing to assume that the details are purely random, we quickly realize that, within only a few lines, we have had references both to a fall caused by a woman with apples and to ultimate redemption: the hour of three o'clock is associated with the end of the darkness at noon that clouded the Crucifixion, and the scene takes place on the day marking Christ's ascension into heaven forty days after Easter.

The allusions of the opening lines are soon borne out by other details: we learn that Anselmus is a student of theology (a detail that justifies the biblical associations), and we follow him as he makes his way to an (actual) amusement park on the banks of the Elbe known as Linke's Paradise. But since as a result of "the fatal step into the basket of apples" (1:279) he has given away the little money he had, he cannot enjoy the coffee and beer to which he had looked forward. Instead, he lies down beneath an elder tree and thinks about the ills that Satan has brought upon his miserable, impoverished life. (There are five references to Satan and the devil within two pages.) As he dozes, he gradually becomes aware of strange sounds beside him in the grass and then in the branches and leaves of the tree above— twittering, then whispering and bell-like sounds. Looking up, he sees what appear to be three small green-gold snakes playing in the branches. At first he believes that the vision is caused by the evening sun glittering in the branches of the tree. But one of the snakes gazes at him with her dark blue eyes, filling him with a sense of supreme bliss, and he hears a voice saying that the fragrance and radiance of which he is suddenly for the first time fully aware is the language of nature when it has been ignited by love. At length the three snakes slip off through the grass and disappear into the river. (They subsequently reappear in Lindhorst's library as his daughters.)

The bundle of biblical allusions—to a woman with apples, a literal "fall" in the streets, a curse, serpents in a tree—signals immediately, as in *Candide,* that we are again dealing with the account of a fall from the innocence of the figure's previous existence. But as the ensuing narrative makes vividly clear, it is a fall with a difference: Anselmus's literal stumbling fall occurs as he is rushing out of town through the Black Gate—in other words, as he is leaving the security of his previous bourgeois life, represented by Veronica and her father, and entering the world of myth and poetry exemplified by Lindhorst and Serpentina. The topography of the story bears out this symbolism: Veronica's house, along with the tavern and other locales of bourgeois existence, are all within the old city of Dresden; whereas the mythic adventures—not just the encounter with Serpentina, but also Veronica's sorcery with the witch—take place outside the city walls, in the realm of nature. Even Lindhorst's mysterious house is located in a remote suburb, far from the bourgeois reality of Deputy Rector Paulmann's family. So when Anselmus rushes out the gate on that fateful day, he is leaving behind the security of his earlier life and entering the realm of poetry and nature that has no place in the bourgeois reality of early-nineteenth-century Dresden.

The plot, which need concern us no further, deals with Anselmus's vacillation between the two realms and with the efforts of the two sides to win him over—Veronica for the sake of her worldly ambitions and Serpentina for the mythic redemption of her father. Ultimately Anselmus succumbs to Serpentina's poetic charms and thus recovers from his initial "fall" to enter the new paradise of Atlantis: the "ascension" promised in the opening lines.

Hoffmann's faith in the power of myth and poetry, in sum, enables him to achieve for his figures the redemption denied to Kleist and his characters. But in both of these powerful and representative works of German Romanticism the image of the biblical Fall is used to signal at the outset that the stories we are reading or viewing amount to far more than their comic or fairy-tale plots might at first glance suggest. We are dealing with the loss of innocence and the emergence into a wholly new world of good and evil (for Kleist) or of myth and poetry (for Hoffmann). (The adaptation of the myth for lighthearted purposes was, of course, not unique to Kleist and Hoffmann. In a scene familiar from Schubert biographies and recorded in a watercolor by Leopold Kupelwieser, for instance, the composer's friends in 1821 at Schloss Atzenbrugg enacted a charade in which the key word for a waterfall was suggested by a *tableau vivant* of the biblical Fall.)

AMERICAN AMBIGUITIES

We know from several studies what a pervasive role religious typology played in early American thought and literature.[17] Among the various typological figures, none was more prominent than Adam, whose centrality is suggested by two major works that appeared in 1860.

Biblical typology provided the perfect vehicle for the themes of cyclical recurrence and the westering of culture that inform much of Walt Whitman's poetry. It is no surprise, accordingly, to find that in the third edition of *Leaves of Grass* (1860) he added a section entitled "Children of Adam," in which both of those themes figure prominently. In "Ages and Ages Returning at Intervals," for instance, the poet sees himself as the eternally recurring "I, chanter of Adamic songs, / Through the new garden the West, the great cities calling." Although Adam is not named in the poem "Facing West from California's Shores," he is clearly implied when the poet, "the circle almost circled," looks out over the Pacific toward "the house of maternity" in Asia.

Long having wander'd since, round the earth having wander'd,
Now I face home again, very pleas'd and joyous,
(But where is what I started for so long ago?
And why is it yet unfound?)

The first and last poems in the section make it clear that the new
Adam is the typological figure whose recurrence and westering
come together in the American poet. The cycle begins as the
poet ascends anew "[t]o the garden the world":

Content with the present, content with the past,
By my side or back of me Eve following,
Or in front, and I following her just the same.

And it ends "[a]s Adam early in the morning, / Walking forth
from the bower refresh'd with sleep," asks the world to acknowledge his presence in mid-nineteenth-century America. It is almost as though Whitman, who presumably never heard of Kleist
or his essay "On the Marionette Theater," had succeeded in
going around the world and entering paradise again through
the back gate.

That same year of 1860 saw the publication of Nathaniel Hawthorne's flawed yet magnificent novel *The Marble Faun*. The
work is so long, and the symbolism so complex, that the Adamic
theme often disappears for pages and chapters on end. And yet
for Hawthorne and his obsession with the consequences of sin
and with guilt, the figure of Adam provides the perfect type,
and it occurs nowhere more explicitly than in *The Marble Faun*.[18]
Set in Rome, the novel features Donatello, a charming and innocent Italian count, who is befriended by three artistic friends:
the American sculptor Kenyon, the gifted New England copyist
Hilda, and the exotic painter Miriam. Miriam, the daughter of
Anglo-Jewish and Italian parents, has a mysterious past that is
involved somehow with a Capuchin monk who shadows her
menacingly. Donatello, falling in love with Miriam and becoming aware of her inchoate desire to be liberated from her tormentor, kills the monk in an act of almost mindless spontaneity,

hurling him from the Tarpeian Rock overlooking the Forum, and then flees to his estate at Monte Beni in the Apennines.

The murder takes place a third of the way into the novel; the remainder of the story deals with the consequences of that deed for the four friends. Donatello is plunged by his guilt from innocence into a new maturity. Deciding to accept responsibility for his act, he returns to Rome, where he surrenders to justice and is imprisoned. Miriam, not technically guilty of murder, takes upon herself a life of renunciation and penance for her part in the crime of her lover. The gentle Hilda, a reluctant witness to the murder, eventually recovers from her shock and marries Kenyon, both of them sobered by the experience they have shared with Donatello and Miriam.

The clarity of denouement is obscured by several factors: for instance, the lengthy disquisitions on art and Roman sights. Some critics have also been put off by the plethora of symbols and allegory. The title, which refers to the Faun of Praxiteles, to which Donatello bears a startling resemblance, suggests that Hawthorne initially planned to emphasize the symbolism of classical mythology. At the same time, the Roman location quite naturally brings in the Catholic Church and its ambiguous attraction for the two young American Protestants, Kenyon and Hilda.

The Adamic theme is introduced relatively late. A preliminary hint occurs in chapter 8 when Donatello meets Miriam on the grounds of the Villa Borghese: the narrator reports that "the scene is like Eden in its loveliness; like Eden, too, in the fatal spell that removes it beyond the scope of man's actual possessions" (632). But at this point the characters themselves, and especially the childishly innocent Donatello, are unaware of the potential symbolism, even when Miriam warns him of her Eve-like perils: "Those who come too near me are in danger of great mischiefs, I assure you. Take warning, therefore!" (636). It is only after the crime, which involves the conspicuous image of a literal fall of the Capuchin's body from the Tarpeian Rock, that the images begin to occur, along with the sudden transformation of Donatello's character from innocence to consciousness (chap. 19). "It had kindled him into a man; it had developed within him an intelligence which was no native characteristic of the Donatello whom we have heretofore known. But that simple and joyous creature was gone forever" (689). Almost immediately, we read, their crime "had wreathed itself . . . like a serpent, in inextricable links about both their souls" (690). In a weird inversion they realize that they have been transported by their crime into a "strange, lonesome Paradise" peopled by "the high and ever-sad fraternity of Caesar's murderers" (691). Meanwhile Hilda, too young and pure to have had any previous experience of sin and guilt, sits listless in her room, pondering the dire lesson commissioned by Providence for her moral edification: "[H]e perpetrates a sin; and Adam falls anew, and Paradise, heretofore in unfaded bloom, is lost again, and closed forever, with the fiery swords gleaming at its gates" (707). Hawthorne's characters, anticipating Kafka's, appear to be burdened by an existential guilt, whether of their own doing or not. It is the destiny of his figures, like Hilda, to relive ever anew the experience of the fall from innocence into the knowledge of good and evil. "While there is a single guilty person in the universe," she tells Miriam, "each innocent one must feel his innocence tortured by that guilt" (712).

Biblical imagery has by this point almost wholly displaced the initial classical mythology. When Kenyon visits Donatello at Monte Beni, he feels "the sensations of an adventurer who should find his way to the site of ancient Eden, and behold its loveliness through the transparency of that gloom which has been brooding over those haunts of innocence ever since the fall" (749). Adam, he reflects, saw it in a brighter sunshine, "but never knew the shade of pensive beauty which Eden won from his expulsion." Unaware of Hilda's troubled broodings, he imagines "the sweet paradise on earth that Hilda's presence there might make" (756). Meanwhile, in a Rome deserted by the multitudes in the pestilential heat of summer, Hilda medi-tates: "What the flaming sword was to the first Eden, such is the malaria to these sweet gardens and groves" (778). A hitherto unknown torpor possesses her, "like a half-dead serpent knot-ting its cold, inextricable wreaths about her limbs," now that she has experienced "that dismal certainty of the existence of evil in the world" (779).

Yet the fall is no unambiguous evil. Looking at Kenyon's bust of Donatello, Hilda realizes that his face, which formerly evinced little more than geniality, now gives "the impression of a growing intellectual power and moral sense" (809). And Mir-iam also wonders whether the crime in which she and Donatello were symbolically wed was not actually a blessing, "a means of education, bringing a simple and imperfect nature to a point of feeling and intelligence which it could have reached under no other discipline" (840). Their romance, she decides, re-peated the story of the Fall of Man. Pursuing the analogy fur-ther: "Was that very sin,—into which Adam precipitated himself and all his race,—was it the destined means by which, over a long pathway of toil and sorrow, we are to attain a higher, brighter, and profounder happiness, than our lost birthright gave?" (840). Indeed, does that idea not account for the very existence of sin and guilt in the world? This is the problematic ambiguity with which Hawthorne's story leaves us. On the one hand, in a veritable Whitmanesque recurrence, the annual Roman Carnival, an exhausted ritual for many, is still new each year for the youthful, "who make the worn-out world itself as fresh as Adam found it on his first forenoon in Paradise" (841). On the other hand, as Kenyon concludes on a positive note, it may be the moral of Donatello's story that man is destined ever anew to fall and thereby to awaken moral and intellectual capa-bilities of which he might otherwise have remained innocent. "Did Adam fall, that we might ultimately rise to a far loftier paradise than his?" (854). With this notion of the *felix culpa*, which can be traced back to the earliest Christian exegetes,

Hawthorne ends his novel and rationalizes the existence of sin and guilt in the world.

WHILE THE notion of the American Adam was pervasive in the nineteenth century, as R.W.B. Lewis demonstrated in a seminal study, no other work after *The Marble Faun* exemplified that figure so powerfully as Herman Melville's *Billy Budd* (1891; first published 1924).[19] Melville's novella has become a central text for exponents of the interdisciplinary field of Law and Literature. Yet the author himself indicated that the biblical analogies are at least as important as its legal implications. "Coke and Blackstone hardly shed so much light into obscure spiritual places as the Hebrew Prophets," he reminds us (chap. 11). And the preface suggests that the year of his narrative involved "a crisis for Christendom." With these signals in mind, then, we approach Melville's account of the innocent sailor, impressed in 1797 onto a British warship, whose personal beauty made him at once a popular figure among his fellow seamen and an object of hatred (actually of a homoerotic love-hatred) for the master-at-arms, John Claggart. We have no need to rehearse in detail a story familiar to most American high school and college students. Billy Budd, handicapped in moments of emotional turmoil by his stutter, is manipulated by the scheming Claggart into a situation in which he strikes the master-at-arms and, by accident, kills him. Despite all his instinctive sympathy for Billy Budd and despite the various legal options at his disposal, Captain Vere, fearing mutiny among his men, sees no alternative to the summary justice of hanging the innocent sailor under the Articles of War.

This basically simple tale is enhanced through a variety of motives: the homoerotic relationship between Budd and Claggart, the self-tormenting ambivalence of Vere, mysterious hints at Budd's paternity, the legal situation of a warship operating under the laws of the Mutiny Act, and others. The story also reenacts, in a manner analogous to Hoffmann's *The Golden Pot*, the movement of the Bible from the Fall to the Ascension. Despite various allusions to classical mythology—Billy is compared to Apollo, to Hercules, and to Achilles—the biblical ones prevail. The typology begins (chap. 2) when the foundling Billy is asked about his paternity: "God knows, sir" is his only response. While unlettered, Billy is said to possess the kind of intelligence and rectitude characteristic of "one to whom not yet has been proffered the questionable apple of knowledge." In his utterly natural demeanor, he is "such perhaps as Adam presumably might have been ere the urbane Serpent wriggled himself into his company." Indeed, his pristine virtue seems "to corroborate the doctrine of man's fall," since it is so totally inconsistent with civilized custom or convention. Only the flaw of his stutter suggests that "the envious marplot of Eden" has had his effect on "every human consignment to this planet of earth." But his nature has not yet experienced "the reactionary bite of that serpent" (chap. 13). Indeed, Captain Vere suggests that Billy "in the nude might have posed for a statue of young Adam before the Fall" (chap. 19).

If these allusions prepare us for events of lapsarian grandeur, the descriptions of the two other major figures complete the scenario. Captain Vere, we learn, is a man with pronounced intellectual proclivities, of settled convictions, of faith in institutions, and without patience for infractions of discipline. If Captain Vere suggests through his attributes a Genesis Yahweh, then Claggart's "natural depravity" and baleful desire to corrupt Budd's innocence, along with his official position as disciplinarian of the warship, suit him perfectly for the role of Satan. His pallid complexion betrays an unnatural "seclusion from the sunlight," and he has under his control "various converging wires of underground influence" (chap. 8). Above all, he exemplifies "the mania of an evil nature" that is not the product of training or corruption but innate (chap. 11). His actions are motivated solely by a cynical disdain for innocence (chap. 13). When Claggart falsely accuses Billy of incitement to mutiny, his eyes undergo a remarkable transformation, losing their human expression and protruding like the eyes of deep-sea creatures. "The first mesmeric glance was one of serpent fascination" (chap. 20). Appropriately, when Vere and Budd try to lift the satanic Claggart, whom Billy has just struck down, "It was like handling a dead snake" (chap. 20).

Leaving aside the complexities of motivation and of law, we readily see that Melville has enhanced and universalized the implications of his simple tale by making it into yet another vehicle for the myth of the Fall: under the stern eye of a law unmitigated by mercy we see that innocence is predestined to be corrupted by a malign and pervasive evil. It is his sudden realization of Claggart's, and the world's, iniquity that destroys Billy's innocence and causes his guilt when he kills the master-at-arms. But if the assumptions of Melville's fable are bleak, its conclusion leaves a certain albeit ambivalent leeway for hope. For Billy's execution is depicted with explicit overtones of the Crucifixion and the Ascension. At the moment of his hanging

> it chanced that the vapory fleece hanging low in the East was shot
> through with a soft glory as of the fleece of the Lamb of God seen
> in mystical vision, and simultaneously therewith, watched by the
> wedged mass of upturned faces, Billy ascended, and, ascending,
> took the full rose of the dawn. (Chap. 26)

At the same time, Melville's comments suggest a certain ironic reservation, for within moments the symbolic fleece of vapor vanishes. Although for the next few years superstitious sailors collect chips of the spar from which Billy was hanged "as a piece of the Cross" (chap. 31), and although an account of his last hours, gospel-like, circulates in the form of a sailors' ballad, it remains a distinct possibility that his ascension is not a true re-demption justifying the initial *felix culpa*, as in Hoffmann's Ro-mantic tale, but merely a rationalization through which the wit-nesses sought for a time to make sense of the fundamentally irrational event of the corruption and destruction of innocence by evil. From Whitman by way of Hawthorne to Melville, in any case, we witness a broad spectrum of Adamic symbolism: from

the optimistic faith in the return to paradise, by way of the ambivalent belief that the fall from innocence is the necessary prelude to the growth of moral intelligence, to the gloomy conviction that innocence is doomed in a world that has recourse only
to rationalizing myths.

Modern Ironies

If the nineteenth-century transformations of the myth of the
Fall end in ambivalence, the twentieth-century plunge from innocence into knowledge begins on a note of utter despair: "Gazing up into the darkness I saw myself as a creature driven and
derided by vanity; and my eyes burned with anguish and anger."
This famous sentence concludes James Joyce's "Araby," one of
the fifteen stories constituting his *Dubliners* (1914) and marking
the transition from the group of three stories about childhood
to the next group portraying adolescence. In the desolate world
of fin-de-siècle Dublin ("Araby" was written in 1905 about events
of 1894) the growth from childhood to adolescence signifies
the loss of hope and innocence as the child becomes fully aware
of the stifling constraints that paralyze the body and soul of
Ireland. Joyce portrays this sudden awareness through the eyes
of a narrator recalling the frustrated puppy love that he felt, as
a boy, for an older girl living next door. When the object of
his inarticulate affection is prevented by a school retreat from
visiting a charity bazaar called Araby, the boy decides to go on
his own and to buy her a present. But he arrives too late; most
of the booths have already closed down for the night; and the
tawdriness of the few still open exposes to him the futility of his
ambition and triggers the collapse of his dreams in the face of
reality.

The few pages in which Joyce communicates this moving
epiphany also manage brilliantly to recapitulate the large biblical movement from Genesis to the New Testament—not, however, to any redeeming ascension, as in *Billy Budd*, but simply to

the moment of the betrayal. How does he do it? We are alerted to the religious implications of the text in the second paragraph, where the narrator tells us that the former tenant of his family's house was a priest, who died in the back drawing room. According to Joyce's system of symbols, that death signals the death of religion and the emptying or secularization of its images. When the paragraph goes on to inform us that "[t]he wild garden behind the house contained a central apple-tree and a few straggling bushes under one of which I found the late tenant's rusty bicycle-pump," we realize that we are being primed for a story about the loss of paradise: the Garden of Eden with its apple tree is now wild and deserted, and even the serpent has been reduced to nothing more than the rubber hose on a rusty pump.[20]

But the expulsion from the paradise of childhood that the boy undergoes leads to no redemption. When he arrives at the bazaar, we are again alerted to the religious symbolism: the deserted hall is dark and pervaded by "a silence like that which pervades a church after a service." This silence is first interrupted by the sound of two men counting money onto a tray. "I listened to the fall of the coins"—like the coins paid to Judas for the betrayal of Jesus. At another booth he overhears a snatch of conversation between two young Englishmen and an Irish girl, one of those configurations through which Joyce signals the political submission of Ireland to England:

—O, I never said such a thing!
—O, but you did!
—O, but I didn't!
—Didn't she say that?
—Yes. I heard her.
—O, there's a . . . fib.

Following the betrayal of Judas, this conversation recapitulates the threefold denial by Peter. The boy is, of course, unaware of these typological dimensions of his experience. His disenchantment with the bazaar, his sudden consciousness of his own

vanity and anguish and anger, is provoked by the confrontration
of his childhood dream of glory and love with the cheap and
tawdry reality of the bazaar and its denizens. In the subtle sym-
bology of Joyce's fictional world there is no promise that *culpa*
is *felix*.

AN undertaking surprisingly analogous to Joyce's, but at considerably greater length, is evident in Hermann Hesse's interna-
tionally and intergenerationally successful novel *Demian*
(1919).[21] *Demian* presents the first-person account of a young
man named Emil Sinclair, who soon after the end of World War
I records certain crucial episodes from his life between the ages
ten and twenty. His boyhood memories are dominated by his
friendship with Max Demian, an older boy who rescues him
from a blackmailing bully and then challenges him to liberate
himself through independent thought from the narrow pietism
of his family. When Sinclair goes off to boarding school, he at
first slumps into profligacy. But the platonic love he conceives
for a girl he glimpses in a park sets him back on the path to self-
discovery, whose goals are brought into focus by the mystical
teachings of a renegade theologian named Pistorius. At the university Sinclair encounters Demian again and enters into an at
least symbolically incestuous relationship with his friend's
mother, who is known to her circle as Frau Eva. This year of
happiness and spiritual maturity is ended by the war, which
soon claims Demian as a victim. Demian's death on the battlefield forces Sinclair to the final stage of spiritual independence,
where he discovers that he no longer has need of external pro-
tectors and mentors to guide him on his way.

Hesse once remarked that he considered the religious impulse the decisive characteristic of his life and works.[22] *Demian*,
which amounts to a veritable encyclopedia of comparative religion, bears out this claim. As the son of missionaries to India,
as an avid reader of contemporary works on religion and myth,
and as the psychoanalytic patient of a disciple of C. G. Jung,

Hesse was well acquainted with the myths from which he appropriated many of the symbols of his novel. But this religious imagery is located within a specifically biblical framework, which begins with the Fall and ends with Revelation. Hesse wrote in a letter of 1930, "The myths of the Bible, like all myths of mankind, are worthless to us as long as we do not dare to interpret them personally, for ourselves and our own times."[23] His essay "A Bit of Theology" (1932) begins with the statement that a belief in the three stages of human development is fundamental, even sacred, in his eyes. "The path of humanization begins with innocence (paradise, childhood, a preliminary stage lacking responsibility). From there it leads into guilt, to the knowledge of good and evil, to the demands of culture, morality, religions, of humanity's ideals" (7:389). For anyone who has reached this stage and lived through it as a differentiated individual, he continues, it ends inevitably in despair, in the insight that there can be no realization of virtue, that justice is unattainable, that goodness is unfulfillable. Up to this point Hesse's scheme sounds like the outline for Joyce's "Araby." But, he goes on, this despair can lead either to self-destruction or to a higher stage of the spirit, to the experience of a condition beyond morality and laws—in short, to faith. Here Hesse seems to be recapitulating two of his favorite writers of German Romanticism, Kleist and Hoffmann. In any case, it is this pattern that underlies the development of Emil Sinclair.

The very first page of the novel acquaints us with the "Two Realms" between which Sinclair, as a ten-year-old, feels torn.[24] At home, in the warm security of his father's house, he has grown up in a "light" world of order and Christian goodness. But that cozy harmony is achieved only through the family's ignoring and denying the "dark" world of sex, violence, and lust that Sinclair encounters whenever he goes down to the servants' quarters or out onto the streets of the town. When he imagined the devil, he recalls, it was always downstairs or outside, but never at home. With the first stirrings of puberty he begins to sense that this "dark" world, rejected so disdainfully by his family, is no less a natural part of life than the "light" world that they have contrived to satisfy their Christian ethics. As Sinclair, tempted by the "dark" world, makes his first tentative moves away from the security of home, he looks back at it longingly as at "a lost paradise." When he is thrust out of this innocence of his childhood, he realizes that "a locked gateway to Eden with its pitilessly resplendent host of guardians" (64) has sprung up between himself and the innocence of his past.

Once home has been established symbolically as the primal paradise, the incident that triggers the fall is Sinclair's attempt to impress some of the rougher boys by claiming to have stolen a sackful of apples from a garden near the mill. The plan misfires when an older boy, Franz Kromer, threatens to expose him as a thief. In the boy's biblically schooled mind—it never occurs to him in his inexperience simply to consult his father or some other adult—he takes Kromer for the devil himself: "It was my sin that I had given the devil my hand"; "his evil eye glittered devilishly"; "the devil could take me, for no way led back." Tormented by fear and anxiety, Sinclair "tasted death for the first time." For several weeks he tries to buy off Kromer with the small change at his disposal, but he always has to "leave the garden" to meet his tormentor. His despair reaches its nadir when Kromer demands that Sinclair bring his sister along to their next meeting: suddenly Sinclair becomes aware of sexuality. "I was still a child, but I knew from hearsay that boys and girls, when they were a bit older, could do certain mysterious, repulsive, and forbidden things together" (30–31). By this point we have all the motifs of the Fall: the theft of apples, the presence of a devilish seducer, the sudden awareness of sexuality, and the threatened loss of paradise. Before that happens, however, Max Demian enters the picture and, by mysterious means, manages to rid Sinclair of his tormentor. Following this first taste of good and evil, Sinclair flees, at least briefly, back into his childhood paradise.

If we turn to the end of the novel, following a series of awakening episodes based on other stories from the Bible (Cain, Jacob and the angel, the Prodigal Son, the unrepentant thief at Golgotha), we find an equally unmistakable biblical allusion. As Sinclair stands on the battlefield in Flanders, he experiences the mortar shell that wounds him as the vision of a great goddess in the sky, crouching to give birth to a new humanity: "Suddenly she cried out and from her forehead sprang stars, many thousands of shining stars that leaped in marvelous arches and semicircles across the black sky. One of these stars shot straight toward me with a clear ringing sound and it seemed to seek me out" (139). Hesse is playing here with John's vision in Revelation (12.1–2):

> And there appeared a great wonder in heaven: a woman clothed with the sun, and the moon under her feet, and upon her head a crown of twelve stars:
> And she being with child cried, travailing in birth, and pained to be delivered.

Wounded by the mortar shell, Sinclair is taken to a field hospital, where he has his final encounter with Demian, who tells him he must now look within himself for spiritual guidance. Hesse knows that few mortals are privileged to reach the third stage envisioned by the Romantics and described in his essay: the return to paradise through a higher consciousness. We can hope at most for moments of visionary ecstasy, like those portrayed by Hoffmann in *The Golden Pot*. Most people, once they have fallen as the result of consciousness out of the paradise of childhood and innocence, are condemned to the second stage of despair. For Hesse as well as Joyce, the Romantic escape from consciousness has given way to an essentially modern despair.

THE tragic nature of the modern consciousness was analyzed most meticulously perhaps by Miguel de Unamuno in *The Tragic Sense of Life* (1913). The "point of departure" for this tragic view of life, as he explains in the second chapter, is the ironic insight that humankind has alienated itself from nature solely by consciousness. Unamuno comes to precisely the opposite conclusion from Byron's Adam, who reasoned that "knowledge is good, / And life is good; and how can both be evil?" (*Cain*, 1.1.37–38). If the animal state of nature represents perfect health, then it follows that consciousness is a disease. "Disease itself is the essential condition of what we call progress, and progress itself a disease" (23). This is the real meaning of what he terms the "mythical tragedy of Paradise." Adam and Eve lived there in a state of perfect health and innocence. But when, tempted by the serpent, they tasted the fruit of the Tree of Knowledge, they became subject to disease as well as death, and to labor and progress. "And thus it was," according to the conventional interpretation, "that the curiosity of woman, of Eve, of the being most subject to organic necessity and the conservation of life, brought about the Fall, man's redemption, which put us on the road to God, to attain to Him and to be in Him." But Unamuno sees the situation in a more ironic light. A perfectly healthy man would be no longer a man but an irrational animal: "irrational for want of any disease to ignite his reason" (25). The desire to know for the sole pleasure of knowing is a disease, which perhaps owes its origin to language. And this disease is tragic because it is in conflict with the desire to live. "For to live is one thing and to know is another" (39). It is our consciousness that makes us aware of death, and as a result of that consciousness we strive to attain personal immortality—specifically through sexual union. This longing not to die and to persevere indefinitely in our own being, in turn, constitutes "the affective basis of all knowledge and the personal inner point of departure for any and all human philosophy" (42). The irreconcilable tension and opposition between vitalism and rationalism, for Unamuno, is the basis for his tragic sense of life.

This tragic view of the fall—that consciousness deprives us of paradise and cuts us off from nature—has persisted down to writers of our own time. A modern analogy to Unamuno's account of the tragic origins of sexual urges is implicit in Mike Figgis's film *The Loss of Sexual Innocence* (1999), in which the story of Adam and Eve prefigures a series of contemporary erotic episodes mirroring that primal fall. A different emphasis obsesses the German writer Günter Kunert, in whose poems and prose sketches the myth of the Fall recurs leitmotivically.[25] In a rumination entitled "Genesis: The Serpent and the Expulsion" Kunert argues that the Fall of Man, usually misunderstood as the violation of a sexual taboo, is actually an unclear memory of the most important event in the history of humankind: the departure from nature.[26] In an interview in 1992 Kunert clarified his idea.[27] The fall, he explains, was involuntary and unconscious. "Our whole present misery and all the problems of industrial civilization stem from the fact that, in a remote dark time, we placed our hopes in the instrumental: that is, at the moment when man used the first firestone as a tool, the Fall took place." At the same time a shift occurred whereby human thinking accommodated itself to this instrumental procedure. "Our brain, our modes of thought, our logic, our reason became what one calls instrumental. That is where the Fall can be found. That is our sin, our exit from animality."

Kunert returns to this theme over and over again, but its most bizarre fictional realization occurs in the gloomy parable "Adam and Evam" (1984).[28] The story is allegedly a first-person account by one of two crew members in a filthy space capsule en route to Sirius. Some years earlier in the course of a routine mission, we learn, the crew, known at the time simply as A. and E., had looked down at earth to see what appeared to be fifteen minutes of lightning, even though there had been no reports of storms. Subsequently all communication with their base fell silent. After forty-eight hours it became clear that a huge cataclysm had destroyed earth and humankind. Following their emergency instructions, the crew diverted their capsule from its earth orbit and set out for Sirius, where they were to begin a new human race. What ensues, however, convinces the narrator that perhaps eventual failure is built into every act of creation.

In order to carry out their mission, the narrator was required to perform a sex-change operation on his partner. The necessary surgical equipment and replacement organs were provided in a secret compartment within the capsule, and the procedure—carried out against the wishes of an anesthetized E.—was at least a partial success. Evam, whose male origin is acknowledged by the final letter of his/her name, is wholly bald but sports a full gray beard, which s/he grooms with bits of paper from the former logbook into a weirdly Assyrian shape. Evam, we learn, initially resisted sexual relations with Adam, who finally convinced him/her with the argument that they were destined to create the world anew. "We are the source of a new race of mankind. We shall not repeat the terrible old mistakes. Neither shall our children be named Cain and Abel, nor shall they ever correspond in character to those names." In time, Evam begins to enjoy their sex and manifests feminine allures in order to entice Adam to bed. But, owing to some technical flaw in the plastic sex-change organs provided, they cannot conceive children. Unable to sleep at night, Adam takes barbiturates, which produce hallucinations in which the cables beneath the oscillograph seem to be transformed into the smooth body of a slender serpent. Thus, thanks to the failure of technology, the new Adam and Evam, cut off totally from earth and its nature but accompanied by a spectral serpent of evil, float off into space and eternity with no hope whatsoever for a new or better humankind.

Two centuries of secularization have brought the modern Adam to a depressing end. From Voltaire's realistic paradise, where humankind at the beginning of the technological age may still tend its garden in peace, the new Adam has come by way of Romantic hopefulness and American ambivalence to a modern despair at the state of a humanity that has lost its spiritual bearings along with any hope of a new paradise. In

Kunert's melancholy parable the new Adam is offered, literally, the opportunity to fly around the universe and to reenter paradise by the back door—only to discover that he is prevented from doing so because of flaws in the very technology that originally caused his fall. Kunert gives voice to the feelings of a generation convinced that the miracles of modern technology have caused us to forget or to lose our place in the natural ecological world and, to the extent that we have left paradise behind, have loosed among us and our hallucinations the threat of evil. But Kunert's shift of the paradigm from the initial consciousness of good and evil to the question of technology and the sins of civilization puts Adam very much in the company of the modern Prometheus.

Fig. 6. Nuria Quevedo, *Prometheus*. From Franz Fühmann,
Prometheus. Die Titanenschlacht. Berlin: Kinderbuchverlag, 1974.
Courtesy of © Middelhauve Verlags GmbH, München für
Der Kinderbuch Verlag, Berlin.

CHAPTER FIVE

The Proletarianization of Prometheus

FROM MYTH TO MARX

D URING late classical antiquity and early Christianity, Prometheus suffered the fate of all pagan deities: he was euhemerized out of divinity into human history and allegorized through the process of iconotropy into co-option by the young church.[1] It was believed by some that the model for the legend was a ruler who fled from Jupiter into the remote Caucasus, where he was tormented by a great bird (eagle or vulture)—that is to say, by his conscience and the misery of his condition. Others saw in him a nephew of the legendary Egyptian king Sesostris, who accompanied his uncle on wars of conquest and was left behind with his troops on the Caucasus to secure Scythia. Still others claimed that he was an astrologer who located his observatory on the Caucasus and subsequently brought his knowledge of the stars to the Assyrians. As far as the Christian exegetes were concerned, he was seen as a pagan counterpart to Adam (because he was the father of mankind and punished for the sin of knowledge), of Noah (because he rescued the human race from destruction by the deity), of Moses (because he liberated humankind from servitude), of Job (because of his tragic suffering), of Jesus Christ (because he took the sins of mankind upon himself and was tortured by a kind of crucifixion), and of God himself (because of his creative powers). By analogy, as Dora and Erwin Panofsky elegantly demonstrated in their renowned *Pandora's Box*, Pandora was transmuted into a pagan Eve. During most of the Middle Ages, however, the figure of Prometheus, along with the other pagan deities, faded from popular as well as intellectual consciousness.

111

The Renaissance retrieved Prometheus from medieval obscurity and provided him with a new dimension that transcended the existing allegorizations. Boccaccio, in his influential mythological handbook *De Genealogia deorum gentilium* (1370), recapitulated the traditional stories and interpretations, including the ancient Christian exegesis of Tertullian—that Prometheus is a symbol of *Deus verus et omnipotens* because he created man from the clay of the earth.[2] But Boccaccio went on to provide a second allegorical reading, more in keeping with the emerging spirit of the Renaissance, according to which Prometheus represents *doctus homo*, who succeeds by his teaching in raising humankind from the rude state of nature to the level of civilized community (*ex naturalibus hominibus civiles facit*), possessing both a moral sense and virtue. Yet despite passing references to Prometheus in the works of such thinkers as Marsilio Ficino, Erasmus, and Francis Bacon—who shared Boccaccio's view of him as the embodiment of the principle of reason, as *homo faber* as well as *homo sapiens*—the Titan played only a peripheral role in the imaginative consciousness of the Renaissance.[3]

The allegorical view of Prometheus as symbolizing the creative human spirit persisted into the Enlightenment, where in the authoritative synthesis of the *Grande Encyclopédie* he was termed "le génie audacieux de la race humaine" (in the article *Grec*).[4] This view was confirmed by Rousseau, even though that skeptic of progress regarded the Titan in a more ambivalent light. Rousseau's prize-winning first *Discours* (1750) features a frontispiece depicting Prometheus offering his torch to an idealized man but warning off a satyr with the words "Satyre, tu ne le connois pas."[5] Rousseau interprets the image at the beginning of Part 2 of his *Discours*, where he cites an ancient tradition that "a God inimical to men's repose was the inventor of the sciences." The accompanying note explains:

It is easy to see the allegory of the Prometheus fable, and it does not appear that the Greeks who nailed him to Mount Caucasus thought any more favorably of him than did the Egyptians of their

112

God Theuth. "The satyr," says an ancient fable, "wanted to kiss and embrace fire the first time he saw it but Prometheus cried out to him: 'Satyr, you will weep the loss of the beard on your chin, for it burns when you touch it.'" This is the subject of the frontispiece.

In his reply to a refutation written a year later, Rousseau explained more specifically "that Prometheus's torch is the torch of the Sciences made to quicken great geniuses; that the Satyr who, seeing fire for the first time, runs toward it, and wants to embrace it, represents the vulgar who, seduced by the brilliance of Letters, indiscreetly give themselves over to study; that the Prometheus who cries out and warns them of the danger is the Citizen of Geneva" (90). In their positive and negative assessments, in sum, both the *Encyclopédie* and Rousseau reflect essentially the same view, going back to the Renaissance, that Prometheus exemplifies the creative spirit, a human analogue to divine creativity.

It was the young literary and social rebels of the German Sturm und Drang who recognized in the Greek Titan the archetype of their own defiance. In his dramatic fragment *Prometheus* (1773) and especially in the concomitant hymnic poem "Prometheus," Goethe gave the defining shape to a Prometheus who opposes himself defiantly to a Zeus who has no further power over him and his creative energies. Zeus may cover his heavens with clouds and exercise his lightning on oaks and mountaintops. But he must leave to Prometheus his earth and his hut, which he built with no help from Zeus, and his hearth, for whose warmth the god envies him. Prometheus knows nothing under the sun more pathetic than the gods, who nourish themselves miserably from sacrifices and prayers and would starve if children and beggars were not such hopeful fools. As a child, he continues, he sometimes raised his eyes to the skies, as though there were someone there to hear his pleas. But nothing rescued him from the arrogance of the Titans, from death, from slavery, but his own glowing heart. Why, then, should he

113

honor Zeus, who never softened his pains nor stilled his tears? It was time and fate that made him into a man. Now he sits on his earth and shapes human beings after his own image: a race that will suffer, weep, enjoy, and rejoice like him—and, like him, pay no heed to Zeus.

> Hier sitz' ich, forme Menschen
> Nach meinem Bilde,
> Ein Geschlecht, das mir gleich sei,
> Zu leiden, weinen,
> Genießen und zu freuen sich,
> Und dein nicht zu achten,
> Wie ich.

The powerfully affirmative concluding *ich* sums up the attitude of a generation that not only venerated the creative power of the individual and the human artist, but also went far beyond past ages in rejecting altogether any notion of a higher instance or deity. This image was so dominant in the life and thought of the young Goethe that scholars have sometimes used it to characterize this entire phase of his life.[6]

Because the purely human energy underlying this new understanding of the rebellious Titan was so central to German thought and literature of the Romantic age, several influential modern thinkers have taken Prometheus to be the governing image of the period and the mythical metaphor of the German psyche. The theologian Hans Urs von Balthasar entitled his study of German idealism *Prometheus* and spoke of a "Prometheus Principle" governing even the many works that did not specifically cite the Titan by name.[7] The philosopher Hans Blumenberg, in a massive tome entitled *Arbeit am Mythos* (1979), used the example of Prometheus to illustrate what he understood under "work on myth." Following a three-hundred-page discussion of the nature of myth and another hundred pages on the myth of Prometheus in antiquity, Blumenberg turned his attention for the remainder of his book to an analysis of

Goethe's poem and drama and, in conclusion, reviewed the role of Prometheus in the thought of three prominent modern German thinkers: Marx, Nietzsche, and Freud.

MODERN METAPHORS

The classically educated Marx concluded the preface of his Jena doctoral dissertation, *The Difference between the Democritan and Epicurean Philosophies of Nature* (*Differenz der demokritischen und epikureischen Naturphilosophie*, 1841), with an allusion to Prometheus that comes straight out of the tradition of defiance initiated by Goethe. Quoting Aeschylus's Prometheus—"In a word: I hate each and every god"—Marx asserts that "Prometheus is the noblest saint and martyr in the philosophical calendar."[8] Only two years later history caught up with myth when the radical liberal newspaper *Rheinische Zeitung*, which Marx edited, was closed down by the censors. On an anonymous handbill allegorically protesting the prohibition a bearded Prometheus-Marx, surrounded by his hapless creatures, is shown chained to a printing press while an eagle wearing the Prussian crown gnaws at his heart.[9] Although the figure of Prometheus does not occur frequently in Marx's works—not until *Das Kapital* does he appear as the prefiguration of the proletariat, "riveted to capital more firmly than the wedges of Hephaestus held Prometheus to the rock"[10]—it has been proposed that the myth of Prometheus's fall, suffering, and ultimate redemption constitutes "the dramatic model underlying and informing Marx's Marxism,"[11] whose scientific logos is grounded in a religious mythos. The revisionist Marxist philosopher Leszek Kolakowski has argued that "Prometheanism" provides one of the three principal motifs of Marxism, along with the Romantic theory of alienation and Enlightenment rational determinism.[12] We shall return later to the Marxian tradition.

There is a neat symmetry in the circumstance that Nietzsche, like Rousseau more than a century earlier, introduced his first work with a frontispiece depicting Prometheus—here a seated Prometheus resting one foot on the eagle that has just been slain by Herakles' arrow and raising his hands, to which his shattered chains still cling. Prometheus turns out to be, along with Dionysos, the true hero of *The Birth of Tragedy* (1872). Nietzsche, a professor of classical philology, had long admired the figure of Prometheus, especially as he knew it from Aeschylus. As a fifteen-year-old schoolboy at Schulpforta, he produced a one-act drama entitled simply *Prometheus* (1859), which begins when Iapetos informs his son Prometheus that he has been forced into a pact to entrust the destiny of men to the gods.[13] In a great monologue, Nietzsche's Titan (like Goethe's Prometheus) expresses his intention to contest Zeus for his power and rule. But the hero, betrayed to the gods, is dashed down to the realm of Orcus, and the drama concludes with a chorus in which humankind acknowledges the impotence of the individual before the might of the gods. (The work continues with a satirical scene in which the author and his audience comment on the play they have just seen.)

In his preface to *The Birth of Tragedy* Nietzsche imagines how the dedicatee, Richard Wagner, will surmise from the image of the unbound Prometheus on the title page that its author is engaged in a serious and urgent undertaking. In the analysis of the myth of Prometheus that constitutes section 9 of *The Birth of Tragedy*, and citing the words of Goethe's Prometheus, Nietzsche argues that Aeschylus's Prometheus represents the "glory of activity" as opposed to the "glory of passivity" that he detects in Sophocles' Oedipus (1:57 ff.). It is the presupposition of the Prometheus myth, he explains, that mankind acquires the best and highest of which it is capable only through a sacrilege and must therefore be prepared to take upon itself the consequences of suffering and grief. "Active" sin, as we noted earlier, is the Promethean virtue in contrast to the passive sin of the Judeo-Christian myth of the Fall. It thereby becomes at once the ethical basis of pessimistic tragedy and the justification of human ills. For Nietzsche, therefore, the Aeschylean Prometheus is a Dionysian mask concealing the Apollonian longing for justice that equally characterizes the Greek dramatist. Prometheus's defiance of Zeus marks for Nietzsche the moment at which the serene Olympian culture of the Greeks is overcome by a darker, more profound worldview. In his *Prometheus Bound* Aeschylus resurrects the earlier age of the Titans from the Tartarus to which it had been banned, and Dionysian truth recaptures the realm of myth as the symbol of its understanding. It is the Heraklean power of music, he concludes, that freed Prometheus from the vultures and transformed myth into a vehicle of Dionysian wisdom.

Freud's most astonishing allusion to Prometheus occurs in his note "The Acquisition and Control of Fire" (1932), written in response to criticisms of his book *Civilization and Its Discontents* (1930). In that work Freud argues that the earliest acts of civilization can be seen in the use of tools, the gaining of control over fire, and the construction of dwellings. "Among these, the control over fire stands out as a quite extraordinary and unexampled achievement" (21:90). He explains that this great cultural conquest is epoch-making because the control of fire requires the renunciation of a powerful instinct. Since, according to Freud, the tongues of flame have a fundamentally phallic significance, a male's extinguishing of fire by urinating on it represents for him a kind of dominating homosexual act. "The first person to renounce this desire and spare the fire was able to carry it off with him and subdue it to his own use. By damping down the fire of his own sexual excitation, he had tamed the natural force of fire." In the later essay Freud responded to his critics by citing as an example the myth of Prometheus (21:187–93). Freud reaches his conclusion by a truly weird series of inversions. He first suggests that the hollow fennel stalk in which Prometheus is reported to have borne away the fire is a penis symbol and that the fire within it is transposed through the inversion of dream into the liquid stream with which the penis quenches the flames. The defrauded gods represent the id, the instinctual impulse deceived when the individual renounces the act of urinating on the fire. And Prometheus's punishment—being gnawed at the liver that represented for the ancients the seat of all passions and desires—symbolizes the resentment that humanity feels against the culture-hero who, by forcing them into civilization, deprived them of a basic instinctual gratification. (Günter Grass's novel *The Flounder* [*Der Butt*, 1977] includes a comically outrageous inversion of Freud's theory of fire.)

It was, of course, not only such thinkers as Marx, Nietzsche, and Freud who conveyed the newly revivified myth of Prometheus down through the nineteenth century into the twentieth.[14] The Titan played a prominent role in German Romantic literature after Goethe from Herder to Heine.[15] In France and Italy the theme produced numerous minor works in addition to the three cantos of Vincenzo Monti's *Prometeo* (1797, 1821, 1832) and Edgar Quinet's poetic trilogy *Prométhée* (1838).[16] Balzac, according to the epigraph to André Maurois's biography, stated a pronouced preference for Prometheus over Faust.[17] In England the myth obsessed not only Byron ("Prometheus," 1816) and Shelley (*Prometheus Unbound*, 1820) but also Mary Shelley in the transformations of her "modern Prometheus" *Frankenstein* (1818).[18] This literary interest was reflected in the other arts as well.[19] Beethoven's music for the ballet *The Creatures of Prometheus* (1800–1801) reflects the heroic spirit of Goethe's hymn, which was also set by Schubert (1821) and Hugo Wolf (1889). At midcentury Liszt composed his symphonic poem *Prometheus* (1850); at the turn of the century Gabriel Fauré premiered a three-act lyric tragedy *Prométhée* (1900; libretto by Lorrain and Hérold). And just before World War I Aleksandr Scriabin based his symphonic "poem of fire" *Prométhée* (1913) on what he called his "mythic" or "Promethean" chord. Striking visual images were rendered by many artists, including Anselm Feuerbach, Arnold Böcklin, Max Klinger, Giorgio de Chirico, and Ernst Barlach.[20]

The very popularity of the theme in the nineteenth century led inevitably to its parody. At the turn of the century André Gide published his *Le Prométhée mal enchaîné* (1899), in which Prometheus, descending from the heights of the Caucasus to the boulevards of contemporary Paris, continues for a time to feed the eagle, now his pet, upon his own liver until, finally, he serves up the bird to his friends in a grand feast. (The author notes in concluding that he has written his little book with a quill plucked from that very eagle.)[21] Just after World War I Franz Kafka set down a brief parable entitled "Prometheus" (1918), which consists of four variant legends concerning the mythic hero.[22] According to the first (the traditional one), because he betrayed the gods to mankind, Prometheus was chained to the Caucasus, and the gods sent eagles who ate away at his ever-regenerating liver. A second account recorded that Prometheus, in agony from the incessant gnawing of the cruel beaks, pressed himself ever more deeply into the cliff until he became one with it. (This version corresponds closely to the images painted by Böcklin and de Chirico.) According to a third version his betrayal was forgotten—by the gods, the eagles, and eventually himself. And in the final version everyone wearies of the affair—the gods, the eagles, and even the wound, which gradually heals. Only the mountain remains unexplained. The legend seeks to explain the inexplicable, says Kafka. Since it comes from a ground of truth, it must end ultimately in the inexplicable.

Kafka's doubts appear to have set the tone for the writers who subsequently turned to the myth of Prometheus. Kafka's French admirer Albert Camus remarks at the beginning of his "essay on man in revolt," *L'Homme révolté* (1951), that his contemporaries like to believe that they live in Promethean times. "But is this really a Promethean age?" (26). Two hundred pages later his analysis of the modern condition has led him to the ironic conclusion that Prometheus himself has been transformed by the humanity he had hoped to lead in an assault against the heavens. Because men are weak and cowardly and love pleasure and

119

immediate rewards, Prometheus has had to become a master to teach them self-denial in order that they may grow up.

> Those who doubt his word will be thrown into the desert, chained to a rock, offered to the vultures. The others will march henceforth in darkness, behind the pensive and solitary master. Prometheus alone has become god and reigns over the solitude of men. But from Zeus he has gained only solitude and cruelty; he is no longer Prometheus, he is Caesar. The real, the eternal Prometheus has now assumed the aspect of one of his victims. The same cry, springing from the depths of the past, rings forever through the Scythian desert. (244–45)

No less ironic is the monologue attributed to Prometheus by Kafka's English translator, the poet Edwin Muir. In "Prometheus" (from *One Foot in Eden*, 1956) the ancient Titan wonders what he can possibly say to the gods when he is freed. He has heard strange reports of lands without gods and words without mystery.

> The shrines are emptying and the peoples changing.
> It may be I should find Olympus vacant
> If I should return.

(215)

For whom will his story have meaning in a world to whom a god has come "[n]ot in rebellion but in pity and love"? In Muir's "The Grave of Prometheus" (216) the "heavenly thief" lies forgotten in his mound; for the company of gods has forsaken Olympus, his fire has been extinguished, and his body has become one with the earth (as in Kafka's parable).

The image has, of course, not vanished completely. In 1950 Oskar Kokoschka was commissioned to execute a large triptych illustrating the myth for a residence in London (the painting is now in the Courtauld Gallery). In 1968 Carl Orff produced an opera *Prometheus*, and shortly before his death in 1990 Luigi Nono completed his postmodern suite *Prometeo*. In 1973 Ted

Hughes published a cycle of twenty-one powerful poems voiced by the Titan, *Prometheus on His Crag.*[23] In 1989 the German writer Otto Mainzer brought out a seven-hundred-page novel *Prometheus,* in which a Jewish psychoanalyst, obsessed with the myth and trapped on the coast of France in August 1939, concludes that Prometheus, unlike other heroes who die a spectacular death for their ideas, ends in a German concentration camp. As recently as 1999 the British filmmaker Tony Harrison produced a *Prometheus* welding together the ancient legend of fire with a contemporary plot set in the postindustrial landscape of the Yorkshire coalfields.

In general, however, the Titan's appearance in Western European literature and culture in recent decades seems to justify the melancholy words with which Raymond Trousson concluded his two-volume study of the myth. Prometheus, he wrote in 1964, has arrived at a crossroads. "In the twentieth century the myth appears to have run its course: one must wish, if it is to be started up again, for a new interpretation, a reincarnation. . . . It depends on us whether Prometheus lives or dies."[24] But the French mythographer is not sanguine about the chances. Recalling that Gilgamesh and Ishtar are no longer vital elements in our cultural imagination, he warns us not to rely on any supposed immortality of myths.

MARXIST MYTHS

But perhaps Trousson was too pessimistic. In at least one postwar European culture Prometheus played a powerfully constitutive role: in the forty-year literature and thought of the German Democratic Republic (1949–1989). For at least two reasons Prometheus emerged smoothly and logically as a central image in that Marxist culture. In the first place, as we have already seen, for Marx himself, as well as for more recent students of his thought, Prometheus symbolized the proletariat in its revolt against the capitalist ruling classes. The association was not lost on subsequent thinkers. John Lehmann, for instance, called his study of Soviet Georgia *Prometheus and the Bolsheviks* (1937) "because Prometheus is the oldest poetic symbol of the Caucasus, and can at the same time be considered as the oldest symbol of what the Bolsheviks have had as their aim: the deliverance of man from tyranny and barbarism by the seizure of material power" (foreword). It was therefore perfectly consistent with the Marxist ideology of the GDR when its writers took up Prometheus as a governing image.

In the second place, the recurrence to classical themes ("Antikewelle") has long been recognized as one of the principal characteristics of literature in East Germany.[25] Among the most familiar examples may be cited Bertolt Brecht's searing adaptation of *Antigone* (1947), Heiner Müller's stage versions in the 1960s of *Philoktetes, Oedipus Rex,* and *Herakles,* and Christa Wolf's feminist re-visions of *Cassandra* (1983) and *Medea* (1996). Various factors account for this turn to myth. One major aim of the East German cultural project was to establish and maintain its continuity out of the German and Western cultural heritage—to demonstrate that the GDR and not the Federal Republic was the legitimate heir of the tradition of progressive bourgeois humanism disrupted by the Nazi years.[26] It was desirable, accordingly, to illustrate the vitality of Greek and Roman classicism by retelling its stories and reinvigorating its poetic forms. At the same time, such adaptations provided the opportunity and the literary means of moving beyond a socialist realism that was rapidly becoming sterile.[27] Classical antiquity, in addition, offered to Marxist writers and critics a test case for the historical-materialist theory of history, exemplifying as it did a dramatic shift from a primitive classless society to the crassest form of exploitive order.[28] Finally, the use of classical myth permitted writers to deal metaphorically with contemporary issues that might have been politically compromising had they approached them directly.

With his impressive Marxist credentials, Prometheus lent himself readily to these needs and purposes. GDR scholars sought to demonstrate how the myth had been interpreted by past generations to suit their own ideological ends, and thereby to expose the profound gap between the bourgeois and the socialist understanding of the world.[29] Yet the adaptation of the myth by writers of the GDR was not unproblematic. The heroic view of Prometheus, which extended from Aeschylus by way of Goethe to Marx (and Nietzsche) and was exploited by early Marxist poets, was subsequently modified by the infusion of a second, more negative view, which came down from Hesiod by way of Rousseau. The melding of these two traditions gradually yielded an ambivalent image that perhaps best exemplifies the most thoughtful and critical writers of the German Democratic Republic.[30]

A typical example of the early (pre-GDR) Marxist adaptation of the myth shows up in the poetry of Wilhelm Tkaczyk (born 1907). A tailor's son who was put to work—first on a farm, then in a factory—directly after completing elementary school, Tkaczyk joined the Metal Workers Union at age fifteen and, four years later, became a member of the German Communist Party (KPD), while publishing his first and evidently auto-biographical poems in Communist newspapers and anthologies. Conspicuous among these is "Prometheus in der Fabrik" (Prometheus in the factory, 1925). The poem, which belongs to the category that might be labeled heroic proletarianism, parades its indebtedness to Goethe's Titan. This worker-Prometheus, pacing like a caged animal within the walls of his factory, feels within himself the power to move the world. Frustrated at the thought that he might waste his life in useless labor, he weeps tears of rage and knots his hands into fists. Wondering whether he should rush like a mad dog into the crowd and be kicked to death, he decides that he would rather stamp out the world.

Lieben, hassen, fluchen, beten:
Jupiter—Zeus, höre mich!
Ich empöre mich!
Ist deiner Schöpfung Ziel
Sklaverei?
Komme, was kommen will,
ich
   mach
      mich
         frei!!!

(20)

(Love, hate, curse, pray: / Jupiter—Zeus, hear me! / I am
enraged! / Is the goal of your creation / slavery? Come what
will, / I shall free myself!!!)

The strategy of the poem is clear: by means of the implicit
allusion in the final lines to Goethe's poem, Tkaczyk enlists
the ideals of classical bourgeois humanism in the service of
his socialist project: to liberate the proletariat and to lay the
foundations for the new socialist society of education and
culture.[31]

We see a variant of the heroic socialist Prometheus in the
poetry of Johannes R. Becher (1891–1958), who sponsored the
young Tkaczyk and published his first volume of poems. Becher,
who began his career as an Expressionist poet and pacifist, was
elected in 1925 to serve in the Reichstag as a representative
of the German Communist Party (KPD). Following his exile in
Moscow during the Nazi years, Becher returned to Germany,
where in 1945 he was appointed president of the Cultural
Union for the Democratic Renewal of Germany and in 1954
Minister of Culture of the GDR. Becher's poem "Prometheus"
(1940), written during his Moscow exile, exemplifies, along
with its socialist appropriation of bourgeois humanism, the
poet's aesthetic conservatism: it consists of twenty-six quatrains
of iambic pentameter with alternating rhyme (612–15).

> Er hing an seinem Felsen wie im Sprung,
> Um von dem Felsen weithin abzuspringen,
> Und warf empor, voll heil'ger Lästerung,
> Das Haupt, um mit der Göttermacht zu ringen.

(He hung from his rock as though poised / to leap far out from his rock, / and held up his head defiantly, full of holy blasphemy, / to wrestle with the godly might.)

Shackled to his mountain, he strains so powerfully at his chains that his arms become raw and the earth trembles. As the vulture swoops to tear at his breast, he shouts defiantly that the gods shall never eradicate his lofty dream of the twilight of the gods (Becher actually uses the Wagnerian term *Götterdämmerung*). Thus the seasons pass until, one spring, he looks down to see the human race lighting bright torches and crying out to him, "Thou mighty Titan!" They appear in honor of the one who taught them the arts and crafts of song, of weaving, of agriculture, of construction, and of navigation. (By this point it is evident that the classically educated Becher is reaching back past Goethe to Aeschylus for his source: these strophes sound like a recapitulation of the Culture Speech.)

> Aus ihren Hütten traten sie hervor.
> Da war ein Sturm. Er sprach im Sturm zu ihnen.
> Es war das ganze Menschenvolk, das schwor,
> Der alten Göttermacht nicht mehr zu dienen.

(They emerged from their huts. / There was a storm, and he spoke to them in the storm. / The entire human race swore / no longer to serve the might of the old gods.)

The Titan's mighty words intimate that the stronghold of the gods is about to fall as the era of human rule approaches. When the gods see what is happening, they summon Power and Violence ("Die Götter riefen *die Gewalt, den Zwang*") and send down swarms of vultures. But Prometheus does not desist from his efforts, and the entire mountain becomes radiant. Looking down from his peak, he sees a vision of himself, striding through godless times; and bound, he greets his future liberated self.

> Wie er hoch oben mit dem Felsen rang,
> Da sah er sich: durch götterlose Zeiten
> Schritt er in einem flügelhaften Gang,
> Und der Gefangne grüßte den Befreiten.

Giving his own twist to Aeschylus's *Prometheus Bound*, Becher uses the traditional myth to express his conviction that the age of the gods (that is, the capitalist oppressors) will soon give way to an era of free men and women. Though less defiantly proletarian in his attitudes than Tkaczyk, Becher shares essentially the same vision of socialist humanism that is characteristic of pre-GDR writers.

For a third example of these preliminary adaptations of Prometheus by pre-GDR socialist writers we can turn to Bertolt Brecht (1898–1956). More even than Tkaczyk and Becher, Brecht was fascinated by the figure of Prometheus, whom he evoked repeatedly in his notes and fragments.[32] But we can detect a pronounced shift in Brecht's attitude, which heralds the GDR ambiguities. As early as 1920, in a short poem entitled "Prometheus," Brecht used the traditional myth to illustrate his youthful sense, familiar from such early dramas as *Baal*, of the menacing pleasures of nature: like Prometheus, the poet feels himself bound to the earth yet threatened by its dark power.[33] Twenty-five years later and only two months after Hiroshima (October 2, 1945) he noted in his work journal that he was contemplating a "Prometheus" of an entirely different sort: the gods would be ignorant and malicious and living off the fat of the land.[34] In Brecht's typically ironic re-vision Prometheus invents fire and then, criminally, hands it over to the gods, who capture and bind him so that he cannot pass it on to humankind. For a long time he hears nothing further about his invention. Finally he sees red conflagrations on the horizon:

126

the gods have used the obviously atomic fire to destroy human-kind, not to benefit it.

The common denominator linking the three pre-GDR social-ist adaptations of the myth is the fact that they share the tradi-tional heroic view of Prometheus in opposition to an oppressive capitalist society: in Tkaczyk's poem the proletarian Titan strains to liberate himself from the capitalist factory; in Becher's poem the bound hero witnesses the benefits his invention has brought to a socialist humanity and envisages his own eventual liberation; and in Brecht's early verses the poet identifies him-self with the hero struggling against the forces of nature. There is little in these rebellious Titans to suggest their sin against knowledge. But in Brecht's later synopsis for the play he never wrote, the Titan—in a cynical inversion of the original moral meaning of the theme—has been duped by the gods and must witness their misuse of his invention for the destruction of hu-mankind. Following these early Marxist mythifications Pro-metheus dropped for fifteen years from the cultural horizon.

GDR Ambiguities

The immediate postwar years (1945–1949), known in histories of the German Democratic Republic as the period of antifascist democratic reconstruction,[35] carried on the efforts of writers like Becher—established writers returning from exile in the So-viet Union, the United States, and other countries—to recap-ture the traditions of German liberal humanism in the interest of political and cultural renewal. Immediately following the for-mal establishment of the GDR in 1949, however, a period of cultural stagnation set in, characterized by the official imposi-tion of a socialist realism modeled after Soviet writing and by strict censure of any deviation from the approved revolutionary perspective. The workers' rebellion of June 1953 and the ap-pointment of Becher as minister of culture brought about a brief "thaw" in the cultural climate—a thaw that lasted only

127

until the harsh repressions following the 1956 revolution in Hungary. The *Bitterfelder Weg* (Bitterfeld Movement) of 1959, which urged writers to go into the fields and factories in order to experience the new socialist reality at first hand, produced a disheartening wave of "tractor poems" and industrial novels. As critics of the regime were imprisoned or prohibited from publishing, many prominent intellectuals fled to the West. Then, in August of 1961, the government erected the notorious Wall— allegedly to prevent false ideas from coming in but actually to reduce the growing tide of emigrations.

It is one of the ironies of GDR history that the Wall produced an easing of the harsh cultural restrictions. Becher, Brecht, and other figures who had dominated the cultural scene during the late 1940s and 1950s were dead. A generation of younger writers with serious literary ambitions and intolerant of versified propaganda now emerged to take their place. The new spirit of cultural independence showed up first in lyric poetry, the literary genre most resistant to official restraints. Almost immediately the figure of Prometheus reasserted itself as a pervasive image— indeed, as the mythic image most frequently summoned up by GDR writers to exemplify the rebellion against oppression and the indignity of unjust punishment.[36] At this point the spirit of rebellion has displaced thematically the sin of knowledge. It is initially the structure of the myth that is appropriated rather than its moral content.

In 1963 the literary journal *Neue deutsche Literatur* published "Prometheus" by Heinz Czechowski (born 1935).[37] The poem is still very much in the tradition of heroic proletarianism initiated by Tkaczyk. Czechowski's Titan is fettered not to his crag but to a steam-clouded boiler, and he defends himself against the eagle with his stirring iron. By preserving the fire, the poem continues, he saves himself and defies the gods. His labor, to be sure, maintains the palatial banks and fine automobiles of the bosses ("Bankpalast und Mercedes"): that is the order of things. How long will he endure his agony? Then suddenly he revolts and shatters his chains. The torment of a thousand years is plunged into the all-preserving fire.

> Und dann: das Sichaufbäumen und Krachen
> der springenden Ketten.
> die tausendjährige Qual
> gestürzt in das alleserhaltende Feuer.

Only a year later that same leading journal published Peter Diezel's poem "Prometheus," in which the Titan is fettered to the walls of the Alps above the Rhine, from which the eagle arises to torment and bend him.

> Prometheus, an die Wände der Alpen geschmiedet,
> blickst du hinunter zum Rhein, dorthin,
> wo jedesmal der Adler aufsteigt,
> dich zu beugen.[38]

While the poem never states it directly, this Prometheus is clearly enchained by the Federal Republic of *West* Germany, which fears his proletarian energies yet cannot succeed in subduing him. "The one in chains, even though he suffers, retains his freedom while those who submit have sold out." ("Der in Ketten / liegt, behielt seine Freiheit, wenn / leidend auch, die / sich aber fügen, sind verkauft.") It is no longer a secret that will overthrow Zeus but a (Marxist) "program." The simple working woman Io (that is, the German people), though raped by Zeus (the capitalist bosses), will soon give birth to the liberator.

We note a subtle modification of the heroic view in the poetry of the critic, translator, and poet Georg Maurer (1907–1971), who reintroduces the moral aspect—the sin of knowledge—with an ironic twist. In his "Prometheus," one of several variations that he wrote on Shakespeare's Sonnet 123 ("No, Time, thou shalt not boast that I do change"), watchmen peer down from their battlements at mists that seem to move and whisper.[39] Gradually the sun reveals the peasants below, clad in their goat hides, who demand a reckoning from the judges, lawyers, field marshals, and admirals who rule them. When the rulers appear, the peasants complain that they have almost nothing while the bosses have much. The bosses try to console them by telling them to count their oxen, their plows, and their trees, but the peasants point out that they have also counted the rulers' money. "And who taught you to count?" When they answer, "Prometheus," the rulers concede that he gave them numbers and the fire with which to forge weapons. But, they continue speciously, life was splendid before Prometheus came. "We were all equal. We plucked fruits from the trees and did not count them." When the enraged peasants threaten to hang the rulers from the trees, the latter argue that they protect society against the barbarians, and the peasants agree that they need weapons and leaders and courts. The rulers contend that all misery has come upon mankind through the guilt of Prometheus, who stole fire from his master and passed it on, whereupon Zeus punished the thief and mankind, who also incurred guilt by accepting stolen goods. In the ensuing tumult no one hears the voice of a single critical individual, who cries out that the masters invented their Zeus just in the nick of time. But the speaker is struck down and now lies stretched out—like Prometheus on his crag. The poem concludes with a translation of Shakespeare's concluding couplet, here addressed to the tyrant Zeus:

> Dieses, Kronide, schwör ich treulich mir:
> Wahr will ich sein, trotz deiner Sens' und dir.

("This I do vow [son of Cronus] and thus shall ever be; / I will be true despite thy scythe and thee.")

Maurer's clever free-verse account parallels the propagandistic process analyzed by contemporary GDR literary scholars, exemplifying the invention of the myth of Prometheus to suit the ideology of the ruling class. Here Prometheus is portrayed by the rulers not as the benefactor of mankind but (in the spirit of Hesiod and Rousseau) as the enemy who brought war and inequality into the once paradisiacal world and produced human misfortune by offending the gods. Only one lonely individual, who must suffer the fate of Prometheus, is perceptive and brave enough to understand that the rulers' Zeus is an idol invented by them to subdue the masses. But the poet swears to remain true to himself despite all threats from the rulers. (In 1970 Maurer wrote another, shorter poem with a similar message, "Bis Prometheus kommt" [Until Prometheus comes].[40] Here the poet affirms the virtue of fire that illuminates rather than reducing to ashes. But mankind tends to dignify as cosmic mist the ashes stirred up by fools fighting among themselves. Only art reveals the truth.)

Maurer's poems signal the emergence of a more ambivalent view. In "Prometheus" (1967), an early poem by the brilliant young poet Volker Braun (born 1939), Prometheus warns humankind against the "blind hope" that fogs up our cities ("Weg, blinde Hoffnung, die unsre Städte / Beschlägt"), obscuring the dangers of the airplanes that fly through the heavens bearing the fire that will extinguish us.

> Die Flugzeuge gehn durch die schwachen
> Lappen des Himmels
> Und das gelegt wird, unser Feuer
> Löscht uns aus. (2:94–95)

Nothing can be saved if we allow ourselves to be distracted by hope or to trust the present times. In a 1972 interview Braun explained that his poem is not so much an adaptation of the myth as an explicit reversal of its meaning: fire is not brought to humankind from the heavens; instead, we create it ourselves and bear it into the skies.[41]

During the late 1960s the younger generation began to scrutinize with a critical eye the role of the intellectual in the GDR, and this reevaluation inevitably affected the image of Prometheus. In 1969 the *poeta doctus* Karl Mickel (born 1935), published his "Entfesselter Prometheus" (Prometheus unbound), which, as he tells us in his notes, was inspired by the attempt of the English Marxist scholar George Thomson to reconstruct Aeschylus's lost play.[42] The poem is presented as a succinct telephone call between Zeus and Prometheus in his prison ("Zuchthaus"). "How's your vulture?" "Being killed." "By whom?" "By Herakles." As the conversation continues, Prometheus explains that the noise Zeus hears (and which in his fear he interprets as the sound of the Titans advancing to overthrow him) is the hoofbeats of the centaur Chiron. Now that Prometheus's liberation is near, Zeus demands that he speak (to reveal the secret he withholds: of the threat to Zeus's rule). Prometheus points out that Zeus really needs the bow of Herakles, not his words. Zeus requires the liberated Prometheus to wear a ring of his fetters in memory of his punishment, and a piece of stone from his crag (which the poet calls "Meiner Mauer Bruchstück"—no doubt an allusion to the Berlin Wall). Mickel's hermetic poem permits various possibilities of interpretation: it could refer to the writers and intellectuals imprisoned by the GDR (or any other socialist totalitarian) government and subsequently released in the face of popular rebellion—writers who refuse to lend their voices to an oppressive regime, suggesting that only force (Herakles' bow) can keep it in power, but also acknowledging that even when freed (and in the West?) they will still bear the traces of their existence behind the Wall.

In any case, by 1971 when the GDR Center for Cultural Work (Zentralhaus für Kulturarbeit) compiled an anthology to commemorate the twenty-fifth anniversary of the founding of the Socialist Unity Party (SED), the image was prevalent and representative enough to justify a section entitled "Comrade Prometheus at Work."[43]

THREE MAJOR RE-VISIONS

During the 1970s the emphasis in GDR literature shifted from the problems of the socialist society to the role of the socialist individual in that society—a shift reflected in typical re-visions of the myth of Prometheus by three of the finest and most prominent writers: a poet, a dramatist, and a novelist. In 1970 Günter Kunert (born 1929), perhaps the leading poet of his generation, whose talents were discovered by Becher and sponsored by Brecht, made use of the myth in a poem in memory of Yannis Ritsos ("Yannis Ritsos nicht zu vergessen").[44] Kunert recounts the occasion of a 1962 tape-recorded conversation in Berlin with the Greek Communist poet (1909–1990), face-to-face in a "symmetry of mustaches." Leaning back in their upholstered easy chairs, they spoke, Kunert recalls, of those things about which fools always speak—the growing power of reason in the world—little suspecting that Ritsos would soon (in 1968) be interned on the prison island of Yiaros by the right-wing military junta for his radical political views.

> Einmal sprachen wir miteinander,
> ehe er endgültig an den Felsen von Jaros
> geschmiedet ward, ausgeliefert
> den Adlern, patriotischen Galgenvögeln,
> gewiß einen Funken Hoffnung nährend, daß
> auch diesmal Herakles auftritt und ihn losmacht—
> erleuchtet von einem Funken Furcht, daß
> der vielseitige Kraftprotz diesmal
> Im Dienst der herrschenden Kerberosmeute wirke
> und würge.

(Once we spoke with one another, / before he was finally forged to the crag of Yiaros, / exposed / to the eagles, patriotic gallows birds, / certainly nourishing a spark of hope, that / this time again Herakles would appear and free him— / illuminated by a spark of fear, that / the versatile muscleman this time / in the service of the ruling Cerberus pack would work / and strangle.)

In Kunert's poem the bringer of fire and culture is transformed into an artist, whose creative powers rapidly dissipate when freedom is suffocated ("daß die Kunst / rasch verfliegt, wo die Freiheit erstickt"), for the one is nothing but the breath of the other.

If Kunert's early poem reinterprets Prometheus to suggest the dependence of the intellectual on society, the Kafkaesque prose sketches that he wrote toward the end of that decade exploit the myth to expose the craven sin of the intellectual clinging to his authority. In one, entitled simply "At the Beginning and End: Prometheus" ("Am Anfang und Ende: Prometheus") the Titan, consumed in body and soul, loses all consciousness of hope "because the law of improbability paralyzed the miracle, which would consist in the fact that a Herakles would come and liberate him."[45] Another, called "Prometheus II," states that mankind is incapable of possessing at the same time both fire, necessary for the maintenance and reproduction of life, and the capacity to recognize the future. For the power of foresight involves not future catastrophes, but the certainty that life is nothing but endless repetitions—a tragic vision irreconcilable with the power and impulse to sustain life.

> Prometheus deprived us of our existential knowledge in order to make us capable of living, but if we have nothing but that capacity without that knowledge, we remain vulnerable to our own blindness, from which with the assistance of the gift that is the basis of all civilizing technology we work at the revocation [*Aufhebung*] of all life. One way or the other we have been betrayed and sold out. For that reason Prometheus was justly punished by the gods.[46]

If in the first sketch Prometheus himself is deprived of all hope and nobility, in the second he is justly punished for placing humankind in the intolerable situation of knowledge without understanding, of rationality without morality.

BY THE early 1970s Heiner Müller (1929–1995) had emerged as East Germany's leading playwright, known in particular for his brilliant adaptations of classical myths, which he employed as vehicles for the critique of contemporary GDR society. In 1968, using an interlinear translation, Müller had adapted Aeschylus's *Prometheus Bound* for the stage. Constrained by the

134

original, he was able to make only modest shifts of emphasis. Nevertheless, while retaining its tragic grandeur, he manages to suggest through subtle linguistic changes a hero representing revolutionary optimism in a context of primal communist circumstances.[47] When he was given the important commission in 1971 to write a play for the Berliner Ensemble, he chose as his source Fyodor Gladkov's classic work of socialist realism, *Cement* (1925). Like Gladkov's novel, Müller's scenic drama deals with the struggles of the working class in the period immediately following the civil war of 1917–1921, when political power was shifting from revolutionary idealism to Soviet bureaucratic rationalizations.[48] The action of the play, with its many characters, revolves around the problematic relationship of the returning soldier Gleb Tschumalow and his wife Dascha, whose personal development into a liberated feminist has left behind the other characters still frozen in their older political forms. But Müller introduces a wholly new device in order to universalize the story of his specific individuals: through the Brechtian technique of alienation the action is commented upon on several occasions by captions with mythological allusions. The scene in which Gleb returns to his wife Dascha, who in her newfound independence has been anything but the faithful spouse, is entitled ironically "The Return of Odysseus"; when Gleb and Dascha are discussing the death of their daughter from neglect, the caption reads, "Medea Commentary"; and so forth.

Early in the play Gleb with the engineer Kleist visits the ruined cement plant in which he once worked.[49] Three years earlier, it emerges, Kleist denounced Gleb and three Communist friends to the Whites. As Gleb, overcome by hatred and lust for vengeance, prepares to strangle the traitor, he recounts the story of Achilles' slaying of Hector. Then he relents, realizing that he needs Kleist's expertise in order to rebuild the plant for the good of the people. At that point Kleist relates—in prose, interrupting the blank verse of the dialogue—"The Liberation of Prometheus."

135

Prometheus, we hear, provided men with lightning but did not teach them how to use it against the gods—for the self-serving reason that he took his meals with the gods, and there would have been less to go around if these had to be shared with mortals as well. For this act of suppression he was forged by Hephaestus to the Caucasus, where a dog-headed eagle daily consumes his liver. His only sustenance is the filth that the eagle evacuates upon him from his bowels, and he transfers it through his own feces onto the rock beneath him. When after three thousand years Herakles approaches to liberate him, he can make out the bound Titan, glittering white with bird dung, from a considerable distance; but he is overcome by such revulsion at the stench that he circles the crag for another three thousand years until, following a five-hundred-year rain, he is able to approach within shooting range. Since he still has to hold his nose against the stench, his first three arrows miss, one striking Prometheus on the foot; but the fourth kills the eagle. Prometheus, the story continues, weeps for the bird, his sole companion for three millennia and his only provider for twice three thousand years. Am I supposed to eat your arrows? he cries, forgetting that he ever knew any other sustenance, and vomits in disgust at the stench still clinging to Herakles from the Augean stables. Herakles urges him to eat the eagle, but Prometheus refuses, believing that the eagle is his last connection to the gods. Instead, he curses his liberator while Herakles examines the chains that time and the weather have rendered indistinguishable from the stone. Eaten through by rust and loosened by Prometheus's violent movements, they could easily have been cast off had Prometheus not feared the eagle. That he fears freedom more than he did the bird is suggested by the fact that he desperately defends his chains against the clutches of his liberator. Howling in the torment of movement with his deadened limbs, he screams for his quiet place on the rock beneath the wings of the eagle. Even when he can again stand upright, he refuses to walk, and Herakles must carry him down the mountain on his shoulders. The gods seek to prevent their descent by hurling huge boulders down upon them while Prometheus loudly proclaims to the heavens his lack of complicity in his liberation. Finally the gods commit suicide by casting themselves out of heaven onto Herakles. Prometheus, working his way onto the shoulders of his liberator, assumes the pose of a victor, riding toward the jubilation of the welcoming populace—Müller's sardonic comment on the liberated intellectual exploiting for his own benefit the strength of the proletarian workers. Müller's treatment represents the sharpest break with the earlier idealizing Marxist view, suggesting as it does that Prometheus is so inextricably linked to bourgeois ideology that Marxists require for their purposes a wholly different mythic image, for which he proposes Herakles.[50]

In his earlier adaptation of Aeschylus's *Prometheus Bound*, Müller still viewed the Titan as a heroic rebel. The later cynical inversion owes as much to Gide and Kafka as to Goethe and Becher. Indeed, Müller's interpretation appears to one GDR critic to be a perfect example of the socialist appropriation of the classical heritage, lying midway as it does between Goethe's idealizations and Kafka's indeterminacies.[51] This Prometheus represents the craven intellectual opportunist who abjectly submits to the humiliations of his masters until finally, when they have been overthrown without his assistance and even over his objections, he eagerly jumps on the bandwagon of the new order, which requires his skills. In the context of Müller's play the re-vision explains the role of many intellectuals during the civil war in Russia; but it applies equally well to the writers and intellectuals in modern tyrannies (whether fascist or communist) who happily accept the benefits lavished upon them by the government as long as they support its policies. However, alongside these cynical re-visions the traditional heroic view persisted.

DURING these same years the East German Children's Book Press (Kinderbuchverlag), planning a collection of the great myths and legends of the world, approached Franz Fühmann to contribute a volume on Prometheus suitable for young readers from the age of eleven on. Fühmann (1922–1984), one of the country's most prominent and prolific novelists and essayists, was known for his skillful adaptations of such classics as the medieval tale of Reineke the Fox, fairy tales based on Shakepeare, and the *Iliad* and *Odyssey*. Having already encountered the legend in connection with his Homer adaptations (where Thersites relates the story of Prometheus to the Greek warriors), Fühmann accepted the assignment.[52] But he promptly ran into difficulties because he became aware that there were two radically different versions of the legend (102–3). Aeschylus had depicted a grandiose rebel against a political usurper, while Hesiod had portrayed a well-meaning swindler who, through his unwanted interventions, drags mankind into a situation from whose consequences we still suffer. In sum, the author was confronted with the two basic models of Marxist adaptation. Which was the genuine Prometheus, Fühmann asked himself, and which the false one? Was the older version more legitimate, or did they both go back to a still earlier Babylonian account? To complicate matters, Plato in his *Protagoras* represented Prometheus as a kind of ideologue of consumption ("Konsumtions-ideologen"), who provides humankind with material comfort but withholds the political virtues that would have redeemed them in the eyes of the gods. Lucian suggested yet a fourth model, a cabinet intrigue between two equally corrupt cliques. And what was one to do with the more recent adaptations by Goethe, Shelley, Gide, Kafka, and others?

Consulting Kerényi's study *Prometheus*, Fühmann concluded that we can never determine the original form of any myth but can only identify the compatible elements that can be distilled from its various versions. This is what he sought to achieve in his *Prometheus: The Battle of the Titans* (1974), which draws upon all the standard classical sources to carry the story from the beginning of time down to Prometheus's creation of man and woman. His adaptation also involves a complex understanding of the nature of myth itself, combining depth psychology and Marxist theory. Fühmann had concluded that it is the unique capacity of myth to provide models by which we can measure individual experience against humanity's experience (96). This insight was buttressed by Jung's theory of the collective unconscious, which proposes that each individual bears within his consciousness a set of archetypes common to the mythic concentrate of human experience. Fühmann admits that he cannot resist the attraction of Jung's theory (105–6). But it occurs to him that this conception of myth is analogous to Lenin's theory of dialectical oppositions, according to which the individual is related to the general and the part to the whole (106–7) in a tension of unity. Each myth thereby becomes both an archetype for the human experience of the individual and a model for the relationship of the individual to society. These views provide the theoretical basis for Fühmann's adaptation of the Prometheus legend, through which he hoped to offer young readers insight into both their personal experience and the society in which they are growing up.

"Many, many years ago, when there were still no human beings and the flowers faded unseen in the thickets, the cosmos with its land and sea was ruled by seven mighty princes, who called themselves the Titans" (7).[53] From this beginning, which offers a sense of the narrative style of the handsomely illustrated work, Fühmann proceeds to describe "The Kingdom of the Titans" (Part 1), "The Overthrow of the Titans" (Part 2)—characterized by one GDR critic as a "genealogy of power" and an "ideological critique" ("Ideologiekritik") of Zeus[54]—and "The Creation of Humankind" (Part 3). Prometheus is utterly different in temperament from his brother, we learn in the opening pages (9–10). While Epimetheus liked to lie around in the grottoes of the Milky Way, recalling the latest feasts of Kronos, Prometheus as the embodiment of dynamic energy preferred to descend to earth and roam jubilantly through the hot steppes of the south or the snowy tundras of the north. He knew that

139

his excursions were forbidden, but could not restrain himself. After the overthrow of the Titans, Hephaestus created a dangerous new weapon-toy for Zeus, who with his lightning bolt caused disasters on earth, destroying the animals with his fire. Prometheus, who helped Zeus to overthrow the other Titans, is now as incapable of aligning himself with the new dictatorship as he had been with the earlier oligarchy. When he reproaches Zeus for breaking his oath to rule justly, Zeus maintains that he made no promises, and that he now possesses the lightning with which he could conquer everything and everyone (246–51). With his Aeschylean bodyguards Kratos and Bia standing behind him, Zeus offers a pact to Prometheus, who assumes that Zeus intends to reassert his former dreams of peace and harmony. Instead, the tyrant expels the troublesome rebel from Olympus, ordering that he is free to live on earth or in Hades but that he may never return to the domain of the gods. Cursing Zeus as a traitor, Prometheus returns to earth and its creatures. Seeking companionship, he eventually creates clumsy figures of clay in his own image (258), but he cannot bring them to life even by breathing upon them. He finally consults with Hermes, who points out that his creatures would be unable to survive in earth's atmosphere with divine breath alone. Prometheus takes the goat Amalthea, and together they breathe simultaneously— divine breath and earthly breath—into the two nostrils of his clay men and women, who gradually come to life. The book ends as the new human beings (*Menschen* in German) get their name from the bleating of the goat Amalthea: "Määhntschen, Määhntschen" (298–99). The future course of events is only hinted at briefly in a vision in which Prometheus sees himself dividing the meat for the feast at Mekone (294).

While Fühmann's spirited and imaginative adaptation of the myth, which incorporates elements from Hesiod, Aeschylus, Homer, Apollodorus, and other sources, is in no way a clumsy politicization of the material, he emphasizes those elements that present Prometheus to his adolescent readers as the heroic rebel against an unjust ruler who has violently seized power after overthrowing the earlier political dynasty, and as the resourceful, active man who devotes his considerable energy and ingenuity to the betterment of life on earth—in short, as an exemplary socialist hero whose knowledge is a benefit to humankind.

THE ENEMY OF THE PEOPLE

By the 1980s, as the ecological movement gained momentum, thoughtful East Germans began to realize that scientific rationality has its dire consequences, that technology produces damages along with its rewards—that, in sum, the sin of knowledge bears guilt in its train.[55] This conclusion was summed up in a witty distich by Rainer Kirsch, who had recently (1979) produced the first East German translation of Shelley's *Prometheus Unbound*:

Groß in Gesängen rühmten die Alten den Schaffer Prometheus,
Weil er das Feuer uns gab; wir heute schlucken den Rauch.

(13)

(Mightily in song the ancients praised the creator Prometheus / because he gave us fire; today we swallow the smoke.)

This is essentially the view developed at much greater length by Peter Hacks in his adaptation of Goethe's *Pandora*, one of the many allegorical masques that Goethe produced for Weimar court festivities, and that he published as a fragment in 1810.

Hacks (born 1928), who was educated and had his first successes in Munich, moved to the GDR in 1955 out of political conviction and rapidly became perhaps the most versatile and productive of its dramatists, with his works regularly performed in both East and West Germany. Hacks was obsessed with Goethe, whom he valued also for his political astuteness, and adapted several of his works for the stage. He enjoyed perhaps

141

his greatest success with the brilliant monodrama *A Conversation in the Stein Residence about the Absent Herr von Goethe* (1974).

The Prometheus of Goethe's *Pandora* (written 1807–1808) bears little resemblance to the Titan that the young genius of Sturm und Drang had imagined thirty-five years earlier. While Goethe had no classical source for the action of his masque, the dialectical opposition of Prometheus and his brother Epimetheus was based on Plato's *Protagoras*. Unlike his youthful ode in free verse, which vaunted sheer creative energy, the masque, written in measured classical trimeter, was intended to represent a reconciliation and synthesis of the forces of thought and action symbolized by the two brothers—but also the exemplary forces of poetry and power exemplified by Goethe himself and Napoleon, whom he met at Erfurt in the fall of 1808. In Goethe's fragment the two poles are represented by the stage set: to the audience's left, "Prometheus's Side" is characterized by a still unshaped nature of rocks and mountains, caverns and crude stone structures, and untamed trees and plants; "Epimetheus's Side" on the right, in contrast, features primitive wooden buildings, cultivated gardens, and a background resembling a landscape by Poussin. The action takes place in the period between Pandora's disappearance, following the opening of her fateful jar, and her return heralding a new era of peace. The reconciliation, which is not achieved in the fragment but suggested in Goethe's notes, was to have been symbolized by the marriage of Phileros and Epimeleia, the son and daughter respectively of Prometheus and Epimetheus.

When Hacks undertook his adaptation in 1980, he was convinced that Goethe's play was no fragment but contained all essential dramatic elements. However, he felt that it required certain changes in order to be made suitable for stage production. In the process, he modified and expanded the setting, the characters, and the action in such a manner as to alter radically Goethe's emphasis and to exploit the play as a critique of GDR society of the 1970s.[56] Basically, Hacks wanted to suggest that the times required a shift from the previous official emphasis on technology and production to a new society of wholeness and harmony. To achieve this goal, he shifted the focus of the masque, which he frankly calls a "drama of ideas,"[57] from Prometheus to Epimetheus. The changes begin with the stage sets themselves: gone are the balanced "sides" of Prometheus and Epimetheus; instead, both acts take place in Epimetheus's realm. The first act depicts a Mediterranean setting before a primitive wooden temple dedicated to the memory of Pandora.

As the action begins, Prometheus and his chorus of ax-bearing men come down from their realm, whose mountains they have denuded in their search for fuel for their ever-hungry fires, and pillage the fruitful landscape of Epimetheus, even going so far as to burn the temple. It becomes evident that Prometheus is no longer the culture-bearer but, rather, an aggressive and strictly utilitarian exploiter who seizes without contest whatever he needs ("Unangefochten nimmt der Kluge, was ihm zweckt"), justifying his actions in the name of right and work.

> Und Holz muß sein:
> Damit von unsern Hebeln Erzes Masse stürzt,
> Geschmolzen fließt, zum Werkzeug umgebildet dann,
> Zur Doppelfaust, bis hundertfältig sei die Kraft,
> Und eigne Kraft und Bruderkräfte mehren wir,
> Werktätig, weisekräftig ins Unendliche.
> Ist bessere Befugnis? Hat nicht Recht, der muß?
> Und heißt der Name unserer frischen Arbeit Raub,
> Heißt solchen Raubes Name Arbeit.
>
> (15)

(And there must be wood: so that masses of ore may plunge and flow molten from our levers, reshaped then into tools that redouble the strength of the fist until our might is hundredfold, and thus, active and resourceful, we increase into infinity our own power and that of our fellows. Is there any better authority? Does not he who must have the right? And if the name of our vigorous work is pillage, then the name of such pillage is work.)

Prometheus has nothing but contempt for the lovely landscapes and dreams of his brother: to call oneself king without forges is empty play. In their dialogue it becomes evident that, while Epimetheus thinks only of past and future—he laments the departure of Pandora and dreams of her return—Prometheus is concerned only with the present. Prometheus's ruthlessless is intensified in the character of his son Phileros, who rapes Epimetheus's daughter Epimeleia before he carries her off as his wife.

The second act takes place in another time and place. The unspecified primeval age has given way to a twentieth century with telephones, automobiles, and power stations; and the setting is a northern landscape featuring a country estate in Grecian taste, whither Epimetheus followed Pandora after her departure from the South. But the human situation has not changed: Prometheus is still ravaging the landscape and polluting the rivers for the sake of his industrial undertakings; and Phileros, now a man of political and industrial power, has deserted his wife Epimeleia for an affair with her sister, Elpore. Rather than bringing about any Goethean reconciliation, the three descendants of the two hostile brothers die in a car accident when they are blinded by the radiance preceding Pandora's return. As her appearance becomes imminent, the brothers realize that she is not returning to Prometheus; the day of ruthless technology has passed, and the future belongs to a humanistic society based on the benefits produced by industry. As Pandora approaches, Prometheus tells his brother:

> Das Ende düster kriegsdurchtoster Männerzeit,
> Vorläufger Kämpfe, engen Eiferns, dummer Hast,
> Der es erfocht, genießen wird ers nicht, nicht er.
> Den Unverdruß, die Niederlagen durchzustehn,
> Die zu dem Siege leiten, hat der Blinde nur.
> Empfange du mein Angehäuftes, Schauender.
> Nicht unstolz auf Vergangnes, schlag ich Künftges aus.
> Das Angenehme, meine Sache war es nie.

(94–95)

144

(The end of grim, war-ravaged masculine time, of preliminary battles, of narrow-minded zeal, of mindless haste—he who brought it about will not enjoy it. Only the blind man has the patience to survive the defeats that lead to victory. May you, visionary one, accept my heaped-up goods. Not lacking pride in the past, I reject what the future brings. Pleasure was never my affair.)

Hacks's adaptation ends, then, not with a Goethean synthesis of the *vita activa* and the *vita contemplativa*, but with a clear rejection of a society driven by technology to destroy both nature and culture (Prometheus) in favor of a new society dedicated in hope (Pandora) to mind and spirit (Epimetheus).

A similar rejection of the Promethean bargain, of knowledge purchased by sin, is widespread in the 1980s. In 1982 Volker Braun wrote a Kafkaesque prose sketch entitled "Prometheus's Trial" ("Verfahren Prometheus").[58] When Prometheus (who is never named in the text) is brought to trial, he is a little old man with white hair and a furrowed face who bears no sign of his previous accomplishments except a violin case that he clutches under his arm. Indeed, he can scarcely remember how his career began. He vaguely recalls that "he was bored to death in the Stone Age," both unsuitable for stonework and afraid in the forests. So he hid behind the bushes and dreamed up inventions, such as fire. Later, in order to justify his ingenuity, this social deviant had to be declared a demigod. As the ages pass—Braun uses a temporal technique resembling that of Virginia Woolf's *Orlando*—a consumer society readily accepted his inventions: axes, timepieces, signal fires. He became the noblest of saints because he created work with his ideas. It was while calculating the transport system for the stones of the pyramids that he first felt a pain in his liver as he watched the sweating backs of the workers. The stab of pain returned when he invented the iron sword, and when he sent men down into the Near Eastern mine shafts. In Rome he rode in carriages, paying no heed to the revolts. And when he created factories where thousands ruined their strength and health, he thought only of the useful products. Though at night he felt palpitations of the heart, every morning he hurried into the laboratories of Bayer-Leverkusen for the great experiments. Ashamed of his secret lust for knowledge, he persevered. And thus it might have continued forever, but unexpectedly he made the discovery that brought honor to his former name: the (atomic) fire of fires. The planet's cries of jubilation and horror announced that he was now immortal; yet playing his violin like a harmless madman, he was no longer able to fend off the vulture of his own agony. So he stands before the tribunal of history: "IT WAS I! IT IS I! I AM DEATH, WHICH PLUNDERS ALL, I AM DARKNESS. Without awaiting the verdict, he goes back through the recoiling crowd to his prison cell, which has assumed the size of the world that he can destroy."

The generational suspicion of Prometheus and his ambivalent knowledge appears in the parable "The Judgment of Prometheus" ("Beurteilung des Prometheus," 1986) by Wilhelm Bartsch (born 1937). Written in the form of a Party political hearing, the parable weighs the pros and cons of "Colleague P.," an activist who from the first showed signs of "anarchosyndicalistic tendencies" and invented means of indulging "collective-egoistical interests" that served his well-known vanity (106–7). His resulting popularity constantly challenged the authority of the leadership, and he persisted in his deviancy despite all their tolerance. Indeed, he stated publicly that he intended to get away with anything he could. While it cannot be denied that he stood in the forefront of the battle against barbarism, he used that fact to justify operating against the directions of the leadership. As a result there were serious disturbances of operations amounting almost to sabotage. As a disciplinary action he was exiled for many years to a remote section of the operation. But despite daily discussions with Colleague Adler ("eagle") he persisted in his idiosyncratic frame of mind. Finally, thanks to the efforts of his colleagues and especially of Worker Hercules, he was reintegrated into the collective in the hope that he

would prove his worthiness. But his individualism remained un-
broken, and his independent actions and criticism now compel
the judges to let P. state his views before the whole workforce.
Prometheus's statement, which follows in the poem "Übungen
im Joch" (which means, according to Bartsch's own commentary, both "Exertions in the Yoke" and "Exercises in Yoga"), is a
simple assertion that he is content to sit on his crag practicing
breathing exercises and restoring his liver through calm, diet,
and contemplation. No one need come to unbind him because
his chains already hang ringing against the rock above an empty
world.

With the works of the 1980s by Hacks, Braun, and Bartsch
the image of Prometheus has been wholly inverted from the
neo-Goethean Titan who once raged in the factories and cried
out for a new society. Now he stands before tribunals, condemned (or condemning himself) for the sin of knowledge:
the very acts that lifted humankind out of barbarism into civilization have also produced the ravages of the atomic age, ecological disaster, and a dehumanizing technologization. Yet the
centrality of the myth in all its ambivalence for the national self-
image is exemplified by the fact that the GDR Cultural Association (Kulturbund der DDR) commissioned works by a number
of painters and composers as well as writers for a project called
simply "Prometheus 1982."[59]

IT IS fitting to round off this survey of the proletarianization of
Prometheus with an autobiographical anecdote that the novelist and scriptwriter Günther Rücker (born 1924) published in
the last year of the GDR in the leading East German journal of
literature and culture.[60] "Prometheus 1937," which consists of
two scenes, begins with Rücker's recollection of a volume of
socialist poetry that his father brought into their Bohemian
home in 1937: marching songs for proletarians bearing ham-
mer and sword; theatrical scenes of workers gazing up at castles
to be torn down in future struggles; and others. Among these
was a poem that he usually skipped—though unnamed, it is

clearly Goethe's "Prometheus"—because of its mythological allusions and free verse. Then one day the thirteen-year-old suddenly realized that the scornful words of the opening lines spoke to him: here someone was taking issue with the Almighty himself. While the other poems spoke of future struggles, here someone was already engaged in a battle against unequal odds. Learning the poem by heart, the boy shouted it aloud, wishing that his voice would carry to the very heavens. When the Germans invaded the Sudetenland in 1938 and the family went into exile, the book was lost along with possessions, country, and people.

The second scene takes place twenty years later in Moscow, where Rücker and three fellow Germans are celebrating the conclusion of a lengthy and difficult assignment. At a neighboring table some fifteen Russians are also celebrating their imminent return to various parts of the country. Then one of the Russians comes over and, in an elegant but antiquated German, invites Rücker and his friends to join them in a toast to a German Communist who did not live long enough to witness their day of justice. As the men raise their glasses to the fallen comrade, the first Russian begins to recite the lines of Goethe's poem: "Who helped me against the arrogance of the Titans? Who saved me from death, from slavery? Did you not do it all yourself, holy-glowing heart?" Rücker ends his account without further commentary. "My heart was beating in my throat."

But we understand that, despite all his metamorphoses— from heroic proletarian revolutionary through problematic ambivalences to enemy of the people—and despite the problematical effect of his knowledge, Goethe's Prometheus retained throughout the entire history of the GDR his power to inspire and unify socialists in their ideal of revolution and humanism. Meanwhile and through a sublime irony, in the country that the GDR anathematized as the exemplification of modern capitalism and its evils, the arch-German legendary figure of Faust was being embraced as the image of that society's own anguish in the face of sinful knowledge.

CHAPTER SIX

The Americanization of Faust

MODERNIZATIONS OF THE MYTH

FOR AT LEAST two centuries Germans have recognized in Faust a psychogram of their national soul. In his lectures on the philosophy of art (1802–1803), delivered only a dozen years after the initial fragmentary publication of Goethe's dramatic poem, Schelling called Faust "the most profound, purest essence of our age" ("die innerste, reinste Essenz unseres Zeitalters").[1] This view of Faust as phenotype generated many literary treatments other than Goethe's and lasted well past World War II, when it produced two symptomatic works that amounted to retractions of Goethe's redemptive ending.[2] Thomas Mann returned to the original chapbook of 1587 for the paradigm of the scholar who sold his soul to the devil in return for knowledge and creative genius. In his novel *Doktor Faustus* (1947) the life and career of the composer Adrian Leverkühn parallels the self-destructive course of Germany in the early twentieth century. Five years later Hanns Eisler, basing his libretto *Johann Faustus* (1952) on the seventeenth-century puppet plays, portrayed Faust at the time of the Peasants' War (1524–1525) in a manner that parodied Goethe's work in almost every scene: the prologue takes place not in heaven but in hell; Faust translates not the Gospel of John but the Book of Job; his actions are aped by his servant, the clownlike Hanswurst; and at the end (after only twelve, not the traditional twenty-four years), he is condemned. The official response to Eisler's work was so violent—it was denounced for its reactionary ideology and negative depiction of the German people, and for its portrayal of an alienated Faust who betrays the masses—that Eisler never went on to compose the music to his libretto.[3] Stage performances of

149

Fig. 7. Rockwell Kent, *Faust and the Earth Spirit.* From Goethe's *Faust,*
translated by Carlyle F. MacIntyre. New York: New Directions, 1941.
Courtesy of The Rockwell Kent Legacy.

the text were prohibited in the German Democratic Republic
for over twenty years.

The worldwide success of Mann's novel and the controversy
surrounding Eisler's libretto in both parts of a divided Germany
explain studies with such titles as Hans Schwerte's *Faust and the
Faustian: A Chapter of German Ideology* (1962) or Klaus Völker's
Faust—A German Man (1975). For the same reasons the com-
piler of the standard four-volume Faust bibliography felt confident in claiming that "the Faust material can be designated as
the national German theme."[4] The figure of Faust has continued
to occupy the German mind—in the brilliant film version of
Goethe's drama by Gustav Gründgens, in puppet shows performed in the marketplaces of many cities, and in museum exhibitions. Restaurants offer wines and menus redolent, however

150

tenuously, of this most famous of German legends.[5] In the 1995–1996 season, productions of *Faust* still outdrew all other nonmusical plays on German stages. In recent years, to be sure, the old theme has usually been demythified, democratized, and popularized in an effort to dedemonize it.[6]

It seems inevitable that a myth so powerful, like those of Adam and Prometheus, should in an era of globalization be internationalized.[7] On the eve of World War II Faust emigrated across the border to France, where in 1940 Paul Valéry drafted two dramatic comedies (published in 1946 under the collective title *Mon Faust*) featuring a Faust who points out to Méphisto-phélès that in the modern world he no longer enjoys the same privileged status as before. René Clair's celebrated film *La Beauté du diable* (1950) begins with a traditional Faust disenchanted with his knowledge. Rejuvenated by Mephisto, he joins a traveling circus featuring Marguerite and her performing dogs. When Faust is accused of murdering his former self, Mephisto assumes the appearance of the elderly Professor Faust to exonerate him. When things go badly for the rejuvenated Faust, he finally agrees to a pact with Mephisto; but his dream of benefiting humanity through his knowledge is shattered when Mephisto shows him, in a magic mirror, the unmistakable cloud of an atomic bomb. Marguerite, accused of sorcery, is persecuted by a mob; but when they catch sight of the pact signed by Faust, they turn their fury upon Mephisto, who has assumed Faust's shape. Following Mephisto's death at the hands of the mob, Faust and Marguerite gaze out upon a sunny landscape where the traveling circus is moving toward the horizon. "It is never too late"—this refusal to accept the yoke of destiny is the tragicomic twist that Clair and his collaborator Armand Salacrou sought to give the traditional legend in the years following World War II and the bomb over Hiroshima (168).

As though to substantiate Valéry's claim that "nothing demonstrates more certainly the power of a creator than the infidelity or insubmissiveness of his creature" (7), Faust quickly showed up in other countries as well. Lawrence Durrell wrote a "morality in nine scenes" entitled *An Irish Faust* (1964), while Mikhail Bulgakov in *The Master and Margarita* (1967) resurrected the Reformation figure in Moscow of the 1920s and 1930s, and Slobodan Snajder's *Croatian Faust* (1987) satirized the co-option of the theater by the Fascists in 1942. In England, Anthony Borrow used the theme, in his dramatization *John Faust* (1958), to depict "the cosmic loneliness of man"; D. J. Enright retold the traditional chapbook life in the seventy-three poems of his *A Faust Book* (1979); Robert Nye traced the erotic adventures of the chapbook Faust from the viewpoint of his assistant Wagner in his picaresque *Faust* (1980); and the protagonist of Emma Tennant's feminist *Faustine* (1992) signs the infernal contract for her rejuvenation in a television sales shop in modern London. (*The Loves of Faustyna* [1994] by the Polish-Irish writer Nina Fitzpatrick catalogs the sexual adventures of a heroine in Communist Poland who is unsuccessfully tempted to become an informer by an intelligence officer whom she knows as Mephisto.) In the past decade theatergoers in Toronto could attend Andrew Kelm's adaptation of a twentieth-century Faust (1993) as well as *Mephisto's Dream* by Richard Niecsczym (1989), in which an aging Quebecois professor searching for his soul is corrupted by an anglophone devil.

Czech humor produced both the bizarre universe populated by animated marionettes of Jan Svankmayer's film *Faust* (1994) and the black comedy of Vaclav Havel's *Temptation* (1986), which appropriates the legend to attack "the pride of that intolerant, all-powerful, and self-serving power that uses the sciences merely as a handy weapon for shooting down anything that threatens it" (100). His Dr. Foustka is a scientist at a research institute dedicated ostensibly to attacking prescientific thinking and rooting out mysticism. When Foustka, who has begun to entertain doubts about the institute's aim, seeks to conjure spirits, he is approached by a disgusting old man named Fistula, who offers to initiate him into the black arts. It turns out that Fistula is an informer who betrays Foustka to the authorities.

The play ends with a costume party in which all the members of the institute show up as revelers at a witches' Sabbath to celebrate Foustka's downfall and their own hypocrisy.

FAUST AND THE BOMB

Despite these instantiations from East to West, nowhere outside Germany has Faust appeared so frequently or in such variegated forms as in the United States. (In fact, he changes his character as frequently as Mephisto changes the spelling of his name.) In poems, novels, and dramatizations, in comic books and musicals, the figure of Faust has emerged as a psychic seismograph of America's shifting dreams and enduring angst since World War II. In 1971 the Minnesota Opera premiered *Faust counter Faust: Collage in Two Acts* by John Gessner and H. Wesley Balk. In the following decade the Opera Company of Philadelphia, sponsored by a group of area businesses that called themselves "The Faust Consortium," mounted a Faust Series featuring the familiar works by Berlioz, Gounod, and Busoni. And not only in our cultural artifacts! For those who have never encountered the original chapbook, Marlowe's tragedy, Goethe's poetic drama, Gounod's opera, or Rockwell Kent's woodcuts and Salvador Dali's etchings, "Faust" and his "bargain" have taken on a metaphorical life of their own, with only the loosest resemblance to the twenty-four years of experience and knowledge for which Faust bargained away his soul. An editorial in the *New York Times* (January 27, 1998) speaks of "the Faustian bargain" that citizens of the United States, overlooking the president's indiscretions for the sake of his political and economic agenda, signed with Bill Clinton. A Jungian analyst proposes Faust, along with Don Quixote and Hamlet, as one of the "three levels of masculine consciousness," in which Faust represents the perfect state of the fully integrated man (an analogy that would have surprised Jung as well as Goethe).[8] And in the personal

153

columns of the *New York Review* (February 27, 1986) a "Gret-chenesque Helena" advertises for a "mature Goethean Faust."

In the westering of the legend, Karl Shapiro's poem "The Progress of Faust" (from *Trial of a Poet*, 1947) plays a transitional role, tracing in its seven octaves of iambic pentameter and with poetic precision the history and migration of the legend (121–22). His Faust, "born in Deutschland" and "graduated in magic from Cracow" in 1505, bargains with the devil for "pleasures intellectually foul" and then wanders around Germany, as reported in the chapbook of the historical Faust, lecturing at fairs, performing minor miracles, and teaching the "black art of anatomy." In 1594 he moves to London where, at the climax of Marlowe's play, he "crashed through the floor." For the next century he tours the Continent, boxing the devil's ears in the puppet plays and publishing "penny poems" about his sins. Shortly before the French Revolution he returns to Germany, where (in Goethe's version) he dallies with "the fair Phrygian" and "called all universities his own." At this point the historical-literary figure emerges as the embodiment of German academic scholarship, preaching "comparative science to the young / Who came from every land in a great throng." In 1939, however, Faust is expelled by the Nazis and disappears for five years,

> appearing on the sixth to pose
> In an American desert at war's end
> Where, at his back, a dome of atoms rose.

With this final strophe, which transposes Faust from Germany to the United States and exposes him in the guise of an atomic scientist, Shapiro—probably unwittingly—is exploiting a theme that dominated the thinking and rationalizations of the makers of the bomb, German and American alike, before and after World War II.[9] The tradition reached a high point at Niels Bohr's Institute of Theoretical Physics in Copenhagen, where in 1932 a parody of Goethe's *Faust* was performed featuring Bohr himself as the Lord, his student Wolfgang Pauli as Mephisto, and Paul Ehrenfest as Faust.[10] The "Prologue in Heaven" contained technical allusions to contemporary cosmological controversies, while other scenes dealt with the discovery of the neutron and the theory of radiation. The scene in Auerbach's cellar was used to poke fun at Einstein's proposals for a unified field theory, and the Walpurgis Night spoofed various versions of quantum theory. What matters in the present context, however, is not the scientific detail but the project itself. In the construction and elaboration of the history of their discipline, atomic physicists have been among the most ingenious mythmakers of the twentieth century, from whom even sophisticated political spin doctors have much to learn. By attaching their science to the legend of Faust, they romanticized and glorified their part in the invention of the atomic bomb.

The parody in Copenhagen antedates the bomb: it is mythification, of course, yet still rather harmless. But after 1945 the allusions to Faust crop up with notable frequency in the memoirs of atomic physicists, where especially J. Robert Oppenheimer is portrayed as the Faustian figure who made a bargain with the devil—an analogy signaled by Oppenheimer himself, who in 1956 reportedly remarked that he and his fellow physicists at Los Alamos "did the devil's work."[11] In his "personal history of the atomic scientists" Robert Jungk established the pattern, describing Oppenheimer's security hearing. "The last act—for the time being—of the Oppenheimer drama is reminiscent, in its simplicity, of the popular ballads and traditional spectacles of earlier centuries, in which Marlowe and Goethe discovered the materials for their tragedies on the theme of Faust" (329). One account of the hearing spoke of those who saw in Oppenheimer the "Faust of the twentieth century [who] had sold his soul to the atom bomb."[12] A few years later Freeman Dyson sought to explain the lure of the "Faustian bargain." "The glitter of nuclear weapons. It is irresistible if you come to them as a scientist. To feel it's there in your hands—to release this energy that fuels the stars, to let it do your bidding."[13] Yet behind these mythifications lurks a more self-serving purpose. To the extent that the bomb can be attributed to Oppenheimer and his pact with the devil, the rest of the scientific community exonerates itself. It was Oppenheimer, looking more like Gründgens's Mephisto than like Faust, who sold his soul to the devil—not the rest of us, who can stand complacently aside and look on raptly as the tragedy unfolds itself before the security board of the Atomic Energy Commission. The frequent allusions of this sort, in any case, betray a pronounced awareness of the American scientific community's discomfort with the wages of the sin of knowledge.

PLAYFUL FAUSTS OF THE FIFTIES

Shapiro wrote his poem before this mythification had taken place and presumably with no awareness of the physicists' earlier caper in Copenhagen. But his very ignorance speaks loudly for the insightfulness of the poetic imagination, which made the association even before the scandals of the 1950s drove the physicists into their spasm of mythmaking. While these early treatments focus explicitly on the sin of knowledge in their appropriation of the myth, George Haimsohn's Madcap Classic *The Bedside Faust* (1952) looks like a defensive response to Shapiro's grim visions. The cartoons present a surprisingly faithful rendition of the legend as familiar from Gounod's opera. But the cartoon version, like all parodies, suggests that in 1952 the story of Faust—whether from Gounod's opera, from Great Books courses at colleges and universities, from Delacroix's lithographs or Rockwell Kent's woodcuts, from the text (or subsequent film) of Marlowe's *Faustus* or the many translations of Goethe's *Faust*, or even from the allusions in the scientific community—was familiar enough in the United States to justify the expectation that parodic adaptations of the theme would be understood and appreciated. And during the 1950s the parodies appeared with a vengeance: two by leading American writers of high and late modernism, and two in the form of successful Broadway plays.

156

Gertrude Stein's operatic libretto *Doctor Faust Lights the Lights* was written in 1938, but because it was not published until 1949 or performed until 1951, it had its effect, like Valéry's *Mon Faust*, in the postwar years. Stein's Faustus is a post-Enlightenment genius, who has sold his soul to Mephisto in order to invent electric light and thereby to illuminate, and symbolically enlighten, the world. As the opera begins, however, he is utterly bored with life: he knows everything and can do everything but now wonders if he ever had a soul to sell to the devil. As Faust sings a duet with his talking dog about the electric lights, which flicker on and off, the heroine of the piece, who bears the double name Marguerite Ida and Helena Annabel, is bitten by a viper and saved by Faust. Still bored and concerned about his own identity, Faust decides that he wants to go to hell. Mephisto tells him that he must first commit a sin by killing his dog and his boy-companion. Thereupon Mephisto rejuvenates Faust and urges him to take Marguerite Ida and Helena Annabel off to hell with him. But she resists his invitation, and as the lights fail, Faust sinks away into the darkness.

The social and political implications of the text are clear: Stein is expressing her doubts about technology in the modern industrialized world as well as her fears about a Europe about to be plunged back into the barbarity of Nazism. She is fully aware, in other words, of the theme of the sin of knowledge that underlies and informs the Faust myth. Her Faust also ruminates on issues of identity and success that were central to her own concerns as a woman and a writer.[14] Beyond that, however, the text with its singing dog, its heroine with the tricky name, its inner rhymes and Stein-patented repetitions, is playful to the point of silliness.

> sold my soul to make it bright with electric light and now no one
> not I not she not they not he are interested in that thing and I
> and I I cannot go to hell I have sold my soul to make a light and
> the light is bright but not interesting in my sight and I would oh
> yes I would I would rather go to hell be I with all might might
> and then go to hell oh yes alright. (232)

157

Precisely this silliness seems to have appealed to Robert Duncan, whose acknowledged admiration for Gertrude Stein manifested itself in the "Imitations" that he wrote in the early 1950s and published in his volume *Derivations* (1968). His *Faust Foutu* suggests through its very title that it intends to outdo even Stein in its playfulness. Duncan was obsessed with the material for most of the decade: the first act was produced in 1954 in a dramatic reading at King Ubu's gallery in San Francisco and the complete "entertainment in four parts" a year later at The Six Gallery in the same city. In addition to the tenuous Faust theme—based on general familiarity and not on Goethe's *Faust*, which Duncan claimed not to have read[15]—the work features Stein-like language and frivolity, an author's apologia, a "soliloquy for five voices," a discussion of "Robert Duncan's work," and pervasive attacks on the war in Korea. In the prologue the Master of Ceremonies introduces Faust by singing:

> in the midst of the war he was a war himself
> looking for the eternal piece of ass.

The Muse, who talks like the cat in Don Marquis's *Archy and Mehitabel*, complains that "us muses is always having to ring the six o'clock in the morning alarm, knock on the bathroom door to interrupt the fun, send notes warning of syphilis schizophrenia or scabies to keep these American beauties alive to the whip of daily living."

Duncan's Faust is a painter whose huge canvas depicts the course of his life. (In 1951 Duncan was living with the abstract expressionist painter Jess Collins, who at the time was experimenting with monumental collages.) The boy with an animal head who visits him reminds us unmistakably of the talking dog and boy who accompany Stein's Faust. Marguerite, whose nurse is the devil speaking in an Irish brogue, goes to bed with Faust and sings a song to "nights of love" (which sounds suspiciously like a parody of *Tristan und Isolde*). In her dreams she sleepwalks

among the celestial stars and encounters Helen of Troy, Brun-
hilde, and Garbo, who speak a weird German/French patois.
Later they show up in Faust's bedroom, where he joins in their
dance and confesses his own desires and his willingness to sell
his soul: "To conquer time, to go farther, to enter the lights"
(again an allusion to Stein's *Faust*). At the end of the first act
Faust meets his aged mother and confesses that for his pride he
fell out of self and from heaven into hell. As they curse each
other for their mutual misunderstanding, the Master of Ceremonies appears again and exclaims: "What the Devil! This isnt
much fun. Everything's gone to hell in my absence." And the
Muse comments that "This Act was bound to have a dismal
close." Like Stein, Duncan has appropriated the Faust theme
as a vehicle for comments on the American soul and on the
contemporary political scene. For all its literariness, however, it
betrays no awareness beyond the bare plot of the underlying
theme of the sin of knowledge. His entertainment takes so
much self-satisfaction in its own linguistic play that continuity
and coherence are sacrificed for the sake of the brilliant scene
or song.

WHILE Gertrude Stein and Robert Duncan adapted the Faust
theme playfully for purposes of serious cultural criticism, other
writers were attracted by the comic possibilities inherent in the
notion of a pact with the devil—a theme whose popularity
suggests a great deal about the values of an America luxuriating
after the Korean War in the security and prosperity of the Eisen-
hower era. Douglass Wallop's best-selling novel *The Year the
Yankees Lost the Pennant* (1954), upon which the musical *Damn
Yankees* was based, tells the tale of a fifty-year-old real-estate sales-
man named Joe Boyd, who is such a passionate fan of the Washington Senators baseball team that he sells his soul to the devil
to help the team. The devil, who appears in the form of a slippery agent-lawyer named Applegate, and who carefully conceals
his cloven hooves and lights his cigarettes by snapping fire out
of his fingers, does not require Boyd to sign his name in blood

"or some phony stunt like that" (33). They simply shake hands on a preliminary two-month contract with an escape clause, whereupon Applegate transforms Boyd into a twenty-two-year-old home-run hitter named Joe Hardy, who leads the Senators into a pennant race with the Yankees. The plot has its complications: Applegate tricks Joe Hardy into a permanent contract and then tries to engineer the defeat of the Senators in the tie-breaking game. Finally, with the help of a devil's helpmeet named Lola, Joe is enabled to escape from his contract, resume his identity, and return to his wife and his former identity. We recognize, in short, the traditional pact with the devil as well as the feats and adventures of the rejuvenated Faust; but, unlike the traditional Faust, Wallop's hero is redeemed and does not have to suffer the consequences of his sin.

The parallels between Wallop's novel (or the musical *Damn Yankees*) and George Axelrod's comedy *Will Success Spoil Rock Hunter?* (first performed in 1955) are conspicuous. Here the victim is a minor newspaper columnist and aspiring playwright named George MacCauley, who initially shakes hands with a literary agent named Irving Lasalle on a deal for a million dollars in return for 10 percent of his soul. Here the plot device involves MacCauley's successively deeper spiritual indebtedness to the devilish agent—50 percent more of his soul for a successful Hollywood screenplay, 10 percent for the love of the movie sex-goddess Rita Marlowe—until finally Lasalle owns "ninety percent of such a wealthy, talented, two-fisted, hard-punching, Academy-Award-winning, poet, lover, adventurer, et cetera, et cetera, et cetera" (119). MacCauley eventually escapes when a friend buys out his contract from the satanic agent, confident that he has the character to resist the final 10 percent: he intends to make it as a writer on his own merits and without the assistance of the devil.

In both of these works a soul is sacrificed for the sake of a good quite different from Faustian knowledge. The structure of the myth is more important to the authors than its thematic content: the sin of knowledge. Yet both of these folksy Fausts acquire moral insights that ultimately justify their mythic experiences, and the use of the myth in works intended for general audiences suggests at least a degree of popular familiarity in the America of the 1950s with the tale of Faust.

A BLUE-COLLAR FAUST

What is interesting about these last two works is not their literary value but their social significance. Both reflect a society worrying that it has bargained away its spiritual values for material success—but a society still hoping to laugh and sing its anxieties away. (Wallop's novel was chosen both as a Book-of-the-Month Club selection and as a Reader's Digest condensed book.) Jack Kerouac had a different view of the theme altogether. Kerouac was a close contemporary of Robert Duncan's—he was born in 1922, three years after Duncan—and later met him in the circle around Kenneth Rexroth and the poetry readings at The Six Gallery in San Francisco (where *Faust Foutu* was first presented). But insurmountable differences, apart from Duncan's political activism and Kerouac's apolitical anarchism, separated the heir of Gertrude Stein's "lost generation," with his self-conscious literary "derivations," from the dharma bum of the Beat Generation. When Duncan tried to talk to Kerouac about his work, Kerouac responded with wisecracks. "In fact he's too decent for me—all I can understand is franticness."[16] So we expect few of the similarities that are evident in the Fausts of Stein and Duncan. The modernists seized upon Faust as a traditional cultural possession through whose deconstruction they were able to make cynical comments on the decline of Western civilization. For Kerouac, in contrast, Faust emerges as a model in the experience of life and, hence, again in his traditional role as the sinner for knowledge.

In *Dr. Sax* (1959), Kerouac's frankly autobiographical novel of boyhood in blue-collar Lowell, Massachusetts, the mysterious titular figure plays Mephisto to the adolescent hero of the account, which bears the subtitle *Faust Part Three*. During the late 1940s Kerouac was obsessed with the notion of writing an autobiography in imitation of Goethe's *Poetry and Truth*.[17] The earliest version of *Doctor Sax*, a short piece written in 1948 and entitled "A Novella of Children and Evil," was begun as a continuation of Goethe's *Faust*.[18] The novel, written in 1952 and heavily colored by the French Canadian patois of Kerouac's family and neighborhood of Pawtucketville, recalls in a linguistically exuberant stream of consciousness the years immediately preceding the great flood of March 1936, which devastated Lowell. The main device of the work is the author's romanticization of his boyhood, which he achieves by projecting onto it a fantasy world fed by the pulp magazines to which Kerouac was addicted; by movies featuring the Marx Brothers and W. C. Fields, and by *The Wizard of Oz*; and by such fabulous characters as The Shadow, Dracula, and—most important—Faust. Kerouac is specific about this influence. Describing Doctor Sax, he writes:

> His shroud flew after him, he stood like a Goethe witch before his furn-forge, tall, emasculated, Nietzschean, gaunt—(in those days I knew Goethe and Nietzsche only from titles in faded gold paint imprinted on the backs of soft brown or soft pale green old velvety Classic books in the Lowell Library—The Cat swished his great tail. (212–13)

While this scene is based on the "Witch's Kitchen" in the first part of Goethe's *Faust*, others look as though they were inspired by the Delacroix lithographs that illustrated many nineteenth-century editions of Goethe's *Faust*. At one point, for instance, Doctor Sax leads the boy on a flight into the sky. "Doctor Sax, elongated like a long scorpion, is flying across the moon like a demented cloud. Fiendish, teeth shining, I fly after him in a minor flare of ink" (210). In another place: "Doctor Sax had knowledge of death . . . but he was a mad fool of power, a Faustian man, no true Faustian's afraid of the dark" (43). While

162

Goethe's *Faust* lends the images that shape many of the principal scenes, in the phantasmagoria of Kerouac's account it is often unclear to what extent the figure is a projection of the boy's own imagination or of the writer looking back fifteen years later. Moreover, even though Doctor Sax, the imaginary companion who accompanies the boy on his way through puberty, is sometimes portrayed as though he were himself Faustian, in the rhetoric of the work he plays the role of the Mephisto who inducts the boyish Faust into experience and knowledge. "I didn't know his name then. He didn't frighten me, either. I sensed he was my friend . . . my old, old friend . . . my ghost, personal angel, private shadow, secret lover" (33–34). It is in this sense that the novel is "Faust Part Three."

Doctor Sax, the (Jungian) shadow, appears with increasing frequency as Ti Jean (Kerouac's own childhood nickname) emerges from childhood into adolescence. In a major scene toward the end Doctor Sax takes the boy on a nighttime tour of Lowell that exposes the town in a magical illumination colored by fantasy and imagination. Made invisible by Sax's "shroudy cape" (201), they peer through a bedroom window at one of Ti Jean's friends, who is reading *Star Western* in bed. Sax chooses this moment to expose a vision of the future to his protégé. "You'll come to angular rages and lonely romages among Beast of Day in hot glary circumstances made grit by the hour of the clock—that is known as Civilization. You'll roll your feet together in the tense befuddles of ten thousand evenings in company in the parlor, in the pad—that is known as, ah, socializing" (202). The bleak account goes on to rehearse old age, maturity, and other experiences that mark human life.

The details of Kerouac's frenzied—at times, indeed, almost incoherent—phantasmagoria are not important here. (Kerouac was notoriously obsessive about the autobiographical particulars of his childhood in Lowell.) What matters is the dominant presence of the Faust theme as the organizing principle of the work. Unlike the playful parodies of Stein and Duncan, unlike the social-critical comedies of Axelrod and Wallop, Kerouac's novel uses the Faust theme, specifically as presented by Goethe and as illustrated by Delacroix, seriously to exemplify the relationship between the boy and the shadow figure of his imagination who tempts him out of the innocence of childhood and into the consciousness of adulthood. Through Sax, the boy becomes aware of the struggle between good and evil, which comes to a climax in the hallucinatory scenes of the final pages, when a great Bird of Paradise comes down to save mankind from the monstrous Snake coiled beneath the castle above Lowell. Sax's final comment, as the Bird carries off the Serpent, is "The Universe disposes of its own evil!" (245). Following this anti-Mephistophilean insight he begins to disappear again from the boy's life. "I have seen Doctor Sax several times since, at dusk, in autumn, when the kids jump up and down and scream—he only deals in glee now" (245).

Kerouac's novel, which—despite his considerable difficulties in finding a publisher and despite the unfavorable reviews—he liked best among his works, is a vivid rendition of youth's constant attempt to romanticize and dramatize the often bleak and tawdry circumstances of everyday life. In the process it revitalizes the Faust myth as a vehicle for the sin of knowledge.

PROFESSORIAL FAUSTS

If in the 1950s the American Faust was in the hands of playful modernists, Broadway entrepreneurs, and earnest beatniks, in the 1960s he returned to the university in several works that, in utterly different ways, are distinctly professorial and, accordingly, reflect the traditional theme of the sin of knowledge. The legend of Faust has belonged since its beginnings to a university setting.[19] The original chapbook of 1587 was among other things an antiuniversity tract: a religious attack on the search for forbidden knowledge. Goethe's *Faust* contains an academic satire so savage that it undermines the beliefs upon which the institution, at least as it was known in the eighteenth century, was founded. In Thomas Mann's *Doktor Faustus* it is at the universities of Halle and Leipzig that Adrian Leverkühn is infected, first, by the theological doctrines that undermine his faith and, second, by the syphilis that is associated in Mann's mind with his genius. From the start, then, the Faust theme has been attached to universities, and hence to knowledge, in such a manner as to subvert the institution and to cast doubt upon its pursuits. In the sixteenth century it was regarded as a place whose knowledge was sinful; in the eighteenth century as a place whose knowledge was worthless; and in the mid–twentieth century as a place whose knowledge is powerless against the forces of evil.

Written in 1951, Elder Olson's "Faust: A Masque" very much exemplifies this last category. Olson was a professor at the University of Chicago and prominently associated with the neo-Aristotelean critics located there. His masque—especially the first of its two scenes with its allusions to Milton and quotations from Marlowe and Goethe—looks like nothing so much as the pastiche of a humanities course on Western literature. His Faust, aged and fearful of death, inhabits a castle whose decay reflects his own decrepitude. The chorus of serving men and peasants has come this evening to watch his window because their fates are "shadows of his fate":

> We watch and whisper in terror of a prophecy
> That tonight of all nights he will fail us.

(4)

Within the castle Faust summons Mephistopheles with a Latin incantation and, when he arrives, tests him with the traditional question regarding the speed and power of the various demons. They finally agree that the fastest devil of all is "as fast as misery follows upon folly" (8). Faust has forgotten why he had wanted to summon the devil:

I had once, I think, some noble motive—I have forgotten it.
But I am human; therefore, let us say,
Lust, greed, ambition, rage, fear.

(8)

As Faust recites his traditional lament over the failure of the faculties, Mephistopheles interrupts his list with words from the famous monologue of Goethe's Faust, first in English and then in German:

> M. And jurisprudence, and have all these years—
> F. Led my students hither and thither by the nose—
> M. "Und bin so klug als wie zuvor."
> F. What is that you are saying? You seem to pluck
>   The words out of my soul. . . . I have a curious
>   feeling, almost a premonition. . . .

(10–11)

Mephistopheles reminds him that it is not a premonition but a memory, that "all human action has been repetition." Indeed, he continues, true damnation is to be condemned to do "over and over again the self-same wrong" (13). When Faust says that he wants to have back his youth, Mephistopheles tells him that he has come only "because the script demands it," but that

> Man is obsolete; he must evolve or die;
> Somehow the new creature must take shape
> To inhabit the altering world—what do you say, will you risk it?

With a passing reference to Milton's fallen angels Mephistopheles promises to restore Faust's youth but then does not do so and remarks in an aside,

> I should think his own words would tell him he is old;
> No young man ever talked so of youth.

(16)

Faust, falsely believing himself rejuvenated, asks if it is possible to see Helen of Troy, whereupon Mephisto quotes Marlowe's *Faustus*:

166

Why not? It's all set down in the old play.
There, now—look at her—look; make the usual speech
Pronounced on this occasion.

(Points; nothing is there.)

What, must I prompt you?
—"Is this the face that launched a thousand ships?"

But Faust has forgotten his own lines and, looking in the mirror, realizes that he is still old. Confronted with his own corrupt flesh, he sends Mephistopheles away and intends to summon up a more powerful devil.

Following the chorus's lament—that humankind slowly emerged from the slime of the swamps, only now to be threatened through a sinful knowledge with a return again to that original bestial condition—Doctor Polio-Anthrax, looking like the caricature of an old-fashioned professor, appears in the second scene and, in a long speech spiced with quotations from Horace and other literary sources, reports to Faust that a drug of his invention has rejuvenated an aged rat, which he has brought along in a small cage. Though it has never been tested upon human beings, Faust eagerly demands the formula—"Quickly; my veins thirst" (31). When Doctor Polio-Anthrax is reluctant, Faust struggles with him and scratches himself with the syringe, whereupon the professor points out to him that he has

Signed—dear, dear! a sort of dreadful contract;
Yes; one might say, a sort of dreadful contract
—Signed with your blood, one might say; yes, with your blood.
You see the drug—well, seems to exact a price
After a certain while.

(33)

The professor leaves without answering Faust's question about the price. When Faust goes back to look at the rejuvenated rat in its cage, he is startled by its appearance and calls back the professor, who explains that the rat will continue to change in

167

a process of regressive evolution. The masque ends as Faust stares at his rapidly aging hands with a fascinated horror. For a cynically embittered Olson, apparently, the recently experienced ravages of World War II with its Auschwitz and Hiroshima tarnished the image of Faust, to the extent that he symbolizes the fate of modern man. This modern Faust, exploiting the tools of science for ignoble ends, avoids the responsibility of progressing into the future and thereby has condemned himself through the sin of knowledge to a return to bestiality.

In the book-length poem *Horatio* (1961) by Hyam Plutzik, an award-winning poet and professor of English at the University of Rochester, Faust has been reduced to a drunken and pedantic old babbler. Following Hamlet's death, his friend Horatio undertakes a pilgrimage across Europe to gather information so that he can carry out the dying prince's commission "[t]o tell my story." In the course of his peregrinations Horatio encounters a rude and ignorant ostler, a condescending French count and countess, a cynical prime minister of Denmark, an innocent shepherd, and other sources. In the twelfth year after Hamlet's death he returns to Wittenberg, where he visits his former teacher, once "wiser and more erudite" than any of Europe's sages, but who now has taken

> The old blasted path into damnation,
> And with his blood, abjuring gentle Christ,
> Matched his indenture with the Prince of Demons.
>
> (135)

But Horatio gets little satisfaction from the pedantic Faust, who sees only abstracts and universals—not living, vital reality.

> For when a man who moved in history
> Enters the universal, passing once
> The abstract symbol before the haughty door
> Of high philosophy, there's no return
> Into the stupid hovel of bone and flesh.
>
> (136–37)

168

Between swallows of his wine, "a prime hog-swill from Saxony," he pompously translates "To be or not to be" into the German dichotomy of *Sein* and *Werden* ("being" and "becoming") and manages, through what he regards as a brilliant conceit, to read the encounter of Hamlet and his father's ghost as an embodiment of the Holy Trinity. Plutzik's brief episode, while it serves the general function within his narrative poem of illustrating once again the gap between perception and reality, reduces the figure of Faust to the role of the unworldly and ridiculous professor, incapable of comprehending the genius of his own former student, Hamlet.

I. A. Richards's "infernal comedy" *Tomorrow Morning, Faustus* (1962) is equally professorial and equally sardonic about the usefulness of academic knowledge. Richards, who taught at Harvard, seems to have been obsessed with the Faust theme— Marlowe's *Faustus*, not Goethe's—during the early 1960s. The poem "Theodicy" (25–32) comprises an "internal colloquy" in which Faustus, "[m]uch learnt since Marlowe's man," debates with Lucifer the merits of consciousness versus innocence and of a society "TV'd beyond concern." In the poem "Faculty Meeting" (61–62) Faustus reviews the various academic subjects— math, physics, political science, psychology, philosophy—only to conclude cynically that all have become "a bag of tricks, a line of talk" eschewing all intellectual and social responsibility. Only theology, "fair abdicated Queen," still holds her old domain. It is hardly surprising, then, that Richards turns in his three-act "infernal comedy" to a reassessment of the theme from a contemporary point of view.

The prologue is spoken by Marlowe's Faustus (237), who tells us that, in an age when "you up-to-dates" learn in preschool years what formerly only erudite scholars knew, it no longer suffices to ridicule the institution—"to laugh at Doctorates." His successor has more ambitious goals. It is the fiction of the play that Satan, chairman of the board of the Futurity Foundation, has called a General Epochal Meeting of his directorate to review the past and plan future action. Mammon, the financier, has contributed to the troubles of the world through overpopulation, overproduction, and depressions, while General Moloch has worked through his wars, his secret police, his concentration camps and genocides. Don Belial did his part with psychoanalysis, juvenile delinquency, TV, resorts, and other time killers, and Beelzebub, managing director of the enterprise, has encouraged standardization, the rule of fashion, and the mills of uniformity. During these proceedings Sophia serves as clerk of the board, whose words appear on a large screen suspended above the boardroom table: only those words that are filtered through her amount to lasting wisdom. Their deliberations expose them as a remarkably bumbling, incompetent group; even Satan concedes that he is "not the Fiend I was" (269). At this point, they conclude, the modern Faustus, this "New Model," is equipped "biologically, ontogenetically, / Psycholo-sociologically" to serve their aims "better than the Marlowe or the Goethe models" (279–80). While they have lost their direction, "[h]ere's Man on Earth making enormous gains / In knowledge and in power every which way" (277). Mammon therefore sends down a "vehicle" in the form of an attractive young career woman to tempt him.

Faustus, meanwhile, has concluded that he has not learned a thing "[s]ince that exalted hour when I called / And they responded" (246). Indeed, his lofty *conjecturing* has been reduced to little more than *conjuring*. When the moment of his death arrives—the "tomorrow morning" of the title—he accepts it calmly and goes to the underworld, where he joins the infernal board at their meeting. Following a discussion in which he and the devils wonder whether they are not actually each a projection of the other, Faust causes Mammon and Moloch to disappear and leaves Beelzebub in charge of administering the world and Belial of redesigning mankind. Then, becoming one with Satan, he sets out on a journey into a new being, "augmented far beyond / Their either compass, now sudden lifted high / Above designs of either," as Sophia observes in her concluding remarks (299).

Richards's play, respectfully reviewed when it was published, is clearly a professorial jeu d'esprit, teeming as it is with literary allusions to Plato, Dante, Milton, Shelley, and Byron as well as hidden quotations from the Bible and other texts. Indeed, many passages sound like versifications of Richards's own *Principles of Literary Criticism* or his *Practical Criticism*. In the end, however, his pontifications sound more like a commentary on the Faust theme than an original contribution to it. At the same time, these professorial variations constitute collectively a remarkable meditation on the disaffections within higher education in the United States during the period of its expansion following World War II, and on the doubts regarding the value—or at least the usefulness—of traditional knowledge in the postwar American society.

IN JOHN HERSEY's novel *Too Far to Walk* (1966), which is set at an American university strongly resembling Yale, the Faust theme is updated to accommodate and explain the mood that contributed to the student unrest of the sixties. The novel features an undergraduate hero named John Fist, who has an admiring friend named Wagner and is so eager for knowledge that he wants to major in everything—even in magic (29–31). But by the beginning of his sophomore year he is so bored with his classes and with traditional institutional learning that he cannot even bring himself to walk to his classes (hence the title). At this point John meets a classmate named Breed, who drives fast cars, exudes an odor of ozone, and belongs to a secret society that wants to make a deal with Fist. They sign a twenty-six-week contract, with the option of a lifetime renewal, according to which Breed will provide Fist with experience—by which these undergraduates of the mid-sixties seem to mean mainly sex and drugs—in return for which Fist agrees to assign his id to them, his "inmost primeval soul" (40). At the end of Hersey's rather predictable novel—the girl that Breed helps him to seduce is, of course, named Margaret—Fist refuses to renew the contract because he realizes that Breed has given

171

him no real experience but only visions and illusions. "I've come to see that there can't be any shortcuts to those break-throughs I yearn for," he concludes (216). Hersey's message to students—essentially, that they should stop experimenting with LSD and go back to class—is consistent with the views of a writer who during the tumultuous 1960s was master of an un-dergraduate college at Yale University: who, in short, was work-ing within the institution and sympathetic to its goals.

The dramatic poem *The American as Faust* (1965) by Lawrence Lee, a professor of literature at the University of Pittsburgh, announces itself as concerned with universals—not with singu-lars, like politics, or with faith, like religion. The three acts in blank verse, which take place mostly in an apartment overlook-ing the Gateway Center in Pittsburgh, portray the responses of three representative men to Margaret, the wife of an indus-trialist identified simply as "A Man from Yale." Her confidant is an unnamed "Artist," who has completed a handsome por-trait of Margaret. And John Faust is a research scientist who has just perfected a new wonder drug that has made him fa-mous. The industrialist, so totally consumed by his business affairs that he has no time for his wife, wants to manage Faust and his new vaccine. A chorus of Newspaper Men and Women, who babble like the birds in Aristophanes, pursue celebrity and deprive Faust of the inner peace he once possessed. Mean-while, the Artist lectures them both. He reminds the indus-trialist of the superiority of art to business: "What would you manage if art did not make?" (3). And he tells Faust that it is not too late to "look at innocence" (21). When the Man from Yale goes to New York on business, Margaret, the embodiment of pure, healthy love, invites "unwise poor Judeo-Christian Faust" to release his body from "the wringing clutch of guilt" (24) and to yield to her love. But Faust, "whose worship is the pompous game called work" (33), is unable to respond, any more than the artist, whom Margaret reproaches with being more of a father to her than a man (34). When Faust seeks to

172

free himself from the pressures of his fame, the industrialist reminds him of their contract. Disappointed, Margaret finally tells them,

> My spirit has stood naked before you three
> And was rejected in its need by each.
>
> (46)

The three men are left behind with their regrets: the industrialist recognizes that "I would be warm but never am"; Faust has learned that "[t]he will of man is all that does man harm" (49). And, as the three of them watch Margaret walk out into a new life, the artist theorizes:

> Now Eve has fled
> To look for God within the living world.
> And Adam, or Faust, at last will lift his head
> To know that he can follow where she led. . .
>
> (50)

This rather ponderous play actually revolves around the figure of Margaret, who embodies Woman, rather than around Faust, who is simply one of the universal aspects of Man (the scientist, the artist, and the manager). But as much as the works of Olson, Plutzik, Richards, and Hersey, it represents a self-consciously professorial approach to one of the canonical themes and texts of world literature. Exemplifying a cynical belief in the willingness of the creative individual to sell his soul—for youth, for power, for experience, for fame—to whatever force in our secularized world represents the devil, they suggest at the same time a certain exhaustion of tradition. While the professors from the security of their chairs in universities tended to look at the America of the fifties and early sixties with poetic and critical detachment, and to deplore the lack of appreciation, in the emerging new society, for traditional forms of knowledge, many writers held a different view of the changing times.

173

FAUSTS OF POLITICS AND POETRY

To writers looking back following the turmoil of the late 1960s the adjective "Faustian" almost ritually came to mind as the fitting designation for those tumultuous years, a designation reflecting the structure of the myth rather than its thematic content. In 1971 Norman Mailer remarked murkily, "We are a Faustian age determined to meet the Lord or the Devil before we are done, and the ineluctable ore of the authentic is our only key to the lock."[20] In an agonizing reappraisal the geneticist Gunther S. Stent, bemused by the beatniks across the bay in San Francisco and traumatized by the 1964 Free Speech Movement at Berkeley, argued that Faustian Man, exemplifying the Nietzschean will to power that had driven the modern era of progress, was being replaced on the evolutionary scale by Polynesian Man (the exemplar of universal leisure) or Mozartian Man (the creative type whose art thrives not on conflict but on sheer joy). And in an elegiac piece on the 1960s Marshall Berman lamented the loss of Faustian vision and energy that had characterized the "collective journey to the underworld" of the decade that had marched on the Pentagon.[21] The booming economy of the postwar era had been the Mephisto that made possible the development of the young Fausts of the 1960s. "In the gray '70s, the devil is very much with us, even though Faust is not" (71).

This explicit politicization of Faust, following the more literary and professorial Fausts of the 1960s and forsaking the theme of knowledge for the sake of plot alone, prepared the way for Burton H. Wolfe's *The Devil and Dr. Noxin* (1973), which takes Marlowe's *Faustus* as the pattern—in explicit detail, down to the same number of scenes and a similar grouping of characters—for a travesty of Richard Nixon's political career. The commentator is a dapper Jehovah dressed in a Norfolk jacket and a turtleneck sweater and sucking meditatively on a briar pipe, who

174

introduces Dr. Noxin, a dental surgeon whose fear of death has led him into various obsessive behavioral patterns as well as the study of theology. With the assistance of two members of the Society of Satan, Noxin learns how to conjure up Lucifer, a streetwise and jazzy black man dressed in a bright red zoot suit. Noxin signs the traditional pact: "Blood is a real special juice. Once you in blood, you a brother. Ain't no other way to become one" (41). In return Lucifer promises to make him president in nine years ("the end of the Democrat cycle"). Noxin needs a helpmeet for his purposes, but when Lucifer shows him the image of a sexy naked woman in his magic mirror, he recoils in disgust. He prefers "a thin, somewhat boyish woman, one who has the appearance of a commanding figure, one no man would dare approach with any thoughts of impropriety" (47). After discussing Martha Washington, they finally settle on a rejuvenated Joan of Arc for the role.

The travesty continues in this vein to recapitulate Nixon's political career. Noxin, aided by a public relations expert with a German name, gets to Congress by exploiting the Communist issue and then makes his reputation with the case of "that State Department communist whose last name had the fortuitous sound of the original evil serpent" (88). He is then nominated as the vice presidential candidate along with an old navy war hero, Hiram O. Hightower, who detests Noxin. But following the famous Bathroom Debate with Premier Boobikov, he fares badly in "The Great TV Match" with the glamorous senator Jacob K. Finkelstein. This failure, plus the assassination of JKF and the succession of his vice president, drives Noxin into depression and psychoanalysis. The psychotherapy works its magic and creates a New Noxin, who becomes president. At this point Noxin tries to weasel out of his contract with Lucifer. He holds a Presidential Prayer Breakfast and proclaims that the whole nation is under God. But Lucifer insists that "[t]he Man Upstairs done decreed it. Ralph Noxin is our property. We takin' you, mother-fucker" (180). The Satanists close in upon him as

175

Noxin, ranting and raving, screams, "You won't have Ralph Noxin to kick around any more" (182). At the end Jehovah appears once more to affirm his own Master Plan, which runs its course despite the futile attempts of mortals to supersede the natural order of things. He makes peace with Lucifer, and as the two of them walk toward the exit, Jehovah says, "This morality play has been presented to you at a critical time in history, so that you may know. . . . America and the world are in a hell of a state" (184–85).

While Burton Wolfe was writing his political satire with its close and often witty parallels to Marlowe's *Faustus*, another American poet turned to that same text for more intensely personal reasons and at the same time restored to the myth its traditional connection to the sin of knowledge. In her remarkable poem "Faustus and I" (from *The Death Notebooks*, 1974) Anne Sexton re-creates Faustus's famous lament on the failure of knowledge ("Settle thy studies Faustus"). However, rather than the academic disciplines that disappoint the scholar, the poet laments the failure of the arts. "I went to the opera and God was not there," the first of the sestets begins (353). At that point, still in her apprenticeship, the relationship between the listener and the voices (probably, though not explicitly, Wagner's *The Flying Dutchman*) constituted "a form of worship"—art as the surrogate for religion. In the next sestet she goes to the galleries, where she also fails to find God—this time in Van Gogh's paintings. Addressing "my Dutchman" (presumably the *other* Dutchman of the opera), the poet concludes that "the crimes . . . that wait within us all / crawled out of that sea long before the fall." After the failures of music and painting the poet goes to the bookstore, "and God was not there." What she finds is a copy of Marlowe's *Doctor Faustus* in a blue binding with the Knopf (Borzoi) dog on its spine (probably the 1928 Knopf edition). In the absence of God she engages in a dialogue with Marlowe's "arch-deceiver." Not in music, not in painting, not in poetry is God to be found. In her desperate search she has even,

Sexton confesses in the last sestet, stolen the Gideon Bible, "Godes Boke," during a love affair in a hotel room. But only the Song of Solomon, underlined by some earlier pair, still had life and meaning. "I am not immortal. Faustus and I are the also-ran." A few months later Sexton, having experienced in her own way the sin and failure of knowledge, took her life.

FAUSTS FOR THE NINETIES

Marshall Berman may have been correct in his gloomy assessment. In any case, the 1980s present us with no literary Fausts to match those of earlier decades. Yet Faust is once again alive and well in the 1990s. In Randy Newman's exuberant rock musical *Faust* (1995), to be sure, the scholar has been considerably diminished in the shadow of a lively Lord and Devil. According to the scenario that accompanies the seventeen songs, this contemporary Faust is a "schizophrenic student from Notre Dame University." "Sometimes you know I think that I / Will surely go insane. / Got suicide and murder / Runnin' in and out my brain," Henry introduces himself to us. Despite the traditional university setting this Faust is not out for knowledge. He is so blatantly power-hungry and ambitious that even the Devil is contemptuous of him. Nevertheless, the Devil hopes to use Henry for his purposes. For he longs to return to heaven: "Can't keep a good man down," he intones on one of his visits to the Lord. They make the traditional wager, and Henry signs his pact without even reading it just because he gets "good vibrations" from the Devil. While Henry falls in love with Margaret, a poor "townie" from South Bend, the Devil has his own affair with her friend Martha, who later dumps him with the result that he is "[b]leeding all over the place." Margaret gets pregnant and drowns the child in a creek. "This is the comic high point of Goethe's original play," notes the scenario, "and one of the most delightfully urbane moments in all of German literature.

177

In a hilarious courtroom sequence, Margaret is convicted of murder and sentenced to die at the Indiana State Prison in Michigan City." But Margaret is saved by the angels. When Henry poisons himself in despair, the Devil gloats that he has won his wager with the Lord. Henry is redeemed, however, and the Devil is denied the victory to which he feels himself entitled. But the irrepressible Devil—with "corruption, seduction, destruction, reproduction" on his mind—recovers his good spirits and goes off to Las Vegas for a "real good time." Newman's playful travesty, which no longer has the least connection with the sin of knowledge, is nevertheless a reminder of the central role of at least the Faust plot in the American popular cultural imagination.

A nice symmetry is apparent in the circumstance that the most recent American Faust, Michael Swanwick's *Jack Faust* (1997), reenacts the historical sequence of Karl Shapiro's "The Progress of Faust" and restores the sin of knowledge in its full force to the myth. The novel stays close to the incidents of the traditional chapbook, but the events are foreshortened historically in such a way that the story beginning in the sixteenth ends in the twentieth century. We first meet Faust, "as learned as any man alive" (15), at the University of Wittenberg shortly after 1500. "Yet all he knew with any assurance was that he knew nothing." During a fever precipitated by a fire in his study, Mephistopheles appears through a window between universes and exposes to the astonished Faust the mysteries of human and celestial creation. Mephistopheles promises to reveal all knowledge to Faust in return for the extinction of the human race. It is intolerable to the devil and his kind that their parallel universe, speeding along at a much faster rate, will grow old and die long before the slower, feebler human race. If Faust accepts the compact, his knowledge will soon choke the race and cause them to destroy themselves. Faust accepts the wager, confident that humankind can endure any truth and that "with the perfection of knowledge we will and must ascend toward the perfection of spirit" (33).

178

As Faust proceeds to invent microscopes, telescopes, the hydrogen balloon, and the periodic table of the elements, his inventions bring him no security or profits. Instead, his creditors drive him out of Wittenberg, and he goes to Nuremberg, where he is attracted by the innocence of Margarete Reinhardt, the daughter of a respectable businessman. Faust sets up a workshop that becomes the intellectual center of the town, and where he continues his inventions: electric generators, repeating rifles, the principle of mass production, refrigeration, and even a giant Ferris wheel to amuse the citizens of the town. When the plague, caused by a pathogenic organism in the groundwater, strikes Nuremberg, Faust invents an antibiotic to treat the patients (and dreams of X rays and CAT scans). The following Easter he delivers a sermon in which he explains that reason can tell us how to make inventions, but not whether or how to use the products. "The problem is that logic does not know *should* or *ought* but only *how*" (163). He concludes with the Nietzschean message that we must follow our will. "Nothing is forbidden. *Do What Thou Wilt* shall be the whole of the law" (164). The townspeople, infuriated by his lack of faith, run him out of town, and Faust flees to London.

Margaret, whom Faust has married and left behind to manage his affairs, creates a new financial instrument, a limited liability corporation, through which her business flourishes. As Margaret's firm prospers, thriving from such new inventions as contraceptive pills, the woman herself, now known as Gretchen, has been increasingly seduced by power and lust. Meanwhile, in England, Faust has been summoned to the Admiralty to aid in the deliberations about the approaching Armada. Publicly Faust is adulated because his inventions enable the English to defeat the great Armada. But privately he is in despair because, at his request, Mephistopheles has exposed to him the truth about history, revealing by means of a vision the meaninglessness and individual suffering in the war.

Gretchen, whose business is plagued by anarchy and labor unionism, has become pregnant out of sheer negligence and goes to an abortionist. Faust, disgusted with his notoriety, flies across the Channel in his experimental biplane. He and Wagner drive through a landscape pockmarked by the shells of the First World War, fighting off their exhaustion with amphetamines. When Gretchen, now imprisoned, is told that she can bribe her way to freedom, she fears that by doing so she would become as corrupt as her oppressors. Instead, she poisons herself with barbiturates just as Faust arrives back in a Nuremberg now governed by the notorious Nazi race laws. When a Jew whom Faust warns asks him why this is happening, Faust tells him that "[t]here is no purpose, no direction, no guidance to events. Nothing means anything. The world is a howling desert of meaninglessness, and reason is useless before it" (328).

Mephistopheles then leads Faust to the Dirigible Field in Nuremberg, where a huge crowd is waiting. "What should I tell them?" he asks the minister of propaganda. "Tell them anything," the minister replies, as the multitudes roar for Faust. In a final vision Mephistopheles shows him that his life's work is nearing its completion: as Faust watches ecstatically, he sees a series of huge atomic explosions destroying the entire continent of Europe. " 'More!' Faust cried. 'More light!' " (328). Following this drastic inversion of Goethe's reputed last words the vision disappears, and Faust is once again a young man in Nuremberg. The future still lies before him, and Faust is eager to start.

> It would be as simple as setting off a nuclear reaction—once critical mass was achieved, all else followed as a matter of course. He had set foot upon the final road. Not all the demons of Hell could turn him away. Heaven itself would be helpless to stop him. (336)

Sadly but symptomatically, Swanwick's Faust has progressed through the sin of knowledge no farther than Shapiro's—to the invention of the bomb.

THE APPEAL of Faust to more than a dozen writers in the United States of the past fifty years conspicuously parallels the reception of Prometheus by their contemporaries in the German

Democratic Republic. There, as we saw, Prometheus played an ambivalent role: as the embodiment of the rebellion against authority (first of bourgeois capitalism and then of the Communist state) and the corrupt intellectual, as the creator of civilization and technology and the destroyer of the very civilization and environment that he created. Here, in an age that has come to equate knowledge with power and by way of such capitalist products as the Broadway theater, academic satires, and best-selling novels, Faust has been revived in his traditional role as a cautionary icon for the society that has sold its soul for personal gratifications: fame and celebrity, political power, or material wealth.

In both cases—Prometheus and Faust—the sin of knowledge has been radically secularized. Yet both Randy Newman and Michael Swanwick leave us, at the end of the twentieth century, where the anonymous author of the chapbook began four hundred years earlier. The spirit of evil, in its secularized and Americanized metamorphoses, is alive and well, and new Fausts stand ever eager to accept his pernicious pact.

On the Uses and Abuses of Myth

W̲ᴇ ɴᴏᴛᴇᴅ at the outset the timeless topicality of the myths of Adam, Prometheus, and Faust. Whether we regard their exploitation in advertising, political cartoons, and comic books as legitimate uses or as abuses, it should be clear to any observer of the contemporary cultural scene that all three are vividly present in the modern imagination as images for various aspects of the sin of knowledge. Our readings have exposed the literary continuity of the myths in several dozen adaptations by prominent writers in Europe and the United States.

The myth of the Fall differs from the other two in one important respect: it has most often not been simply retold but adapted in typological postfigurations. It is, of course, not the case that there have been no straightforward retellings. But these have tended, at least since the end of the eighteenth century, to be satirical or comical. Jens Baggesen, an influential anti-Romantic critic who served as a literary and intellectual mediator between Germany and Denmark, wrote a "humoristic epic" *Adam und Eva, oder die Geschichte des Sündenfalls* (Adam and Eve, or the story of the Fall, 1826), which amounts in part to a satire against the contemporary philosophies of Fichte and Schelling. The "Historical-Critical Introduction" states that, while people have generally portrayed world history as dry and tedious, it is filled with comical stories worthy of a Cervantes. Human history begins with a tale that exceeds in humor anything that Rabelais invented: the Fall. The first of the twelve cantos proceeds to describe the Creation parodistically according to Fichte's notion of objective reality as being the projection of a positing subject and to Schelling's theory of identity. The temptation is carried out by a cavalier serpent, who kisses

POSTLUDE

Eve's foot, and to whose blandishments Adam and Eve succumb largely out of boredom. The first couple is finally escorted out of Paradise by a benign God who promises to watch over them during their life in the world. In another account entitled *Der erste Mensch und die Erde* (The first man and Earth," 1828), the book-dealer and popular writer August Gottlob Eberhard locates Adam in the realm of classical deities, where he falls in love with Venus and reconciles himself to earthly existence only when the goddess provides him with a human woman created in her image. Mark Twain's *The Diaries of Adam and Eve* (written 1893–1905) purport to represent parallel accounts of the same Genesis incidents from the radically different perspectives of a timorous, privacy-seeking Adam and his talkative, sociable mate. When Adam finds Eve climbing the forbidden tree, he tries to "emigrate" from the garden; but after Eve eats the fruit, the hitherto peaceful animals begin to fight, and the horse on which he is trying to escape is eaten by a tiger.

To move to our own century, John Erskine's playfully erotic novel *Adam and Eve, Though He Knew Better* (1927) depicts the prelapsarian life of a rather dull-witted Adam torn between two women: the seductive but soulless Lilith and the plainer but soulful Eve, who bears him children, keeps house, cooks, and makes clothes that she primly insists he wear. At the end of the novel a complacent Adam expresses his satisfaction that their first child is a boy. "After all, this is a man's world." Peter Hacks, regarding it as "a responsibility of Marxist art to save Christianity from the Christians,"[1] enjoyed considerable success with his blank-verse comedy *Adam und Eva* (premiered in 1973), which concludes with Adam's insight that the Garden of Eden is by definition a place from which one is exiled, and that thereby guarantees human freedom. Had he stayed in the garden, he would have remained a creature without free will; only through his striving to achieve again that paradisiacal state can he affirm his freedom.

Not all the nineteenth-century treatments are trivial. In Imre Madách's dramatic poem *Az Ember Tragédiája* (*The Tragedy of*

184

Man, 1861), which enjoys the classic status of a Hungarian *Paradise Lost* or *Faust,* God and Lucifer compete after the Fall for the soul of Adam. In eleven episodes Lucifer shows the exiled Adam scenes depicting the future of humanity from ancient Egypt down to the present. The scenes, featuring Adam himself in roles ranging from that of a tyrannical pharaoh by way of rulers of classical antiquity and the Middle Ages down to Danton in the French Revolution, are so depressing that Adam wants to commit suicide rather than condemn his descendants to such a future. He is saved by the love of Eve, who points out that it will be the eternal destiny of humankind to struggle between the opposing forces of God and Lucifer. In general, however, most serious adaptations of the myth have tended to be postfigurations.

This is not really unexpected. Most of the memorable modern literary adaptations of biblical materials have been typological in form.[2] The poignancy of John Steinbeck's *The Grapes of Wrath* (1939) is intensified by the pattern of the biblical Exodus underlying the migration of the Joad family. Many of the finest works of modern fiction, from Ignazio Silone's *Bread and Wine* (1936) and Graham Greene's *The Power and the Glory* (1940) to William Faulkner's *A Fable* (1954) and Günter Grass's *Cat and Mouse* (1961), are fictional transfigurations using the events of the gospel narrative as the model for wholly secularized actions set in the twentieth century. As we observed earlier, typological thinking is a mode of thought directly related to biblical exegesis; so we are not surprised to find it employed in the modern adaptations of themes from the Old and New Testaments. Seeing no need to rewrite the canonical text of the Bible, but unwilling to eschew its familiar ethical associations, writers in a secular age have with varying ingenuity exploited the ancient exegetical technique to gain biblical reverberations for their modern stories.

Accordingly, the works that we considered from Voltaire's *Candide* to Kunert's "Adam and Evam" were in every case postfigurations: that is, works in which the modern action is prefigured by the biblical account. What is striking about the myth of the Fall, however, in contrast to the gospel narrative, is the circumstance that it is rarely used as the pattern for an entire action: that turned out to be the case only in Kleist's tragicomedy. As Kleist's play and the humorous works mentioned earlier suggest, it may well be that the comic implications of the theme become too tempting if it is displayed in its entirety. Instead, allusions to the myth often show up in the opening pages of a story—as in Voltaire, Hoffmann, Melville, Joyce, and Hesse—to signal a specific aspect of the work: the fall of a young hero out of a state of innocence into consciousness and the knowledge of good and evil. Even in Hawthorne's novel, where the myth is not limited to its opening pages, its motifs are cited to highlight the fall of all four central figures out of their former Edenic innocence into a new moral awareness of evil. Sometimes, as we saw, it is coupled with motifs from the New Testament in such a manner as to suggest the entire biblical history of humanity from Fall to Redemption (*The Golden Pot, Billy Budd, Demian*) or, more pessimistically, from Fall to Betrayal ("Araby").

The adaptations of Prometheus and Faust, in contrast, have for the most part been reworkings of the legends from a modern point of view. Postfigurations, inspired by the epoch-making model of Joyce's *Ulysses*, do occur: for example, Thomas Mann's *Doktor Faustus* and John Hersey's *Too Far to Walk*. But by far most of the examples we encountered are modernizing adaptations—reworkings that, in contrast to the Adamic theme, make use of an imaginative variety of literary genres, including novels, plays, and poems. It is obvious, but still bears mentioning, that such adaptations are inevitably also secularizations: the modern Prometheuses and Fausts no longer serve as vehicles for the often religious meaning of their original Greek and Reformation contexts. The myths have been abstracted from their original contexts in such a manner as to liberate their structures or plots for new meanings with which later writers and societies have invested them. Of course, if Prometheus is transformed

186

into a socialist hero and Faust into a capitalist antihero, the sin of knowledge must be appropriately modified.

Adaptations of classical and postclassical myths are alluring for the writer because, unlike the Bible, there is no canonical text. As Franz Fühmann explicitly stated, the modern writer adapting the story of Prometheus has first of all to decide which version to foreground: Hesiod's trickster or Aeschylus's culture-hero. And the writer reworking the theme of Faust needs to determine which source to use: the chapbook, Marlowe's tragedy, or Goethe's redemptive poetic drama. It is precisely this malleability of the myths that has made them attractive to many writers of the past half-century.

Our review of the relevant texts exposed occasional overlaps between the two myths. Both figures, as creative scientists, are sometimes made responsible for the atomic bomb: Prometheus in Brecht's scenario as well as Volker Braun's poem and story, and Faust in Karl Shapiro's poem as well as Jack Swanwick's novel and the mythmaking of the physicists. But such occasional overlaps are incidental. The essential difference between the two myths is evident if we consider what appears on the surface to be another similarity: their themes of rebellion.

Prometheus rebels against higher authority for the sake of humankind, whereas Faust's pact is only incidentally a rebellion against God; it is first and foremost an action intended for personal advantage (the acquisition of forbidden knowledge or power). It is for this fundamental reason that Prometheus and Faust have exercised such different popular appeals. Prometheus is located within a social and political context and Faust within a private ethical one. Even on the few occasions when Prometheus is accused of moral weakness—compromising with the rulers—he does not sell out for the sake of greater knowledge and experience. Rather, as in Brecht's plot outline or Heiner Müller's play, he bargains away his knowledge (and the people's welfare) for the sake of personal security and comfort.

Accordingly, Prometheus is always viewed and judged, whether positively or negatively, in a social context. Already in Marx's thinking he emerged as a martyr for the proletariat. The first pre-GDR poets appropriated the heroic image that had come down to them from Aeschylus by way of Marx, and that same social-political myth provided the basis for the early GDR works portraying Prometheus as the proletarian hero rebelling against the capitalist bosses, and contributing through his enlightenment to the new socialist society. But as early as 1945 Brecht anticipated the ambivalence that would characterize subsequent depictions of the Titan. During the 1970s, as criticism of the GDR began to be voiced, a more Aeschylean Prometheus began to speak up as an opponent of the regime. But as the problems of technology gradually became apparent—the ecological ravages produced as a by-product of the very fire that Prometheus had brought—Hesiod's view began to intrude. Prometheus was reviled as the mindless technologist whose projects work against the socialist society whose achievements he had once exemplified.

Faust, in contrast, is not a social hero but an individualist—the successor to Prometheus, as it were, who emerges when knowledge itself, having been assured, has become problematic. It is symptomatic that the earliest as well as the most recent American Fausts—those of Karl Shapiro, Gertrude Stein, and Jack Swanwick—are carried to the moment when their personal quests for knowledge have led to the bomb and to the darkness of a new barbarism.

It appears that Faust can only with difficulty escape the edifying context of his mythic pattern. Strikingly, the American works aimed at the broadest public—the Broadway plays of Wallop and Axelrod, John Hersey's popular novel, and Randy Newman's rock musical—all display a radically secularized version of the same preacherly impulse as Spies's original chapbook. In every case, to be sure, the writers soften the message by means of happy endings and convey essentially the New Testament message on the title page of the chapbook: "Resist the devil and he will flee from you." In both *Damn Yankees* and *Will Success Spoil Rock Hunter?* as well as *Too Far to Walk* the Faustian heroes escape from their fiendish contracts and return to their former lives, and the undergraduate hero of Randy Newman's *Faust* is redeemed. The baby-boomer audiences of rock musicals in the 1990s are evidently no more eager to confront hell-fire and damnation than was the Broadway public of the 1950s. At the same time, all of these works amount to criticisms of a prosperous society that has put success and personal satisfaction, achieved by devilish and immoral means, above all other considerations.

The professorial Fausts of the sixties reveal further dimensions of the pattern, for the professors leave no analogy uncommented. The fact that the works are so heavily laden with literary associations suggests that their authors are laboring self-consciously, and sometimes pedantically, under the burden of a Great Classic. Elder Olson uses the theme, as did Gertrude Stein, to voice a cynical comment on a society that he saw regressing into bestiality after World War II. But whereas for Stein's Faust the motive is the quest for knowledge and "light," for Olson it has been degraded into the selfish craving for youth. Plutzik and Richards both appropriate the myth for purposes of academic satire; Plutzik's Faust is a babbling pedant, and Lee's is reduced to little more than the "type" of the Scientist, as incapable of true love for Margaret as are the Industrialist and the Artist. The association of Faust and the university, as we noted, has been implicit in the myth since its inception, but the skepticism about the knowledge purveyed there has been translated into twentieth-century terms.

In the entire catalog of postwar American Fausts, only two rise above social and political and academic satire to embody what appears to be a personal ethical meaning: Kerouac's novel and Sexton's poem. For Kerouac, Goethe's poetic drama provides the pattern—as for Goethe a nontragic one—determining the education of the youth who is introduced by his Mephisto into a new world of adult experience and knowledge. And in

189

her profoundly poignant poem Anne Sexton reenacts the lament of Marlowe's tragic hero, plunged into despair by the failure of traditional knowledge—a failure that led Faustus into his
pact, and that evidently left Sexton with no option but her own
death. Yet the prevalence of the myth is a social marker that
cannot be ignored.

The choice of mythic models and images reveals a great deal
about a society's aspirations and anxieties. Societies that envi-
sion themselves as Promethean—and this applies equally well
to Aeschylus's Greece, Sturm-und-Drang Germany, and the
twentieth-century GDR—are those that see themselves as engaged in a heroic struggle against social and political oppression, whether against ancient feudal lords, eighteenth-century
despots, or modern capitalists. Already well acquainted with the
knowledge of good and evil, they are concerned at their relative
stage of historical development with the translation of the
knowledge acquired through that dear purchase into a better
society.

Societies attracted by Faust, in contrast, are societies with a
guilty conscience: political security and social prosperity have
become so prevalent—Prometheus has achieved his goals so ef-
fectively—that life now looks dull and human beings complacent. So the individual makes a pact with the devil: for a sports
victory, for a literary success, for sexual conquest. Civilizations
are Faustian, in Freud's catchy phrase, when they have become
aware of their discontents. The wistful longing of writers like
Norman Mailer and Marshall Berman for the Faustian energies
of the 1960s differs in grandeur but not in kind from the wishful
projections of Marlowe and Goethe. When knowledge has been
achieved, whether the four faculties of the early modern world
or the sophisticated sciences of the twentieth century, the modern Faust succumbs to the moral temptations of lust, of wealth,
of power.

This observation differs from, and is much narrower than,
Spengler's broad characterization of postmedieval Western society as Faustian. At different stages in its development the same

society can see itself as Adamic, Promethean, or Faustian. A society emerging from innocence into consciousness tends to imagine itself in terms of the Fall. Striving to liberate itself from tyranny and to build, or become part of, a better world, the same society projects itself in attitudes of Promethean heroism. Finally, sated with the satisfactions of that achieved civilization with its science and technologies and lusting for more, even at the risk of destroying ourselves through moral degradation or our societies by such devices as the bomb, we detect our inner Faust. A nineteenth-century America newly conscious of its lost innocence turned, with Whitman, Hawthorne, and Melville, to the image of Adam and the Fall. The enormous industrial success of the United States in the first half of the twentieth century was proclaimed symbolically by such works as Paul Manship's looming sculpture of Prometheus at Rockefeller Center and Rockwell Kent's powerful woodcut of 1938. A postwar America forced to confront the problematics of technological success and economic prosperity—the bomb, ecological disaster, political corruption, the drug culture, moral laxity—recognized itself in the image of Faust.

It is perhaps a final commentary on the cultural exhaustion of modern civilization, whether Adamic, Promethean, or Faustian, that we have liberated ourselves so totally from any sustaining culture that we have become incapable of generating original myths of our own. We reach instead with a certain nostalgic desperation into the past for the stories that we tell ourselves to bestow meaning upon our lives, to give shape to our dreams and dreads. Societies that have so objectified themselves that they can reach for foreign myths as mirrors of their goals and anxieties have also reached a level of sophistication at which the penalties for knowledge have been sublimated. We relieve our anxieties and uneasy consciences by off-loading them onto such mythic scapegoats as Faust. We observed this pattern with the atomic physicists and then repeatedly in the later adaptations of the Faustian theme. But as the history of the now completed twentieth century has taught us with depressing regularity—from Nazi Germany and the Stalinist Soviet Union down

191

to the most recent savagery in other parts of our contemporary world—the sin of knowledge, whether it manifests itself as the Adamic critical consciousness of good and evil, as Promethean rebelliousness and technological progress, or as the Faustian desire for unrestrained knowledge and experience and power, still leads with an almost mythic inevitability to anxiety, doubt, and guilt or, at worst, to exile, imprisonment, and death.

✳ *Notes* ✳

PRELUDE

1. Steiner, *Prometheus*, 11.
2. Germany has a long tradition of comic book treatments of Faust. See Frank Schönfeld, "Mini-Faust, Krankenstein und Lucifera: Comics machen Literatur," in Möbus, *Faust. Annäherung an einen Mythos*, 285–98.

CHAPTER ONE
ADAM: THE GENESIS OF CONSCIOUSNESS

1. Graves and Patai, *Hebrew Myths*, 67.
2. Grabar, *Christian Iconography*, 12–13.
3. Stone, *A History of the Literature of Adam and Eve*, 6–41; and Levison, *Portraits of Adam in Early Judaism*, 163–90.
4. Kirchner, *Die Darstellung des ersten Menschenpaares in der bildenden Kunst*.
5. Röhrich, *Adam und Eva*.
6. Pagels, *Adam, Eve, and the Serpent*, has traced early Christianity's use of the story as a metaphor for its own thinking about sexuality, freedom, and human nature.
7. Julien Riese, "The Fall," in *The Encyclopedia of Religion*, 5:256–67, esp. 256–57.
8. Frazer, *Folk-Lore in the Old Testament*, 1:5–29; and Loretz, *Schöpfung und Mythos*, 109.
9. "Fall, The," in *The Interpreter's Dictionary of the Bible*, 2:235–36; Graves and Patai, *Hebrew Myths*, 60–81; and Damrosch, *Narrative Covenant*, 88–143.
10. I refer to the translation by Speiser in Pritchard, *The Ancient Near East*, 1:40–75.
11. "On the Psychology of the Trickster-Figure," in Jung's *Archetypes and the Collective Unconscious*, 255–72; here 260.
12. See also Graves and Patai, *Hebrew Myths*, 78–79.
13. I cite Speiser's translation in Pritchard, *The Ancient Near East*, 1:76–80.
14. *The Golden Legend* for May 3: "The Invention of the Holy Cross."

15. *The New Golden Bough*, 106–24.

16. *The Encyclopaedia of Religion and Ethics*, 5:702.

17. Davidson, *Genesis 1–11*, 35. See also Engelberg, *The Unknown Distance*, 29–30.

18. Frazer, *Folk-Lore in the Old Testment*, 1:47–52.

19. Albert de Pury, "Yahwist ('J') Source," in *The Anchor Bible Dictionary*, 6:1012–20; and Damrosch, *Narrative Covenant*, 157–73.

20. Bloom, in *The Book of J*, goes even further, arguing that the author was an aristocratic woman of ironic disposition living at the court of Solomon and Rehoboam.

21. Damrosch, *Narrative Covenant*, 149–57.

22. Butler, *Myth of the Magus*, 35–43.

23. Bloom's reading of this episode as "a children's story" (*Book of J*, 186) composed by an ironic mother figure deprives it of all moral grandeur.

24. Damrosch, *Narrative Covenant*, 139, suggests plausibly that the alienation of man from God begins already when the Lord, failing to understand Adam's needs, initially creates animals as his helpmates rather than a woman.

25. Loretz, *Schöpfung und Mythos*, 112.

26. Ricoeur, *The Symbolism of Evil*, 242.

27. Kant, *Political Writings*, 226.

Chapter Two
Prometheus: the birth of Civilization

1. Trousson, *Le Thème de Prométhée*, 1:3–9, reviews theories regarding the origin of fire-myths. See also Bachelard, *La Psychanalyse du feu*, 17–27.

2. Trousson, *Le Thème de Prométhée*, 1:8–9.

3. Kerényi, *Prometheus*, 59–66; Wutrich, *Prometheus and Faust*, 7–22; Trousson, *Le Thème de Prométhée*, 1:3–9.

4. Thomson, *Aeschylus and Athens*, 317–18; editor's notes to Hesiod, *Theogony*, 60–61.

5. Editor's introduction to Hesiod, *Theogony*, 7–8.

6. Dietz, *Prometheus*, 49–52.

7. Thomson, *Aeschylus and Athens*, 317, whose reading is based on his Marxist view of class struggle.

8. Bianchi, *Prometeo, Orfeo, Adamo,* 216, compares the Fall of Man in Hesiod with that of Genesis; but while stressing the trickster aspect of Prometheus, he does not make the connection with the serpent but, instead, defines the differences vis-à-vis Adam. Dietz, *Prometheus,* 72–75, comes closer to my own interpretation when he refers to the "Luzifer-Prinzip" in the Old Testament and the Prometheus legends; but the fire-stealing trickster of Hesiod is still far from the light-bringing Lucifer of the Judeo-Christian tradition. Headlam, "Prometheus and the Garden of Eden," 65, goes farther than either, equating Prometheus's fire with the Tree of Knowledge and, if only tentatively, Prometheus with the serpent. But his lecture notes do not develop either thought.

9. Editor's introduction to Hesiod, *Theogony,* 4–5.

10. See Trousson, *Le Thème de Prométhée,* 1:57–83.

11. Lecourt, *Prométhée, Faust, Frankenstein,* 27.

12. Trousson, *Le Thème de Prométhée,* 1:40–55.

13. Editor's introduction to Aeschylus, *Prometheus Bound,* 3.

14. Thomson, *Aeschylus and Athens,* 315.

15. The arguments are recapitulated in the editor's introduction to Aeschylus, *Prometheus Bound.*

16. Herington, *Aeschylus,* 161, 175.

17. Editor's appendix to Aeschylus, *Prometheus Bound,* 281–83; Dietz, *Prometheus,* 53; and Wutrich, *Prometheus and Faust,* 41. Most editions reprint the extant fragments of both plays.

18. Herington, *Aeschylus,* 166.

19. Wutrich, *Prometheus and Faust,* 31.

20. Editor's commentary to Aeschylus, *Prometheus Bound,* 242.

21. Dietz, *Prometheus,* 248–56.

22. Thomson, *Aeschylus and Athens,* 327.

23. Lecourt, *Prométhée, Faust, Frankenstein,* 43.

24. Gadamer, "Prometheus und die Tragödie der Kultur," in *Kleine Schriften II,* 71.

25. Thomson, *Aeschylus and Athens,* 321–22.

26. Herington, *Aeschylus,* 160.

27. For the following paragraphs see Herington, *Aeschylus,* 15–27; Thomson, *Aeschylus and Athens,* 85–94; and Wutrich, *Prometheus and Faust,* 26–30.

28. Diels, *Fragmente der Vorsokratiker,* 2:37–40 (frags. 11–14).

29. Herington, *Aeschylus,* 26.

30. E.g., Diels, *Fragmente der Vorsokratiker,* 2:5 and 8 (frags. 1 and 2).

31. Schelling, *Philosophie der Mythologie,* 482.

CHAPTER THREE
FAUST: THE AMBIVALENCE OF KNOWLEDGE

1. On Faust, Don Juan, and Don Quixote see Watt, *Myths of Modern Individualism*; on Faust and Don Juan see Butler, *Fortunes of Faust,* and Smeed, *Faust in Literature.*

2. See *Der Tübinger Reim-Faust von 1587/88.*

3. The passages from Luther's *Tischreden,* as well as the following historical references to Faust, are conveniently available in Palmer and More, *Sources,* 81–125, where they are cited both in the Latin or German original and in English translation. See also Butler, *Myth of the Magus,* 121–44; Mahal, *Faust, der Mann aus Knittlingen,* 6–20; and Wutrich, *Prometheus and Faust,* 73–77.

4. But see Baron, who in *Faustus. Geschichte, Sage, Dichtung* and elsewhere has argued that Faust was in fact a man named Georg von Helmstadt, born ca. 1466–1467 near Heidelberg.

5. Palmer and More, *Sources,* 83–86; see also Farouk Grewing, "Über den 'Fürsten der Nekromanten': Johannes Trithemius an den Magister Johann Virdung von Haßfurt," in Möbus, *Faust. Annäherung an einen Mythos,* 28–30, who reproduces a facsimile of the famous letter.

6. Notably by Mahal, *Faust, der Mann aus Knittlingen,* 15–17.

7. Bengt Fuchs, "Doctor Johann Faust und die Justiz um 1500," in Möbus, *Faust. Annäherung an einen Mythos,* 51–58.

8. Butler, *Myth of the Magus,* 215–42 and 261–63.

9. Günther Mahal, "Faust und Alchymie," in Möbus, *Faust. Annäherung an einen Mythos,* 21–27.

10. Notably Baron and Mahal.

11. Christoph Daxelmüller, "Teufelspakt. Gestalt und Gestaltungen einer Idee," in Möbus, *Faust. Annäherung an einen Mythos,* 11–20; here 17.

12. Gerald Strauss, "How to Read a *Volksbuch*": The *Faust Book* of 1587," in Boerner and Johnson, *Faust through Four Centuries,* 27–39; here 30–31.

13. Baron, *Faustus on Trial,* 4; see also 135.

14. Butler, *Myth of the Magus,* 143–44.

15. The tales from the so-called Erfurter Reihe are reproduced in *Historia*, 152–63.

16. Palmer and More, *Sources*, 129–30.

17. *Das Faustbuch nach der Wolfenbüttler Handschrift*, v–xviii.

18. See Baron, *Faustus on Trial*, 192–209, for a bibliography of works published by Spies from 1580 to 1590.

19. Frank Möbus, "Kein Meister über die Geister: Doctor Fausti 'Höllenzwänge,' " in Möbus, *Faust. Annäherung an einen Mythos*, 36–50.

20. Strauss, "How to Read a *Volksbuch*," in Boerner and Johnson, *Faust through Four Centuries*, 27.

21. I quote in my own translation from the critical edition of the *Historia von D. Johann Fausten* by Füssel and Kreutzer. The English *Historie of the damnable life, and deserued death of Doctor Iohn Faustus* (1592) often changes and colors the German original.

22. The chapbook *Historia* has been variously evaluated by discriminating scholars. For a negative view of its literary merit see Butler, *Myth of the Magus*, 121–44; for a positive view, Hoelzel, *Paradoxical Quest*, 23–44.

23. See the editor's afterword to the *Tübinger Reim-Faust*.

24. Dédéyan, *Le Thème de Faust*, 1:98–105.

25. The relevant passages from the secondary sources are reproduced in *Historia*, 217–96.

26. Kreutzer's postscript to the *Historia*, 335.

27. Strauss, "How to Read a *Volksbuch*," in Boerner and Johnson, *Faust through Four Centuries*, 34–35.

28. Erich Heller, in his otherwise brilliant article "Faust's Damnation" (in *The Artist's Journey into the Interior*, 7–8), is mistaken when he assigns this shift in emphasis to the later English translation of the *Historia*.

29. Baron, *Faustus. Geschichte, Sage, Dichtung*, 88–89; Kreutzer's afterword to the *Historia*, 333–34.

30. *Historia*, 186.

31. The relevant passages are reproduced in Palmer and More, *Sources*, 12–41.

32. Ibid., 99.

33. Ibid., 41–58.

34. Ibid., 58–77.

35. Examples printed in ibid., 237–69; see also Butler, *Fortunes of Faust*, 69–110.

36. I base my discussion on the B-text, with the now conventional division into acts and scenes.

37. Text reproduced in Palmer and More, *Sources*, 134–231. See also Butler, *Fortunes of Faust*, 31–41; Hoelzel, *Paradoxical Quest*, 45–46.

38. See the representative "Extracts from Earlier Critics, 1797–1946" in Jump's *Casebook*, 23–45.

39. J. C. Maxwell, "The Sin of Faustus," in Jump's *Casebook*, 89–94; Harry Levin, *The Overreacher: A Study of Christopher Marlowe*, cited in Jump's *Casebook*, 134–64, here 137; Cleanth Brooks, "The Unity of Marlowe's *Doctor Faustus*," in Jump's *Casebook*, 208–21; and elsewhere.

40. Wilbur Sanders, "Doctor Faustus's Sin," in Bloom, *Marlowe's Faustus*, 27–45; here 34.

41. Hoelzel, *Paradoxical Quest*, 48–49.

42. Sewall, *Vision of Tragedy*, 58.

43. From his *Meditationes Sacrae. De Haeresibus*, in *Works* 7:241.

44. Hoelzel, *Paradoxical Quest*, 62–63.

45. See especially D. J. Palmer, "Magic and Poetry in *Doctor Faustus*," in Jump's *Casebook*, 188–203.

46. See especially Kirschbaum, "Marlowe's Faustus."

47. I am not persuaded by the many other analogies to Prometheus advanced by Wutrich, *Prometheus and Faust*, 77–104.

INTERLUDE
FROM MYTH TO MODERNITY

1. See in this connection the six categories proposed in Shattuck, *Forbidden Knowledge*, 327–37. Shattuck, as his title suggests, is concerned mainly with the nature of the knowledge itself, from pornography to modern science policy, and less so with the character and psychology of the knowledge-seekers or the structure of the myths.

CHAPTER FOUR
THE SECULARIZATION OF ADAM

1. See the essays in Miner, *Literary Uses of Typology*.
2. Auerbach, *Scenes from the Drama of European Literature*, 53.
3. Brumm, *American Thought and Religious Typology*.

4. Ziolkowski, *Fictional Transfigurations of Jesus*, 41–43.

5. Gillispie, *Genesis and Geology.*

6. Eissfeldt, *The Old Testament: An Introduction*, 2–3.

7. Eichhorn, *Einleitung*, 2:274–86 (= §416 a–b).

8. Kant, *Political Writings*, 226–27.

9. Lanson, *Voltaire*, 145–46.

10. Hacks, *Adam und Eva*, 104.

11. Kleist's play exists in two versions: the published version of 1811 and a considerably longer stage version (known simply as the "Variant"), which contains a number of clarifying details of plot that were cut from the published version.

12. Ziolkowski, *The Mirror of Justice*, 194–214; esp. 207–9.

13. See especially Delbrück, "Zur dramentypologischen Funktion," and Michelsen, "Die Lügen Adams und Evas Fall."

14. It has been persuasively argued that this otherwise unspecified morning song contains an allusion to one of the most familiar texts of the early Reformation: Lazarus Spengler's popular hymn "Durch Adams Fall ist gantz verderbt / menschlich Natur und Wesen!" ("Through Adam's Fall is wholly spoiled / human nature and being!"). The hymn ends with the statement that God's holy word is a glowing lamp, like the morning star, that shows the way for the sinner's feet ("Mein'n Füssen ist dein heilges Wort / ein brennende Lucerne, / ein Licht, das mir den Weg weist fort; / So dieser Morgen-Sterne . . ."). Günter Hess, " 'Durch Adams Fall ist ganz verderbt . . . ' Richter Adams Morgenlied," 152–59.

15. Graham, *Heinrich von Kleist*, 14.

16. Letter of January 12, 1802, to his sister Ulrike; 2:714–15. This is not to suggest that Kleist refers in this context either to Voltaire or to *Candide*.

17. Brumm, *American Thought and Religious Typology*, and Bercovitch, *Typology and Early American Literature*.

18. Lewis, *The American Adam*, 117.

19. I refer to the "Harvard" edition (as reprinted in most conveniently available editions), with preface and thirty-one chapters, rather than to the shorter Chicago edition.

20. Ben L. Collins, " 'Araby' and the 'Extended Simile,' " in Garrett, *Twentieth Century Interpretations of "Dubliners"*, 93–99.

21. For a full interpretation of *Demian* see Ziolkowski, *The Novels of Hermann Hesse*, 87–145.

22. Letter of December 17 to Wilhelm Kunze; 7:497.

23. Letter of April 13, 1930, to H.S.; 7:488.

24. I quote from the English translation of *Demian,* adjusting where necessary for precision.

25. Dunne, *Der Sündenfall.*

26. "Erstes Buch Mose: Die Schlange und die Vertreibung," in *Die letzten Indianer Europas,* 36–41.

27. Quoted in Dunne, *Der Sündenfall,* 18–19.

28. Kunert, *Zurück ins Paradies,* 151–63.

CHAPTER FIVE

THE PROLETARIANIZATION OF PROMETHEUS

1. Many of the most familiar euhemerisms and allegorizations are recapitulated by Hederich, *Mythologisches Lexikon,* 2096–98. See also Trousson, *Le Thème de Prométhée,* 1:59–82.

2. Trousson, *Le Thème de Prométhée,* 1:87–89.

3. Ibid., 100–120.

4. Ibid., 215.

5. The frontispiece is reproduced in Gourevitch's edition of Rousseau's *Discourses,* 2.

6. E.g., Butler, *Tyranny of Greece,* 85–93; Rehm, *Griechentum und Goethezeit,* 76–78.

7. The first edition of Balthasar's work was called simply *Apokalypse der deutschen Seele* (1937); it was only after World War II that he retitled the (unchanged) work *Prometheus.*

8. Marx, *Promotion,* "Vorrede."

9. The cartoon is reproduced as the frontispiece in Wessell, *Prometheus Bound.*

10. Marx, *Capital,* 799 (= vol. 1, pt. 7, chap. 25). See Wessell, *Prometheus Bound,* 144–89: "The Proletariat as Prometheus Bound."

11. Wessell, *Prometheus Bound,* 64.

12. Kolakowski, *Main Currents of Marxism,* 408–16.

13. Nietzsche, *Jugendschriften,* 62–73.

14. See the texts anthologized in *Mythos Prometheus.*

15. Blumenberg, *Work on Myth,* 561–626; Trousson, *Le Thème de Prométhée,* 1:269–91, 2:295–309;

16. Trousson, *Le Thème de Prométhée,* 2:335–42, 351–59.

200

17. Maurois, *Prométhée ou la Vie de Balzac*: "Entre Faust et Prométhée, j'aime mieux Prométhée."

18. See Trousson, *Le Thème de Prométhée*; Kreutz, *Das Prometheussymbol in der Dichtung der englischen Romantik*; Kreitzer, *Prometheus and Adam*; and Ziolkowski, "Science, Frankenstein, and Myth."

19. Kreitzer, *Prometheus and Adam*, 103–10.

20. On Böcklin and De Chirico, see the catalog for the exhibition *Eine Reise ins Ungewisse*; Barlach's drawing of 1910 is in private possession.

21. Gide, *Romans*, 301–41.

22. Kafka, *Sämtliche Erzählungen*, 306. In 1937 the painter Max Ernst created a *frottage* illustrating Kafka's parable.

23. For other examples see Goetsch, "Die Prometheusmythe in der englischsprachigen Literatur nach 1945," who concludes that in postwar English literature Prometheus has become an exhausted image through which writers conceal rather than express their situation.

24. Trousson, *Le Thème de Prométhée*, 2:487. Kreitzer's survey of twentieth-century adaptations, in *Prometheus and Adam*, also cites few examples after 1945, and none from the GDR.

25. Among the many studies see especially Mittenzwei, "Die Antikerezeption des DDR-Theaters," in his *Kampf der Richtungen*, 524–56; Gericke, *Rezeption des Altertums*; Riedel, *Literarische Antikerezeption*, 183–312; and Bernhardt, *Odysseus' Tod—Prometheus' Leben*, who discusses Herakles and Sisyphus in addition to his title figures.

26. Scharfschwerdt, *Literatur und Literaturwissenschaft in der DDR*, 135–39.

27. Mittenzwei, "Antikerezeption," 545–46.

28. Riedel, *Literarische Antikerezeption*, 11–12.

29. Träger, "Prometheus—unmittelbare und mittelbare Produktion der Geschichte," 187 ff., 285 ff.; and Braemer, *Goethes Prometheus und die Grundpositionen des Sturm und Drang*, 335–65. Turato, *Prometeo in Germania*, makes essentially the same point from a non-Marxist point of view.

30. Riedel, "Aspekte der Prometheus-Rezeption in der Literatur der DDR," in Gericke, *Rezeption des Altertums*, 33–50, and in his *Literarische Antikerezeption*—esp. 13–15, 185–87, 262–65—has stressed the exemplary nature of the Prometheus myth in GDR writing. See also Christoph Trilse, "Prometheus in der sozialistischen Literatur der

DDR," in Schmidt, *Aischylos und Pindar*, 339–50; and Bernhardt, *Odysseus' Tod—Prometheus' Leben*, 71–117.

31. Scharfschwerdt, *Literatur und Literaturwissenschaft in der DDR*, 21–26: "Die sozialistische Bildungs- und Erziehungsgesellschaft."

32. Riedel, *Literarische Antikerezeption*, 185, cites several fragments from the Bertold-Brecht-Archiv in the Akademie der Künste in Berlin.

33. Brecht, *Gesammelte Werke*, 8:87.

34. Brecht, *Arbeitsjournal*, 2:758.

35. Flores, *Poetry in East Germany*, 4–16; Demetz, *After the Fires*, 109–42; Fehervary, "The Literature of the German Democratic Republic."

36. Riedel, "Aspekte der Prometheus-Rezeption," in Gericke, *Rezeption des Altertums*, 33.

37. *Neue deutsche Literatur* 11 (August 1963): 86.

38. *Neue deutsche Literatur* 12 (November 1964): 65.

39. Maurer, *Werke*, 2:45–46.

40. Ibid., 453–54.

41. Bernhardt, *Odysseus' Tod—Prometheus' Leben*, 89.

42. Mickel, *Odysseus in Ithaka*, 108 and 167–68.

43. Bernhardt, *Odysseus' Tod—Prometheus' Leben*, 114.

44. Kunert, *Warnung*, 42–43.

45. Kunert, *Camera obscura*, 98.

46. Kunert, *Verspätete Monologe*, 189–90.

47. Trilse, "Prometheus in der sozialistischen Literatur der DDR," in Schmidt, *Aischylos und Pindar*, 345; and Bernhardt, *Odysseus' Tod—Prometheus' Leben*, 99–104.

48. Wieghans, *Zwischen Auftrag und Verrat*, 181–99.

49. Müller, *Stücke*, 343–44.

50. Riedel, "Aspekte der Prometheus-Rezeption," in Gericke, *Rezeption des Altertums*, 40. Bernhardt, *Odysseus' Tod—Prometheus' Leben*, 118–32, discusses the emergence of Herakles as an image of the worker in GDR literature.

51. Rüdiger Bernhardt, "Heiner Müller's 'Prometheus' (nach Aischylos)—eine Neudeutung," in Gericke, *Rezeption des Altertums*, 51–68; here 51.

52. The following discussion is based on Fühmann's essay "Das mythische Element in der Literatur," in his *Essays*, 82–140.

53. Fühmann, *Prometheus*.

54. Riedel, "Aspekte der Prometheus-Rezeption," in Gericke, *Rezeption des Altertums*, 42.

55. Scharfschwerdt, *Literatur und Literaturwissenschaft in der DDR*, 145–50: "Wissenschaftlich-technische Rationalität und ästhetische Ganzheit."

56. For a complete discussion see Riedel, *Literarische Antikerezeption*, 273–93.

57. Hacks, *Pandora*, 136: "Ideendrama."

58. Braun, *Texte*, 8:263–65.

59. Bernhardt, *Odysseus' Tod—Prometheus' Leben*, 146.

60. *Sinn und Form* 41 (1989): 353–56.

CHAPTER SIX
THE AMERICANIZATION OF FAUST

1. Schelling, *Philosophie der Kunst*, 90.

2. See Butler, *Fortunes of Faust*, and Smeed, *Faust in Literature*.

3. See Bunge's *Dokumentation*.

4. Hans Henning, "Faust im zwanzigsten Jahrhundert: ein Versuch," in Birven, *Faust im zwanzigsten Jahrhundert*, 7–21; here 22.

5. Peter Boerner, "Faust 1987: Alive and Well in East and West," in Boerner, *Faust through Four Centuries*, 263–72.

6. C. Bernd Sucher, "*Faust*-Inszenierungen in Deutschland, Frankreich und Italien seit 1980," in Brown, *Interpreting Goethe's "Faust" Today*, 262–70.

7. See Andreas Anglet, "*Faust*-Rezeption," in *Goethe-Handbuch*, 2:478–513; Eric Blackall, " 'What the Devil?'—Twentieth-Century Fausts," in Boerner, *Faust through Four Centuries*, 197–212; Dédéyan, *Le Thème de Faust*, 415–520; Smeed, *Faust in Literature*; and Mahal, "Faust im 20. Jahrhundert. Ein erster Überblick," in *Faust. Untersuchungen*, 527–39.

8. Johnson, *Transformation*. Goethe's Faust is famously riven by the "two souls" within his breast. Jung, who was convinced that Goethe was his ancestor, regarded it as his personal responsibility to atone for the evil act that Faust committed against Philemon and Baucis at the end of Goethe's play.

9. Holton, "Einstein and the Cultural Roots of Modern Science," writing of scientists' interest in Goethe, has noted that quotations of his poetry are to be found in the technical writings of such physicists as Ludwig Boltzmann, Hermann von Helmholtz, Erwin Schrödinger, Wilhelm Wien, Max Born, Arnold Sommerfeld, and Albert Einstein,

among others. As Volker Zimmermann—" 'Den Menschenstoff ge-
mächlich komponieren': Vom Homunkulus zur Gentechnik," in
Möbus, *Faust. Annäherung an einen Mythos*, 343–56—has shown, the
episode depicting the creation of Homunculus has enjoyed particular
metaphorical favor in connection with modern gene technology and
DNA research.

10. Werner Heisenberg, "Über eine Faust-Parodie der Atom-Phy-
siker," in Birven, *Faust im zwanzigsten Jahrhundert*, 63; and Jungk,
Brighter Than a Thousand Stars, 38–40.

11. Quoted in Jungk, *Brighter Than a Thousand Stars*, 333.

12. Major, *The Oppenheimer Hearing*, 61.

13. Quoted in Knust, "From Faust to Oppenheimer," 129.

14. Hoffman, *Gertrude Stein*, 83–85.

15. Johnson, *Robert Duncan*, 60.

16. Charters, *Kerouac*, 273.

17. Clark, *Jack Kerouac*, 67, 76.

18. Charters, *Kerouac*, 97.

19. Ziolkowski, "Faust and the University," 74–77.

20. Quoted in Berman, *All That Is Solid*, 37.

21. Berman, "Sympathy for the Devil," 38.

POSTLUDE
ON THE USES AND ABUSES OF MYTH

1. Hacks, *Adam und Eva*, 103.

2. See Ziolkowski, *Fictional Transfigurations of Jesus*.

* *Bibliography* *

(This list contains all works mentioned and cited by volume and page number. It excludes those readily available in several convenient editions and cited by verse or chapter.)

Aeschylus. *Prometheus Bound.* Edited by Mark Griffith. Cambridge: Cambridge University Press, 1983.

The Anchor Bible Dictionary. Edited by David Noel Freedman. 6 vols. New York: Doubleday, 1992.

Auerbach, Erich. *Mimesis: The Representation of Reality in Western Literature.* Translated by Willard Trask. Garden City, NY: Doubleday Anchor, 1957.

———. *Scenes from the Drama of European Literature: Six Essays.* New York: Meridian, 1959.

Augustinus. *Confessiones/Bekenntnisse.* Edited and translated by Joseph Bernhart. Munich: Kösel, 1955.

Axelrod, George. *Will Success Spoil Rock Hunter?* New York: Random House, 1956.

Bachelard, Gaston. *La Psychanalyse du feu.* Paris: Gallimard, 1949.

Bacon, Francis. *Works.* Edited by James Spedding. 7 vols. London, 1859–1870.

Balthasar, Hans Urs von. *Prometheus. Studien zur Geschichte des deutschen Idealismus.* 2d ed. Heidelberg: Kerle, 1947.

Baron, Frank. *Faustus. Geschichte, Sage, Dichtung.* Munich: Winkler, 1982.

———. *Faustus on Trial: The Origins of Johann Spies's "Historia" in an Age of Witch Hunting.* Tübingen: Niemeyer, 1992.

Barth, Karl. *From Rousseau to Ritschl.* Translated by Brian Cozens. London: SCM, 1959.

Bartsch, Wilhelm. *Übungen im Joch. Gedichte.* Berlin: Aufbau, 1986.

Becher, Johannes R. *Gedichte 1936–1941.* Vol. 4 of *Gesammelte Werke.* Berlin and Weimar: Aufbau, 1966.

Bercovitch, Sacvan, ed. *Typology and Early American Literature.* Amherst: University of Massachusetts Press, 1972.

Berman, Marshall. *All That Is Solid Melts Into Air: The Experience of Modernity.* New York: Simon, 1982.

Berman, Marshall. "Sympathy for the Devil: Faust, the '60s and the Tragedy of Development." *American Review* 19 (1974): 23–75.

Bernhardt, Rüdiger. *Odysseus' Tod—Prometheus' Leben. Antike Mythen in der Literatur der DDR*. Leipzig and Halle: Mitteldeutscher Verlag, 1983.

Bianchi, Ugo. *Prometeo, Orfeo, Adamo. Tematiche religiose sul destine, il male, la salvezza*. Rome: Edizioni dell'ateneo & bizzarri, 1976.

Birven, Henri, ed. *Faust im zwanzigsten Jahrhundert. Festschrift für Karl Theens*. Knittlingen: Freunde der Faust-Gedenkstätte, 1964.

Bloom, Harold, ed. *Christopher Marlowe's Doctor Faustus*. New York: Chelsea House, 1988.

Blumenberg, Hans. *Work on Myth*. Translated by Robert M. Wallace. Cambridge: MIT Press, 1985.

Boerner, Peter, and Sidney Johnson, eds. *Faust through Four Centuries: Retrospect and Analysis*. Tübingen: Niemeyer, 1989.

The Book of J. Translated by David Rosenberg. Introduced by Harold Bloom. New York: Grove, 1990.

Braemer, Edith. *Goethes Prometheus und die Grundpositionen des Sturm und Drang*. Weimar: Arion, 1959.

Braun, Volker. *Texte in zeitlicher Folge*. 10 vols. Halle and Leipzig: Mitteldeutscher Verlag, 1989–1993.

Brecht, Bertolt. *Arbeitsjournal*. Edited by Werner Hecht. 2 vols. Frankfurt am Main: Suhrkamp, 1973.

———. *Gesammelte Werke in zwanzig Bänden*. Frankfurt am Main: Suhrkamp, 1967.

Brown, Jane K., ed. *Interpreting Goethe's "Faust" Today*. Columbia, SC: Camden House, 1994.

Brumm, Ursula. *American Thought and Religious Typology*. New Brunswick, NJ: Rutgers University Press, 1970.

Bunge, Hans, ed. *Die Debatte um Hanns Eislers "Johann Faust": Eine Dokumentation*. Berlin: BasisDruck, 1991.

Butler, E[liza] M[arian]. *The Fortunes of Faust*. 1952. Paperback ed. Cambridge: Cambridge University Press, 1979.

———. *The Myth of the Magus*. Canto ed. Cambridge: Cambridge University Press, 1948.

———. *The Tyranny of Greece over Germany*. 1935. Boston: Beacon, 1958.

Camus, Albert. *The Rebel: An Essay on Man in Revolt*. Translated by Anthony Bower. New York: Vintage, 1959.

Charters, Ann. *Kerouac: A Biography*. New York: St. Martin, 1994.

Clair, René. *Comédies et commentaires.* Paris: Gallimard, 1959.

Clark, Tom. *Jack Kerouac.* New York: Harcourt, 1984.

Damrosch, David. *The Narrative Covenant: Transformations of Genre in the Growth of Biblical Literature.* San Francisco: Harper, 1987.

Davidson, Robert. *Genesis 1–11: Commentary.* Cambridge: Cambridge University Press, 1973.

Dédéyan, Charles. *Le Thème de Faust dans la littérature européenne.* 2 vols. Paris: Lettres modernes, 1967.

Delbrück, Hansgerd. "Zur dramentypologischen Funktion vom Sündenfall und Rechtfertigung in Kleists 'Zerbrochnem Krug.'" *Deutsche Vierteljahrsschrift* 45 (1971): 706–56.

Demetz, Peter. *After the Fires: Recent Writing in the Germanies, Austria, and Switzerland.* New York: Harcourt, 1986.

Diels, Hermann. *Die Fragmente der Vorsokratiker.* 9th ed. 3 vols. Berlin: Weidmann, 1959.

Dietz, Karl-Martin. *Prometheus—vom göttlichen zum menschlichen Wissen.* Vol. 1 of *Metamorphosen des Geistes.* Stuttgart: Freies Geistesleben, 1989.

Duncan, Robert. *Faust Foutu. A Comic Mask. Act one of four acts, 1952–54. With decorations by the author.* [Santa Barbara, CA]: White Rabbit, 1958.

———. *Faust Foutu. An Entertainment in Four Parts.* Stinson Beach, CA: Enkidu Surrogate, 1959.

Dunne, Kerry. *Der Sündenfall: A Parabolic Key to the Image of Human Existence in the Work of Günter Kunert 1960–1990.* Frankfurt am Main: Lang, 1995.

Eichhorn, Johann Gottfried. *Einleitung in das alte Testament.* 3d ed. 3 vols. Leipzig, 1803.

Eissfeldt, Otto. *The Old Testament: An Introduction.* Translated by Peter R. Ackroyd. New York: Harper, 1965.

The Encyclopedia of Religion. Edited by Mircea Eliade. 16 vols. New York: Macmillan, 1987.

The Encyclopaedia of Religion and Ethics. Edited by James Hasting. 13 vols. New York: Scribner, 1908–1927.

Engelberg, Edward. *The Unknown Distance: From Consciousness to Conscience. Goethe to Camus.* Cambridge: Harvard University Press, 1972.

Das Faustbuch nach der Wolfenbütteler Handschrift. Edited by H. G. Haile. Heidelberg: Winter, 1995.

Fehervary, Helen. "The Literature of the German Democratic Republic (1945–1990)." In *The Cambridge History of German Literature*, edited by Helen Watanabe-O'Kelly, 393–439. Cambridge: Cambridge University Press, 1997.

"Flix." *Who the Fuck Is Faust?: Comic-Tragödie in 7 Tagen.* Frankfurt am Main: Eichborn, 1998.

Flores, John. *Poetry in East Germany: Adjustments, Visions, and Provocations, 1945–1970.* New Haven: Yale University Press, 1971.

Frazer, James G. *Folk-Lore in the Old Testament.* 3 vols. London: Macmillan, 1918.

———. *The New Golden Bough.* Edited by Theodor H. Gaster. New York: New American Library, 1964.

Freud, Sigmund. *The Standard Edition of the Complete Psychological Works.* Edited by James Strachey. 23 vols. London: Hogarth, 1953–1966.

Fühmann, Franz. *Essays, Gespräche, Aufsätze 1964–1981.* Rostock: Hinstorff, 1983.

———. *Prometheus. Die Titanenschlacht.* Illustrated by Nuria Quevedo. Berlin: Kinderbuch, 1974.

Gadamer, Hans-Georg. *Kleine Schriften II: Interpretationen.* Tübingen: Mohr, 1967.

Garrett, Peter K., ed. *Twentieth Century Interpretations of "Dubliners".* Englewood Cliffs, NJ: Prentice-Hall, 1968.

Gericke, Horst, ed. *Rezeption des Altertums in modernen literarischen Werken.* Wissenschaftliche Beiträge 1980/36. Halle: Martin-Luther-Universität, 1980.

Gide, André. *Romans, récits et soties. Oeuvres lyriques.* Edited by Maurice Nadeau. Paris: Pléiade, 1958.

Gillispie, Charles Coulston. *Genesis and Geology: A Study in the Relations of Scientific Thought, Natural Theology, and Social Opinion in Great Britain, 1790–1850.* New York: Harper, 1959.

Goethe-Handbuch in vier Bänden. Edited by Bernd Witte. Stuttgart: Metzler, 1997.

Goetsch, Paul. "Die Prometheusmythe in der englischsprachigen Literatur nach 1945." In *Klassiker-Renaissance. Modelle der Gegenwartsliteratur,* edited by Martin Brunkhorst, Gerd Rohmann, and Konrad Schoell, 31–51. Tübingen: Stauffenburg, 1991.

Grabar, André. *Christian Iconography: A Study of Its Origins.* Bollingen Series 35/10. Princeton, NJ: Princeton University Press, 1968.

Graham, Ilse. *Heinrich von Kleist. Word into Flesh: A Poet's Quest for the Symbol.* Berlin: De Gruyter, 1977.

Graves, Robert, and Raphael Patai. *Hebrew Myths: The Book of Genesis.* Garden City, NY: Doubleday, 1964.

Hacks, Peter. *Adam und Eva. Komödie in einem Vorspiel und drei Akten.* Illustrated by Albert Ebert. Düsseldorf: Claassen, 1976.

———. *Pandora. Drama nach J. W. von Goethe.* With an essay. Berlin: Aufbau, 1981.

Haimsohn, George. *The Bedside Faust.* Madcap Classics. New York: Perigree, 1952.

Havel, Vaclav. *Temptation. A Play in Ten Scenes.* Translated by Marie Winn. New York: Grove, 1986.

Hawthorne, Nathaniel. *The Complete Novels and Selected Tales.* Edited by Norman Holmes Pearson. New York: Modern Library, 1965.

Headlam, Walter. "Prometheus and the Garden of Eden: Notes for a Lecture." *Classical Quarterly* 28 (1934): 63–71.

Hederich, Benjamin. *Gründliches Mythologisches Lexikon.* 1770. Reprographic reproduction. Darmstadt: Wissenschaftliche Buchgesellschaft, 1996.

Heller, Erich. *The Artist's Journey into the Interior.* New York: Vintage, 1968.

Herington, John. *Aeschylus.* New Haven: Yale University Press, 1986.

Hersey, John. *Too Far to Walk.* New York: Bantam, 1967.

Hesiod. *Theogony. Works and Days. Shield.* Translated and edited by Apostolos N. Athanassakis. Baltimore and London: The Johns Hopkins University Press, 1983.

Hess, Günter. " 'Durch Adams Fall ist ganz verderbt . . .' Richter Adams Morgenlied." *Kleist Jahrbuch 1993*, 152–59.

Hesse, Hermann. *Demian: The Story of Emil Sinclair's Youth.* Translated by Michael Roloff and Michael Lebeck. New York: Bantam, 1968.

———. *Gesammelte Schriften.* Frankfurt am Main: Suhrkamp, 1952–1957.

Historia von D. Johann Fausten. Kritische Ausgabe. Edited by Stephan Füssel and Hans Joachim Kreutzer. Stuttgart: Reclam, 1988.

Hoelzel, Alfred. *The Paradoxical Quest: A Study of Faustian Vicissitudes.* New York: Lang, 1988.

Hoffman, Michael J. *Gertrude Stein.* Boston: Twayne, 1976.

Hoffmann, E.T.A. *Poetische Werke in sechs Bänden.* Berlin: Aufbau, 1958.

Hoffmann, E.T.A. *Tagebücher.* Edited by Friedrich Schnapp. Darmstadt: Wissenschaftliche Buchgesellschaft, 1971.

Holton, Gerald. "Einstein and the Cultural Roots of Modern Science." *Daedalus* 127 (1998): 1–44.

Hughes, Thomas P. *Rescuing Prometheus.* New York: Pantheon, 1998.

The Interpreter's Bible. Edited by George Arthur Buttrick. 12 vols. Nashville: Abingdon, 1952–1957.

The Interpreter's Dictionary of the Bible. Edited by George Arthur Buttrick. 4 vols. New York and Nashville: Abingdon, 1962.

John Paul II. *The Gospel of Life (Evangelium Vitae).* New York: Random, 1995.

Johnson, Mark Andrew. *Robert Duncan.* Boston: Twayne, 1988.

Johnson, Robert A. *Transformation: Understanding the Three Levels of Masculine Consciousness.* San Francisco: Harper, 1991.

Jump, John, ed. *Marlowe: Doctor Faustus. A Casebook.* London: Macmillan, 1969.

Jung, C. G. *The Archetypes and the Collective Unconscious.* Translated by R.F.C. Hull. Bollingen Series 20/9:1. 2d ed. Princeton, NJ: Princeton University Press, 1971.

———. *Memories, Dreams, Reflections.* Translated by Richard and Clara Winston. New York: Random, 1963.

Jungk, Robert. *Brighter Than a Thousand Suns: A Personal History of the Atomic Scientists.* Translated by James Cleugh. New York: Harcourt, 1958.

Kafka, Franz. *Sämtliche Erzählungen.* Edited by Paul Raabe. Frankfurt am Main: Fischer, 1970.

Kahler, Erich. *The Orbit of Thomas Mann.* Princeton, NJ: Princeton University Press, 1969.

Kant, Immanuel. *Political Writings.* Edited by Hans Reiss. Translated by H. B. Nisbet. 2d ed. Cambridge: Cambridge University Press, 1991.

———. *Werke in zehn Bänden.* Edited by Wilhelm Weischedel. Darmstadt: Wissenschaftliche Buchgesellschaft, 1964.

Kerényi, Karl. *Prometheus. Die menschliche Existenz in griechischer Deutung.* Hamburg: Rowolt, 1959.

Kerouac, Jack. *Doctor Sax. Faust Part Three.* New York: Grove, 1959.

Kirchner, Josef. *Die Darstellung des ersten Menschenpaares in der bildenden Kunst von der ältesten Zeit bis auf unsere Tage.* Stuttgart: Enke, 1903.

Kirsch, Rainer. *Kunst in Mark Brandenburg. Gedichte.* Munich: Hanser, 1989.

Kirschbaum, Leo. "Marlowe's Faustus: A Reconsideration." *Review of English Studies* 19 (1943): 225–41.

Kleist, Heinrich von. *Sämtliche Werke und Briefe.* Edited by Helmut Sembdner. 2d ed. 2 vols. Munich: Hanser, 1961.

Knoll, Robert E. *Christopher Marlowe.* New York: Twayne, 1969.

Knust, Herbert. "From Faust to Oppenheimer: The Scientist's Pact with the Devil." *Journal of European Studies* 13 (1983): 122–41.

Kolakowski, Leszek. *Main Currents of Marxism: Its Origins, Growth and Dissolution.* Translated by P. S. Falla. Oxford: Oxford University Press, 1978.

Kreitzer, Larry. *Prometheus and Adam: Enduring Symbols of the Human Situation.* Lanham, MD: University Press of America, 1994.

Kreutz, Christian. *Das Prometheussymbol in der Dichtung der englischen Romantik.* Palaestra 236. Göttingen: Vandenhoeck, 1963.

Kunert, Günter. *Camera obscura.* Munich: Hanser, 1978.

———. *Die letzten Indianer Europas. Kommentare zum Traum, der Leben heißt.* Munich: Hanser, 1991.

———. *Verspätete Monologe.* Munich: Hanser, 1981.

———. *Warnung vor Spiegeln. Gedichte.* Munich: Hanser, 1970.

———. *Zurück ins Paradies. Geschichten.* Munich: Hanser, 1984.

Lagerfeld, Karl. *Faust.* Göttingen: Steidel, 1998.

Landes, David S. *The Unbound Prometheus: Technological Change and Industrial Development in Western Europe from 1750 to the Present.* Cambridge: Cambridge University Press, 1969.

Lanson, Gustave. *Voltaire.* Translated by Robert A. Wagoner. New York: Wiley, 1966.

Lecourt, Dominique. *Prométhée, Faust, Frankenstein. Fondaments imaginaire de l'éthique.* Paris: Les Empêcheurs de Penser en Rond, 1996.

Lee, Lawrence. *The American as Faust.* Pittsburgh: Boxwood, 1965.

Lehmann, John. *Prometheus and the Bolsheviks.* London: Cresset, 1937.

Levison, John R. *Portraits of Adam in Early Judaism: From Sirach to 2 Baruch. Journal for the Study of the Pseudepigrapha.* Supplement Series 1. Sheffield: Sheffield Academic Press, 1988.

Lewis, R.W.B. *The American Adam: Innocence, Tragedy and Tradition in the Nineteenth Century.* Chicago: University of Chicago Press, 1958.

Loretz, Oswald. *Schöpfung und Mythos. Mensch und Welt nach den Anfangskapiteln der Genesis.* Stuttgarter Bibelstudien 32. Stuttgart: Katholisches Bibelwerk, 1968.

Lucian of Samosata. *Works.* Translated by H. W. Fowler and F. G. Fowler. 4 volumes. Oxford: Clarendon, 1905.

Mahal, Günther. *Faust, der Mann aus Knittlingen. Dokumente, Erläuterungen, Informationen.* Pforzheim: Dettling, 1980.

———. *Faust. Untersuchungen zu einem zeitlosen Thema.* Neuried: ars una, 1998.

Mainzer, Otto. *Prometheus.* Basel and Frankfurt am Main: Stroemfeld/ Roter Stern, 1989.

Major, John. *The Oppenheimer Hearing.* New York: Stein and Day, 1971.

Marx, Karl. *Capital: A Critique of Political Economy.* Introduced by Ernest Mandel. Translated by Ben Fowkes. Vol. 1. New York: Vintage, 1977.

———. *Die Promotion von Karl Marx—Jena 1841.* Edited by Erhard Lange et al. Berlin: Dietz, 1983.

Maurer, Georg. *Werke in zwei Bänden.* Edited by Walfried Hartinger et al. Halle: Mitteldeutscher Verlag, 1987.

Maurois, André. *Prométhée ou la Vie de Balzac.* Paris: Hachette, 1965.

Mayer, Hans. *Doktor Faust und Don Juan.* Frankfurt am Main: Suhrkamp, 1979.

Melville, Herman. *Billy Budd and Other Tales.* Edited by Willard Thorp. New York: Signet, 1979.

Michelsen, Peter. "Die Lügen Adams und Evas Fall. Heinrich von Kleists *Der zerbrochne Krug.*" In *Geist und Zeichen. Festschrift für Arthur Henkel,* edited by Herbert Anton, 268–304. Heidelberg: Winter, 1977.

Mickel, Karl. *Odysseus in Ithaka. Gedichte 1957–1974.* Leipzig: Reclam, 1976.

Miner, Earl, ed. *Literary Uses of Typology from the Late Middle Ages to the Present.* Princeton, NJ: Princeton University Press, 1977.

Mitchell, Michael. *Peter Hacks: Theatre for a Socialist Society.* Scottish Papers in Germanic Studies 10. Glasgow, 1990.

Mittenzwei, Werner. *Kampf der Richtungen: Strömungen und Tendenzen der internationalen Dramatik.* Leipzig: Reclam, 1978.

Möbus, Frank, Friederike Schmidt-Möbus, and Gerd Unverfehrt, eds. *Faust. Annäherung an einen Mythos.* Göttingen: Wallstein, 1996.

Muir, Edwin. *Collected Poems 1921–1958.* London: Faber, 1960.

Müller, Heiner. *Stücke.* Berlin: Henschel, 1975.

Mythos Prometheus. Texte von Hesiod bis René Char. Edited by Wolfgang Storch and Burghard Damerau. Leipzig: Reclam, 1995.

Newman, Randy. *Faust.* New York: Reprise, 1995.

Nietzsche, Friedrich. *Jugendschriften.* Edited by Hans Joachim Mette. Vol. 1 of *Historisch-Kritische Gesamtausgabe.* Munich: Beck, 1933.

———. *Werke in drei Bänden.* Edited by Karl Schlechta. Munich: Hanser, 1954–1956.

Olson, Elder. *Plays and Poems, 1948–58.* Chicago: University of of Chicago Press, 1958.

Pagels, Elaine. *Adam, Eve, and the Serpent.* New York: Random, 1988.

Palmer, Philip Mason, and Robert Pattison More. *The Sources of the Faust Tradition from Simon Magus to Lessing.* New York: Oxford University Press, 1936.

Panofsky, Dora and Erwin. *Pandora's Box: The Changing Aspects of a Mythical Symbol.* Bollingen Series 52. 2d ed. New York: Pantheon, 1962.

Plato. *The Collected Dialogues.* Edited by Edith Hamilton and Huntingdon Cairns. Bollingen Series 71. Princeton, NJ: Princeton University Press, 1963.

Plutzik, Hyam. *The Collected Poems.* Foreword by Anthony Hecht. Brockport, NY: Boa, 1987.

Pritchard, James B., ed. *An Anthology of Texts and Pictures.* Vol. 1 of *The Ancient Near East.* Princeton, NJ: Princeton University Press, 1958.

Rashi. *The Torah: With Rashi's Commentary.* Translated and edited by Yisrael Isser Zvi Herzog. 3 vols. Brooklyn: Mesorah, 1995.

Rehm, Walther. *Griechentum und Goethezeit. Geschichte eines Glaubens.* 2d ed. Leipzig: Dieterich, 1938.

Eine Reise ins Ungewisse: Arnold Böcklin, Giorgio de Chirico, Max Ernst. Edited by Guido Magnaguagno and Juri Steiner. Catalog of exhibitions at Kunsthaus Zürich, Haus der Kunst München, Nationalgalerie Berlin, October 1997–August 1998.

Richards, I. A. *Internal Colloquies. Poems and Plays.* New York: Harcourt, 1976.

Richardson, Alan. *Genesis I–XI. Introduction and Commentary.* London: SCM, 1953.

Ricoeur, Paul. *The Symbolism of Evil.* Translated by Emerson Buchanan. New York: Harper, 1967.

Riedel, Volker. *Literarisches Antikerezeption. Aufsätze und Vorträge.* Jenaer Studien 2. Jena: Bussert, 1996.

Röhrich, Lutz. *Adam und Eva. Das erste Menschenpaar in Volkskunst und Volksdichtung.* Stuttgart: Müller und Schindler, 1968.

Rousseau, Jean-Jacques. *The Discourses and Other Early Political Writings.* Edited and translated by Victor Gourevitch. Cambridge: Cambridge University Press, 1997.

Rücker, Günther. "Prometheus 1937." *Sinn und Form* 41 (1989): 353–56.

Scharfschwerdt, Jürgen. *Literatur und Literaturwissenschaft in der DDR. Eine historisch-kritische Einführung.* Stuttgart: Kohlhammer, 1982.

Schelling, F.W.J. *Einleitung in die Philosophie der Mythologie.* Vol. 1 of *Philosophie der Mythologie.* Darmstadt: Wissenschaftliche Buchgesellschaft, 1966.

———. *Philosophie der Kunst.* Darmstadt: Wissenschaftliche Buchgesellschaft, 1960.

Schmidt, Ernst Günther, ed. *Aischylos und Pindar: Studien zu Werk und Nachwirkung.* Schriften zur Geschichte und Kultur der Antike 19. Berlin: Akademie, 1981.

Schwerte, Hans. *Faust und das Faustische. Ein Kapitel deutscher Ideologie.* Stuttgart: Klett, 1962.

Sewall, Richard B. *The Vision of Tragedy.* New Haven: Yale University Press, 1959.

Sexton, Anne. *The Complete Poems.* Foreword by Maxine Kumin. Boston: Houghton, 1981.

Shapiro, Karl. *Selected Poems.* New York: Random, 1968.

Shattuck, Roger. *Forbidden Knowledge: From Prometheus to Pornography.* Harvest ed. New York: Harcourt, 1997.

Smeed, J. W. *Faust in Literature.* London: Oxford University Press, 1975.

Stein, Gertrude. *Selected Operas and Plays.* Edited by John Malcolm Brinnin. Pittsburgh: University of Pittsburgh Press, 1970.

Steiner, Reinhart. *Prometheus. Ikonologische und anthropologische Aspekte der bildenden Kunst vom 14. bis zum 17. Jahrhundert.* Munich: Boer, 1991.

Stent, Gunther S. *The Coming of the Golden Age: A View of the End of Progress.* Garden City, NY: The Natural History Press, 1969.

Stone, Michael E. *A History of the Literature of Adam and Eve.* Atlanta, GA: Scholars, 1992.

Swanwick, Michael. *Jack Faust.* New York: Avon, 1997.

Tezuka, Osamu. *Neo-Faust.* Tokyo: Asahi Shimbun, 1989.

Thomson, George. *Aeschylus and Athens: A Study in the Social Origins of Drama.* 1940. New York: Haskell, 1972.

Tkaczyk, Wilhelm. *Der Tag ist groß. Gesammelte Werke in einem Band.* Halle: Mitteldeutscher Verlag, 1972.

Toynbee, Arnold J. *A Study of History. Abridgement of vols. I–VI* by D. C. Somervell. New York: Oxford University Press, 1947.

Träger, Claus. "Prometheus—unmittelbare und mittelbare Produktion der Geschichte." In *Literaturgeschichte als geschichtlicher Auftrag. Werner Krauss zum 60. Geburtstag,* edited by Werner Bahner, 187–283. Berlin: Rütten & Loening, 1961.

Trousson, Raymond. *Le Thème de Prométhée dan la littérature européenne.* 2 vols. Geneva: Droz, 1964.

Der Tübinger Reim-Faust von 1587/88. Edited by Günther Mahal. Kirchheim/Teck: Schweier, 1977.

Turato, Fabio. *Prometeo in Germania. Storia della fortuna e dell'interpretazione del Prometeo di Eschilo nella cultura tedesca (1771–1871).* Florence: Olschki, 1988.

Twain, Mark. *The Diaries of Adam & Eve.* Edited by Don Roberts. San Francisco: Fair Oaks, 1997.

Unamuno, Miguel de. *The Tragic Sense of Life in Men and Nations.* Translated by Anthony Kerrigan. Bollingen Series 85/4. Princeton, NJ: Princeton University Press, 1972.

Valéry, Paul. *Mon Faust (Ébauches).* Paris: Gallimard, 1946.

Völker, Klaus. *Faust—Ein deutscher Mann. Die Geburt einer Legende und ihr Fortleben in den Köpfen.* Berlin: Wagenbach, 1975.

Voltaire. *Candide or Optimism: A New Translation, Backgrounds, Criticism.* Edited by Robert M. Adams. New York: Norton, 1966.

———. *Romans.* Edited by Roger Peyrefitte. Paris: Livre de poche classique, 1961.

Wallop, Douglass. *Damn Yankees.* New York: Norton, 1994. Reprint of *The Year the Yankees Lost the Pennant.* 1954.

Watt, Ian. *Myths of Modern Individualism: Faust, Don Quixote, Don Juan, Robinson Crusoe.* Canto ed. Cambridge: Cambridge University Press, 1997.

Wessell, Leonard P., Jr. *Prometheus Bound: The Mythic Structure of Karl Marx's Scientific Thinking.* Baton Rouge: LSU Press, 1984.

Widmann, Georg Rudolf. *Fausts Leben.* Edited by Adelbert von Keller. 1880. Reprint, Hildesheim: Olms, 1976.

Wieghans, Georg. *Zwischen Auftrag und Verrat. Werk und Ästhetik Heiner Müllers.* Frankfurt am Main: Lang, 1984.

Wolfe, Burton H. *The Devil and Dr. Noxin.* San Francisco: Wild West, 1973.

Wutrich, Timothy Richard. *Prometheus and Faust: The Promethean Revolt in Drama from Classical Antiquity to Goethe.* Westport, CT: Greenwood, 1995.

Ziolkowski, Theodore. "Faust and the University: Pedagogical Ruminations on a Subversive Classic." In *Texte, Motive und Gestalten der Goethezeit. Festschrift für Hans Reiss,* edited by John L. Hibberd and H. B. Nisbet, 65–79. Tübingen: Niemeyer, 1989.

———. *Fictional Transfigurations of Jesus.* Princeton, NJ: Princeton University Press, 1972.

———. *The Mirror of Justice: Literary Reflections of Legal Crises.* Princeton, NJ: Princeton University Press, 1997.

———. *The Novels of Hermann Hesse: Themes and Structures.* Princeton, NJ: Princeton University Press, 1965.

———. "The Responsibilities of Knowledge." *University: A Princeton Magazine* 95 (1981): 1–4.

———. "Science, Frankenstein, and Myth." *Sewanee Review* 89 (1981): 34–56.

Acts of the Holy Apostles, 57
Adam. *See* Fall, myth of
Adapa, 16, 18
Aeschylus, 38–42; *Eumenides*, 40; *Prometheus Bound*, 33–38, 40, 42, 45, 71, 115–17, 125–26, 138, 140, 187–88
Agrippa von Nettesheim, Cornelius, 46, 63
Anacreon, 40
Anaxagoras, 41–42
"Antikewelle," 122
Apocalypse of Moses, 11–12
Apollodorus, 140
Aristophanes, *The Birds*, 32, 172
Aristotle, 41
Athens, 39–41
Auerbach, Erich, 78
Augustine, Saint, 22, 56
Axelrod, George, *Will Success Spoil Rock Hunter?*, 160–61, 164, 188–89

Bachelard, Gaston, 37
Bacon, Francis, 66, 112
Bacon, Roger, 49
Baggesen, Jens, *Adam und Eva*, 183–84
Balk, H. Wesley, 153
Balthasar, Hans Urs von, 114, 200n.7
Balzac, Honoré de, 118
Barlach, Ernst, 118
Baron, Frank, 196n.4
Barth, Karl, 80
Bartsch, Wilhelm, "Judgment of Prometheus," 146–47
Becher, Johannes R., 124, 128; "Prometheus," 124–27, 137
Beethoven, Ludwig van, 118
Begardi, Philip, 51
Berlioz, Hector, 153

Berman, Marshall, 174, 177, 190
Bernhardt, Rüdiger, 201n.25, 202n.50
Bernstein, Leonard, 75
Bianchi, Ugo, 195n.8
biblical criticism, 80–81
Bloom, Harold, 194nn. 20 and 23
Blumenberg, Hans, 114–15
Boccaccio, Giovanni, 112
Böcklin, Arnold, 118–19
Bohr, Niels, 154
Borrow, Anthony, 152
Brant, Sebastian, 53
Braun, Volker, "Prometheus," 131, 187; "Prometheus's Trial," 145–47, 187
Brecht, Bertolt, 122, 128, 187–88; "Prometheus," 126–27
Breker, Arno, 4
Bulgakov, Mikhail, 152
Busoni, Ferruccio, 153
Butler, E. M., 197n.22
Byron, George Gordon, Baron, 118, 171; *Cain*, 106

Cagliostro, Count Alessandro, 48
Calderón de la Barca, Pedro, 57
Calvin, Jean, 79
Camerarius, Joachim, 48
Camus, Albert, *L'Homme révolté*, 119–20
Cervantes Saavedra, Miguel de, 75, 183
chapbook, 164, 181, 187–88. See also *Historia von D. Johann Fausten*
Chirico, Giorgio de, 118–19
Clair, René, *La Beauté du diable*, 151
Cleisthenes, 40
Clementine Recognitions, 57
Collins, Jess, 158

contract with devil. *See* pact with devil

Cranach, Lucas, *Adam and Eve*, 2–3, 12

"Culture Speech" (in *Prometheus Bound*), 34, 38, 42, 125

curiositas, 56, 62, 65

Cyprian, Saint, 57

Czechowski, Heinz, "Prometheus," 128–29

Dali, Salvador, 153

Damn Yankees, 159, 189

Damrosch, David, 194n.24

Dante Alighieri, *Divine Comedy*, 17, 70, 171

Dart, Raymond A., 4

David, King, 19–20

Debucourt, Louis-Philibert, 82

Delacroix, Eugène, 156, 162, 164

Dickens, Charles, 75

Dietz, Karl-Martin, 195n.8

Diezel, Peter, "Prometheus," 129

Don Juan, 6, 43, 45

Don Quixote, 6, 43, 45, 153

Duncan, Robert, 158, 161, 163; *Faust Foutu*, 158–59

Dürer, Albrecht, 53

Durrell, Lawrence, 151–52

Dyson, Freeman, 155

Eberhard, August Gottlob, *Der erste Mensch und die Erde*, 184

Edwards, Jonathan, 79

Ehrenfest, Paul, 154

Eichhorn, Johann Gottfried, 80

Eisler, Hanns, *Johann Faustus*, 149–50

Elucidarius, 55

Emerson, Ralph Waldo, 23–24, 79

Enright, D. J., 152

Ephialtes, 40

Erasmus, Desiderius, 112

Erskine, John, *Adam and Eve*, 184

etiology, 13, 21, 23

Fall, myth of: in "Araby," 100–102; in *Billy Budd*, 97–100; in *The Broken Pitcher*, 82–87; in *Candide*, 75–77; comic retellings of, 183–84; composition of, 18–19; in *Demian*, 102–5; and Faust, 69–72; in Genesis, 9–11; in *The Golden Pot*, 87–92; in *Leaves of Grass*, 92–93; in *The Marble Faun*, 93–97; medieval adaptations of, 12; modern postfigurations of, 185–86; Near Eastern sources of, 13–16; in New Testament, 11, 13; Nietzsche's view of, 25; in Old Testament, 12–13; popularity of, 3–4, 6; and Prometheus, 31–32, 69–72; Unamuno's view of, 105–6

Fauré, Gabriel, 118

Faust, myth of: in academic satires, 164–65, 189; and atomic bomb, 154–56, 187; in chapbook, 52–60; development of, 49–52; in Kerouac's *Dr. Sax*, 161–64; and myth of Fall, 69–72; in Marlowe's *Faustus*, 60–68; in 1950s, 156–61; in 1960s, 174–77; in 1990s, 177–91; as phenotype in Germany, 149–51; popularity of, 5–6, 151–53; in professorial works, 165–73; and Prometheus, 69–72, 181–82, 187; as rebel, 187–88; sources of, 45–52

Feuerbach, Anselm, 118

Fichte, Johann Gottlieb, 183

Ficino, Marsilio, 112

Figgis, Mike, *Loss of Sexual Innocence*, 74, 107

figuralism, 11. *See also* typology

Fitzpatrick, Nina, 152

"Flix," *Who the Fuck Is Faust?*, 5

forbidden knowledge, 71–72

Frazer, James G., 18

Freud, Sigmund, 115, 190; "Acquisition and Control of Fire," 117–18; *Civilization and Its Discontents*, 21–22

Fühmann, Franz, 137–38; *Prometheus*, 138–41, 187
Fürwitz, 56. See also *curiositas*

Gadamer, Hans-Georg, 39
Gast, Johannes, *Sermones Convivales*, 51
GDR (German Democratic Republic), 127–38, 132
Genesis. *See* Fall, myth of
Gessner, John, 153
Gide, André, *Le Prométhée mal enchaîné*, 119, 137–38
Gilgamesh, epic of, 14–16, 71
Gladkov, Fyodor, *Cement*, 135
Goethe, Johann Wolfgang von, 118, 125, 137–38, 162; *Faust*, 153, 156, 163–64, 166, 185, 187, 189; *Pandora*, 141–42; *Prometheus*, 113; "Prometheus," 113–15, 124, 148–49; *Sorrows of Young Werther*, 79
Goetsch, Paul, 201n.23
Golden Age, myth of, 19
Gounod, Charles, 153, 156
Grande Encyclopédie, cited, 112
Grass, Günter, 75, 118, 185
Greene, Graham, 185
Gründgens, Gustav, 150, 156

Hacks, Peter, 141–42, 147; *Adam und Eva*, 81–82, 184; adaptation of Goethe's *Pandora*, 142–45
Haimsohn, George, *The Bedside Faust*, 5, 156
Hamlet, 6, 43, 45, 153, 168–69
Harrison, Tony, 121
Havel, Vaclav, *Temptation*, 152–53
Hawthorne, Nathaniel, 79, 99, 191; *The Marble Faun*, 93–97, 186
Headlam, Walter, 195n.8
Heine, Heinrich, 118
Heller, Erich, 65, 197n.28
Helvetius, Claude-Adrien, 87
Henning, Hans, cited, 150
Herder, Johann Gottfried, 118
Herodotus, 41

Hersey, John, 173; *Too Far to Walk*, 171–72, 186, 188
Hesiod, 27–28, 30, 41, 70, 130, 138, 140, 187–88; *Theogony*, 28–29; *Works and Days*, 29–32
Hess, Günter, 199n.14
Hesse, Hermann, *Demian*, 102–5, 186
Heyne, Christian Gottlob, 80
Hipparchus, 40
Hippias, 40
Historia von D. Johann Fausten, 43–45, 52–60. *See also* chapbook
Historie of the damnable life . . . of Faust, 61
Hoelzel, Alfred, 197n.22
Hoffmann, E.T.A., 87–88, 103; *The Golden Pot*, 88–91, 97, 99, 105, 186
Holton, Gerald, 203n.9
Homer, 27, 140
Hughes, Ted, 120–21
Hughes, Thomas P., 4

Institoris, Heinrich, 50

Jacobus de Voragine. See *Legenda Aurea*
Jerome, Saint, 79
Jerusalem, 19–23, 40
John Paul II (pope), 5
Jonson, Ben, 67
Joyce, James, "Araby," 100–103, 186; *Ulysses*, 186
Jung, Carl Gustav, 14, 102, 139, 203n.8
Jungk, Robert, 155

Kafka, Franz, 95, 120, 138; "Prometheus," 119, 137
Kant, Immanuel, 86; "Conjectures on the Beginnings of Human History," 23, 81, 87–88
Kelm, Andrew, 152
Kent, Rockwell, *Faust and the Earth Spirit*, 150, 153, 156; *Prometheus*, 191

219

Kerényi, Karl, 138
Kerouac, Jack, 161–62; *Dr. Sax*, 161–64, 189
Kirsch, Rainer, 141
Kleist, Heinrich von, 85–87, 92, 103; *The Broken Pitcher*, 82–85, 87, 186; "On the Marionette Theater," 85–86, 93
Klinger, Max, 118
Klopstock, Friedrich, 77
Kokoschka, Oskar, 120
Kolakowski, Leszek, 115
Kreitzer, Larry, 201n.24
Kunert, Günter, 107; "Adam und Evam," 107–9, 185; prose sketches, 134; "Yannis Ritsos nicht zu vergessen," 133
Kupelwieser, Leopold, 92

Lagerfeld, Karl, *Faust*, 5
Landes, David S., 4
Lavater, Ludwig, *Von Gespänsten*, 51
Lee, Lawrence, 172; *The American as Faust*, 172–73, 189
Legenda Aurea, 17, 57
Lehmann, John, 122
Lenin, V. I., 139
Lercheimer, Augustin, *Christlich bedencken*, 51–52
Le Veau, Jean Jacques, 82
Lewis, R.W.B., 97
Liszt, Franz, 118
Lucian, *Prometheus on Caucasus*, 27, 31–32, 138
Luther, Martin, 49–50, 58, 79; *Table Talks*, 45, 55

Madách, Imre, *The Tragedy of Man*, 184–85
Mailer, Norman, 174, 190
Mainzer, Otto, 121
Malleus Maleficorum, 50
Manlius, Johannes, 45–46, 48
Mann, Thomas, *Doktor Faustus*, 149–50, 165, 186

Manship, Paul, *Prometheus*, 4, 191
Marlowe, Christopher, 60–61, 63; *The Tragical History . . . of Doctor Faustus*, 49, 61–68, 153, 156, 165, 169, 174, 176, 187, 190
Marquis, Don, 158
Marx, Karl, 115, 118, 121, 188
Masaccio (pseud. for Tomaso Guidi), *Expulsion from Paradise*, 3
Mather, Cotton, 79
Mather, Samuel, 79
Maurer, Georg, "Prometheus," 129–31
Maurois, André, 118
Melanchthon, Philipp, 45–46, 50, 52, 57
Melville, Herman, 79, 191; *Billy Budd*, 97–100, 186
Mickel, Karl, "Entfesselter Prometheus," 131–32
Milton, John, *Paradise Lost*, 12–13, 17, 77, 165, 171, 185
Monti, Vincenzo, 118
Muir, Edwin, 120
Müller, Heiner, 122, 134–35; "The Liberation of Prometheus," 135–37, 187
myth: modernizing adaptations of, 186–87; as reflections of society, 190–91

Napoleon, 142
Newman, Randy, *Faust*, 177–78, 188–89
Niecsczym, Richard, 152
Nietzsche, Friedrich, 115, 118; *The Birth of Tragedy*, 21, 25, 116–17
Nixon, Richard, 174–75
Nono, Luigi, 120
noûs, 38, 41–42
Nye, Robert, 152

Olson, Elder, 165; "Faust: A Masque," 165–68, 173, 189

Oppenheimer, J. Robert, 155–56
Orff, Carl, 120

pact with devil, 57
Pagels, Elaine, 193n.6
Palma-Cayet, Pierre Victor, 54
Panofsky, Dora and Erwin, 111
Paul, Saint, 11, 17
Pauli, Wolfgang, 154
Peisistratus, 40
Pericles, 40
Plato, 171; *Protagoras*, 39, 138, 142
Plutzik, Hyam, 168; *Horatio*, 168–69, 173, 189
Poussin, Nicholas, 142
Prometheia, 33
Prometheus, myth of: in Aeschylus's *Prometheus Bound*, 32–39; and atomic bomb, 187; and Fall, 31–32, 42, 69–72; and Faust, 69–72, 181, 187; in GDR, 127–47, 188; in Hesiod, 27–32; history of, 111–18; Marxist view of, 121–27; Nietzsche's view of, 25; popularity of, 4–6; as rebel, 187–88; sources of, 25–27; as trickster, 31, 37, 39

Quevedo, Nuria, *Prometheus*, 110
Quinet, Edgar, 118

Rabelais, François, 183
Rashi, 22
Rasputin, Grigori, 48
Rexroth, Kenneth, 161
Richards, I. A., 169; *Tomorrow Morning, Faustus*, 169–71, 173, 189
Ricoeur, Paul, 17
Riedel, Volker, 201n.30, 202n.50
Ritsos, Yannis, 133
Rosshirt, Christoph, 52
Rousseau, Jean-Jacques, 21, 87, 130; first *Discours*, 112–13
Rücker, Günther, "Prometheus 1937," 147–48
Rufus, Conrad Mutianus, 48–49

Sachs, Hans, 12
Salacrou, Armand, 151
Schedel, Hartmut, *Buch der Chroniken*, 55
Schelling, F.W.J., 42, 149, 183
Schubert, Franz, 92, 118
Schwerte, Hans, 150
Scot, Michael, 49
Scriabin, Aleksandr, 118
Sexton, Anne, "Faust and I," 176–77, 189–90
Shakespeare, 129–30. *See also* Hamlet
Shapiro, Karl, "The Progress of Faust," 154, 156, 178, 187–88
Shattuck, Roger, 198n.1
Shelley, Mary, 118
Shelley, Percy Bysshe, 118; *Prometheus Unbound*, 138, 141, 171
Silone, Ignazio, 185
Silvester II (pope), 49
Simonides, 40
Simon Magus, 57
Snajder, Slobodan, 152
Solomon, King, 19–20
Sophocles, *Antigone*, 37; *Oedipus Rex*, 83, 116
Spengler, Oswald, 5, 45, 190
Spies, Johann, 53, 188. See also *Historia von . . . Fausten*
Sprenger, Jakob, 50
Stein, Gertrude, *Doctor Faust Lights the Lights*, 157–59, 161, 163, 188–89
Steinbeck, John, 185
Stent, Gunther S., 174
Svankmayer, Jan, 152
Swanwick, Michael, *Jack Faust*, 178–80, 187–88

Taylor, Edward, 79
Tennant, Emma, 152
Tertullian, 112
Tezuka, Osamu, *Neo-Faust*, 5
Theophilus, 57

Thomson, George, 132, 194n.7
Thucydides, 4
Tkaczyk, Wilhelm, "Prometheus in der Fabrik," 123–24, 126–27
Toynbee, Arnold, 24
trees, in folkore, 17–18
trickster, myth of: 14, 70–71; in Fall, 17, 23, 27, 39; and Faust, 60–61; and Prometheus, 31, 37, 39
Tritheim, Johannes, 46–47, 49
Trousson, Raymond, 121, 194n.1
Twain, Mark, *The Diaries of Adam and Eve*, 184
typology, 11, 77–80, 185–86

Unamuno, Miguel de, *The Tragic Sense of Life*, 105–6
Ussher, James (bishop), 80

Valéry, Paul, *Mon Faust*, 72, 151, 157
Van Gogh, Vincent, 176
Vega, Lope de, 12
Virdung, Johannes, 46–47
Vita Adae et Evae, 11–12
Völker, Klaus, 150
Voltaire (pseud. for François Marie Arouet), 79, 81, 87–88; *Candide*, 75–77, 89, 91, 108, 185–86

Vondel, Joost van den, *Adam in Exile*, 12, 77

Wagner, Richard, 116; *The Flying Dutchman*, 176; *Tristan and Isolde*, 158
Wallop, Douglass, *The Year the Yankees Lost the Pennant*, 159–61, 164, 188–89
Weber, Max, 21
Weier, Johannes, *De Praestigiis Daemonum*, 51
Whitman, Walt, *Leaves of Grass*, 92–93, 99, 191
Widman, Georg Rudolff, 45
Wolf, Christa, 122
Wolf, Hugo, 118
Wolfe, Burton H., *The Devil and Dr. Noxin*, 174–76
Woolf, Virginia, *Orlando*, 145
Wutrich, Timothy R., 198n.47

"Yahwist," 19–23, 31, 40–41, 70

Zimmermann, Volker, 204n.9
Zimmern, Count Froben Christoph von, 46
Zimmersche Chronik, 46, 50
Zschokke, Heinrich, 82, 85